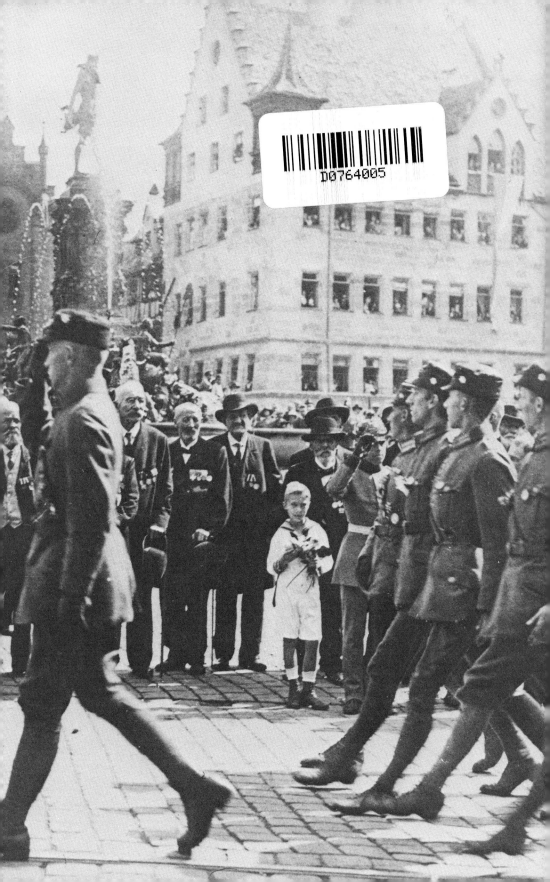

Alex de Jonge has been fascinated by
Weimar Germany and Berlin in the 1920s
ever since he can remember, a fascination
that was sparked by his parents who made
Berlin between the wars a part of his
childhood. Born in 1938, he is currently a
Fellow and Tutor of New College,
Oxford. He has contributed to *The Times
Literary Supplement* and *The New York
Review of Books* and is the author of
*Baudelaire: Prince of Clouds, Dostoevsky
and the Age of Intensity* and *Nightmare
Culture: Lautréamont and "Les Chants de
Maldoror."*

The Weimar Chronicle

The first press photograph of Adolf Hitler taken on September 5, 1923 —
Great German Day in Nuremberg.

The Weimar Chronicle

PRELUDE TO HITLER

ALEX de JONGE

PADDINGTON PRESS LTD
PRESS LTD

NEW YORK & LONDON

For My Parents

Library of Congress Cataloging in Publication Data
De Jonge, Alex, 1938–
 The Weimar chronicle.

 Bibliography: p.
 Includes index.
  1. Germany—History—1918–1933.   2. Berlin
—History—1918–1945.   I.   Title
DD237.D38   944.081'5   78–6952
ISBN 0 7092 0136 2
ISBN 0 448 22188 8 (U.S. and Canada only)

Filmset in England by Vantage Photosetting Co. Ltd.,
Southampton, Hants.
Printed and bound in the United States

Designed by Colin Lewis
Endpapers: Great German Day In Nuremberg.
Demonstrators marching past one of their leaders
Herr Adolf Hitler (marked with a cross), September
15th, 1923. *The Press Association.*

In The United States
PADDINGTON PRESS
Distributed by
GROSSET & DUNLAP

In The United Kingdom
PADDINGTON PRESS

In Canada
Distributed by
RANDOM HOUSE OF CANADA LTD.

In Southern Africa
Distributed by
ERNEST STANTON (PUBLISHERS) (PTY.) LTD.

Contents

Preface

OTHERS SEE historians, and perhaps they see themselves, as having the impossible task of establishing the truth. They make a discriminating selection from carefully sifted sources to ensure that they strike the right balance, that nothing of importance has been omitted from their comprehensive and undistorted account. Then, if they have the audacity, they may even review the material they have so carefully assembled and make a tentative interpretation of it on their readers' behalf.

The Weimar Chronicle is less ambitious. The book was born of an interest in Weimar Germany and Berlin in the 1920s that has been a part of me for as long as I can remember. I have tried to recapture something of an atmosphere which has been the basis of a strange pseudo-nostalgia for events which took place before I was born, events which were not always pleasant ones. *The Chronicle* is not the work of a historian, who sifts and analyzes. As the title implies, it is the work of a chronicler, one who records what he knew or thought or heard had happened. As such, *The Chronicle* is an assembly of voices: extracts from diaries, newspaper reports, eyewitness accounts, memoirs and reminiscences which have been largely allowed to speak for themselves. I have used primary sources for my material, in the sense that I have made little direct use of books about books. Rather than interpret my material, I have tried simply to edit it, and as an editor I am as interested in what people thought they saw as I am in what "really" happened; such distortions are sometimes more valuable than the truth itself when it comes to eliciting the feel of a period.

It would be foolish to pretend that an editor can be unbiased. Bias is reflected in his choice of material, in his comments on it too, so that prejudices are best confessed to from the outset. The reader may well detect a pro-German, anti-French bias in the account of the French occupation. Yet it seems to me that anyone conversant with the facts would find it hard to maintain that French conduct was exemplary. Equally there is a profound prejudice against any political movement opposed to social democracy based upon free elections and universal sufferage — although the Social Democrats of the Weimar republic do not always compel one's admiration. A more irrational prejudice (and one which has, I hope, been kept under control) is a preference for Prussians over Bavarians. This, I admit, is inexplicable.

Although *The Chronicle* covers a lot of ground it does not cover it all. Little is said of Freikorps action in the Baltic provinces or Upper Silesia. The taking of the Annenberg goes uncelebrated. The *Länder* and life in the country feature scarcely at all. More important, *The Chronicle* has been designed, in more ways than one, to culminate with the torch-light procession which celebrated Hitler's assumption of office on January 30, 1933. I have tried to show why so many Germans welcomed it; why, on that night, total strangers embraced one another on the subway exclaiming, "At last we are safe." This intention has given the book much of its focus. Consequently, it has not dealt at all with those aspects of official Weimar politics which, thanks to Hitler, failed to grow a future. There is no mention here of the achievements of Stresemann. For other reasons the "high culture" of Weimar — its music, science, literature, its intelligentsia — is scarcely touched upon. It has been dealt with extensively elsewhere, and to readers unfamiliar with its detail any account of it must seem like an unending list of unfamiliar, though much praised, names.

The Chronicle is an attempt to bring a certain Germany back to life, and more particularly a certain Berlin. Amazingly violent, unbridled, often exuberant, often full of a strange and clumsy poetry, regularly very hungry and very sad, with touches of high lunacy and crankiness. The story of Weimar teaches us that old habits die hard. Just after the war Germany made a tremendous effort to free herself from a certain passion for militarism and the crack of firm government. For a few years there was an extraordinary flowering, a sense of release from author-itarian constraint on every level, together with a belief, in certain quarters, in republicanism and the rule of law. These were hard-won achievements which were all too easily lost because a combination of tradition and circumstance played in certain ways upon the hearts and minds of too many people. The moment of that loss is captured per-fectly in the final picture of *The Chronicle*. Originally entitled "The Last Chance," this photograph of Hitler on an election tour, leaning out of his carriage window to be greeted by a small boy held up by an SS man, might be thought of as symbolizing German manhood commending its young republic to the loving care of Papa Adolf.

A great many people have helped me with this book — not least my parents, who made Berlin between the wars a part of my own childhood. My greatest immediate debt is to Lutz Becker, who loves the period even more than I do. His help with the illustrative material and his comments on the text have been invaluable; I cannot thank him enough. I would also like to thank Frau Boucholz-Starck, Eric Christiansen, Barbara Deavin, Sefton Delmer, Herr Dreyfus, Dr. Heck, Herr Huber, Christopher Isherwood, Dick Jenkins, Fräulein Müller of Ullstein in West Berlin, Gerda Redlich, Professor Reiff, Frau Steck of the Landesbildestelle in West Berlin, Count Nicholas Sollohub, Alec Swan, Herr Wallenberg, the marvelously helpful staff of the Wiener Library in London, and last but by no means least Gordon Wetherell, who arranged so much for me and who was so generous with his hospitality. I would also like to thank David Bowie for inviting me to watch him recreate something of the atmosphere of the old Sportpalast, electronically amplified.

A Note on Sources

THE READER WILL encounter a number of more or less familiar names and voices in *The Chronicle*. Most of these are the authors of memoirs or diaries, the titles of which may be found in the bibliography. One of the most important source books is the diary of Count Harry Kessler, the "Red Count," Red because he actually supported the Weimar Republic. He was a highly civilized and usually balanced observer of events, and a great patron of the arts. He kept a careful diary, which he sometimes wrote with the sound of civil war outside his apartment windows. He knew most of the important figures in politics and the arts, and his diary makes for fascinating reading.

The readers will also encounter some names which do not feature in the bibliography, and the following cast list may tell them something of who they are.

Alexandra Bodryeva A Russian *émigrée* living in Berlin. She ran a successful *haute couture* business, and had many friends in diplomatic and journalistic circles. She met Hitler on numerous occasions and got on particularly well with his chauffeur. Shortly after Hitler came to power, she gave a dinner party for Goering in her apartment, in the course of which her parrot "disgraced itself" all over the future Reichsmarschall's uniform. The parrot survived.

Helena Boucholz-Starck The widow of the German abstract painter Eric Boucholz, who was a close friend of Klee, Kandinsky and the Bauhaus circle. Herself of Prussian aristocratic background, she still lives and works in Berlin.

Sefton Delmer His father was a professor of English at Berlin University before World War I. He went to school in Berlin until 1916, before he and his mother were repatriated. He returned to Berlin as a news-

9

paperman in the twenties and got to know the Nazi leaders better than any other correspondent. He has written a remarkable book about his memories of Berlin and the Spanish Civil War. He is a brilliant and unorthodox observer of Weimar and its immediate aftermath.

Gerda Redlich An Austrian, the daughter of the architect who, together with Hans Poelzig, designed Max Reinhardt's Grosses Schauspielhaus. She attended the Max Reinhardt drama school in Vienna and came to Berlin where she appeared in productions by Reinhardt and Piscator, among many others. She knew and worked with Brecht, and was in the movie of *The Threepenny Opera*. She was also the little girl with the balloon who was murdered off screen by Peter Lorre in Fritz Lang's *M*. She worked in cabarets such as Katakombe and is still actively involved in the theater in the north of England.

Professor Reiff Now a retired professor of economics, he fought in World War I and lived in Berlin during the Weimar period. The son of a trade unionist, he lived in Berlin during its "golden twenties", and is happy to recall that they were indeed golden for him.

Alec Swan An Englishman who went to school in Brünn (now Brno) when it was a part of the Austro-Hungarian Empire. He came to live in Bonn, in the French occupied zone, in 1923 because life was so much cheaper than it was in England. Later he went to Berlin to work with the movie company UFA.

Herr Wallenberg His father was a journalist with the house of Ullstein, and Wallenberg followed in his footsteps. He saw active service in both wars, the second time on the side of the Allies. A keen observer of the Weimar scene, he now works for the Axel Springer group.

1

The Collapse

BY THE MIDDLE of 1918 it was becoming increasingly clear that the Central Powers were going to lose the Great War. This sad truth was kept from the home front, obscured by persistently optimistic communiqués put out by the High Command in an anticipation of what Goebbels would euphemistically refer to in early 1945 as "poetic truth."

Both at the front and at home, discipline had remained remarkably good, but the German nation had sacrificed its wealth and its health to the war effort. The Allied blockade had put Germany on, or just beyond, the hunger line, though it had not made the nation defeatist. Helena Boucholz-Starck grew up in those years. Never, she says, has she been as hungry as she was then, not even in the dying moments of World War II.

The popularity of Kaiser Wilhelm II was on the wane, however, witness the bitter joke in circulation about him and his six sons: "What family is going to survive the war with all six sons alive?" [1] Indeed, by late 1918 that peculiarly vain, hollow and remote leader— "the hare that roars like a lion", as Count Kessler described him [2] — was beginning to feel the strain of leading his nation into total war. The writer Carl Zuckmayer saw him at a decoration ceremony, in close-up, and was frightened by the gray and frozen face with its mustaches apparently fixed by glue and its wide sightless eyes. He felt he was looking at a walking corpse. [3]

The kaiser's popularity with the troops had been open to doubt for some time. When he came to inspect a front line regiment in late 1917, the men were ordered to unload all weapons and hand in ammunition and bayonets, an instruction greeted with hoots of laughter. [4] But the kaiser was not the only member of the royal family to inspire mixed feelings in the men. His son Crown Prince Willy had his own, rather special way of raising morale. The troops did not necessarily object to him watching their return from the front at the bedroom window of his

HQ, in pajamas with one or sometimes two mistresses looking over his shoulder.[5] But at a time when the army was taking punishing losses in the Argonne, it is hard to imagine the thoughts of the men in one particular regiment as they beheld Crown Prince Willy who had come to see them off: in white flannels and waving a tennis racket.[6]

By the autumn of 1918 the army was beginning to show signs of coming apart. Discipline in the rear areas was deteriorating fast. The gap between officers and men, notably reserve officers, was proving much too great for the morale of the men, and the High Command seems to have recognized this. One of the strangest things about the November 1918 Revolution was the speed with which the soldiers' and workers' soviets, or councils, mushroomed all over Germany in a matter of days. Of course, there was the example of Soviet Russia. But rather more to the point was the fact that many such soviets were formed on instruction. From conversations with veterans of the Western Front, it emerges that someone, doubtless the High Command, issued orders in late September 1918 for soviets of officers and men to be formed, presumably to prevent the total breakdown of military discipline.

Of course by no means all soviets were formed in this way. Carl Zuckmayer, a young artillery officer at the time, had returned to the front after a week in an army hospital. He had not yet recovered from a bad head wound, but a captain of the medical corps had declared him healthy enough to get himself killed: "That's what we need young officers for now." Despite an offer from an ex-NCO of his, now an innkeeper, to hide him till the end of the war, he eventually rejoined his unit in early November and found his men in the process of forming a soviet to which they proposed to elect him. His senior officers threatened to have them all shot. The threat was met with laughter, and the disconsolate officers drove off in a divisional car, leaving behind them the placid but allegedly mutinous troops singing not the "Internationale" but nostalgic songs about the Homeland.

The irony of the situation is that Zuckmayer was elected to the soviet because the "mutineers" felt it essential that they should be led by an officer. The point is characteristic of the whole German revolution. Time and again we shall see revolutionary spirit qualified by an inherent need for order and decorum.

Zuckmayer ends his account of military collapse with another equally characteristic expression of pride in the quality of his men. "Starving, beaten, *but with our weapons*, we marched back home" (italics added).[7]

The kaiser's commanders had told him that the war was irrevocably lost, but he hung on for weeks at his headquarters in Spa hoping for something to turn up. General Groener, who had taken over command from Hindenburg and Ludendorff, suggested to the kaiser that he might still secure his position were he to go to the front line and allow himself to be wounded, but he rejected the idea out of hand.

On November 9, 1918, an armistice was announced. Groener ordered the army to withdraw under command of its leaders and officers, informing the kaiser that it would no longer obey his orders and that it no longer stood behind him. The German emperor reluctantly accepted that he would have to abdicate. He had hoped at first to remain king of Prussia, but it was made clear to him that even this was not possible.

The month before, Friedrich Ebert, leader of the Socialist party, the SPD, had urged Groener to secure the abdication of the kaiser and the crown prince. Then, and only then, he said would the survival of the monarchy under a regent be ensured. These were strange words to come from the man who was to become the first president of the Weimar Republic.

It is impossible to overestimate the impact of armistice and abdication upon the German people. Together they play a vital role in the destruction of that inherited framework of beliefs and certainties which had given Germany its particular reassurance: one which derives from a supreme confidence in a nation's collective values. It is the loss of that confidence which will explain the extraordinarily extreme and violent characteristics of Weimar culture.

Service to the kaiser had been the cornerstone of Wilhelmine Germany for teachers, civil servants and above all for the nation's élite, the officer caste. They had been taught that it was the supreme birthright and honor of a gentleman to defend and, if necessary, to die for the kaiser. His abdication destroyed "the foundation stone of what had been the edifice of our public morals".[8] An ensign in a crack regiment, the elder brother of Baldur von Schirach, future leader of the Hitler Youth, shot himself because he could not tolerate the abdication, the collapse of Germany and the end of the officer caste.[9]

There were attempts to explain the kaiser's action away. One loyal pastor in Homburg tried from the pulpit to convince his flock that it was the *German people* who had abandoned their emperor in his hour of need.[10] Abdication, however, was generally regarded as the ultimate betrayal: dishonor flowing from the very fountainhead of honor. Even Hitler would stand and die in Berlin, and it is reasonable to suppose that he was influenced by the kaiser's negative example. Professor Reiff, whose father was a trade union man and no monarchist, well remembers his reaction to the abdication. He felt it to be a shameful act, and, in an echo of Groener's advice, felt that Wilhelm II should have ensured

13

that he die a hero's death on the Western Front.

The loss of the war was a shattering experience for the obvious reasons—and for others. When Reiff and his brother returned home from the front, they found their father in a state of bewilderment which he must have shared with most of the civilian population. He was quite unable to reconcile defeat with the optimistic communiqués sent back from the front. It took the concerted efforts of his two serving sons to make him accept that the military situation was hopeless. It was not that such truths were unpalatable to a patriot, but worse than that. If what his sons had told him was true, then it was the communiqués which had been false; and "Prussian officers do not lie," he kept repeating incredulously.

Reiff's father was an intelligent man and a democrat, but even he found difficulty in accepting such a monumental betrayal of the code of honor. Small wonder then that hundreds of thousands could never accept it at all. They preferred to believe in the "*Dolchstosslegende*," the "Legend of the Stab in the Back," whereby the German army had never been defeated, but rather had been betrayed from within by Red revolutionaries, stabbed in the back by republicans. The legend remained an enduring comfort to Germans who found the alternative impossible to accept. It was cheerfully endorsed by Hindenburg and Ludendorff, Germany's erstwhile warlords.

The abdication of the kaiser was rapidly followed by that of all the other crowned heads of Germany. They seem to have felt they were encountering something rather like a repeat of the Russian Revolution. However, once again, order and decorum prevailed.

In the palace of Potsdam the crown princes waited trembling for the mob, with thoughts of Marie Antoinette and Ekaterinburg. An old servant approached with a shaking voice to announce the leader of the Potsdam revolutionary soviet. He entered, clicked his heels and asked in the name of the soviet whether their Imperial Highnesses felt safe enough, reporting that he had posted a squad of revolutionary soldiers to protect them. [11]

When revolution broke out in Dresden, the king of Saxony left in disgust, telling his subjects in broad Saxon to "*Mach Euren Dreck alleene*"—"Do your dirt alone." Ludwig III of Bavaria fled from Munich on November 7, and overnight tradespeople with the coveted title of *Hofsliferant* (supplier to the court) rapidly obliterated the royal warrant from their shop fronts. The next day, from one of his castles near Salzburg, Ludwig addressed his people:

All my life I have worked for my people. I always strove for the well-being of my beloved Bavaria. After the events of the last few days, I am no longer able to govern, and therefore I relieve all civil servants, officers and men from their oath of loyalty. [12]

The new Bavarian government gave the royal house permission to reside in Bavaria indefinitely, with the proviso that they agreed not to conspire against the state.

The rule of Wilhelmine law was breaking down all over Germany. The collapse had begun in North Sea ports with a naval mutiny. The image of truckloads of revolutionary sailors tearing through the streets of Germany with their cry of "Clear the streets! Shut the windows!" is one of the most powerful and distinctive of all the impressions left by the November Revolution. The immediate cause of the mutiny was a proposed final stand by the Imperial Navy. It planned to send the fleet, preceded by a screen of U-boats, to lure out the British navy and torpedo it to the bottom; the intention was to improve negotiating terms for the armistice. Unfortunately, the sailors refused to sail. Instead they mutinied, and occupied the city.

Lübeck, November 5, a proclamation:
From this evening Lübeck is in our hands. Our cause is just, both at the front and at home. The corrupt military of yesterday must go, root and branch. Our aim is immediate armistice and peace. We request the people of Lübeck to remain calm. We shall do nothing to disturb the peace. Everything will be as before. We expect the population to cooperate. We assure them that whatever changes have occurred have been made without bloodshed. We hope to continue as we have begun. We warn you that violence, looting and robbery will be punishable by death. The civil authority will remain responsible for food supplies. — The Military Soviet [13]

Soviets were forming all over the country, often encouraged by the first of the returning troops, wearing red armbands and still carrying their rifles, which they wore slung upside-down as a sign that they had become revolutionaries.

Hamburg, November 1918 — The town was alive and full of excitement! Crowds of troops were arriving continuously from the railway stations! But they were carrying bright red bows on their rifles and red cockades on their caps. Motor lorries were surging through the streets filled with soldiers, sailors, workers. They were carrying red flags and posters with inscriptions: "Long Live the Revolution," "All Power to the Workers' and Sailors' Soviet...." Wherever we went we saw crowds of soldiers and sailors wearing red armbands. They were armed with rifles and heavy-caliber revolvers. They were tearing the medals and shoulder straps from officers' uniforms. [14]

The animosity of the revolutionaries was focused upon their officers, but instead of lynching them as had happened in Russia, they contented themselves with cutting off their insignia and confiscating their swords. Young cadets such as Ernst von Salomon experienced the action as a form of moral rape, but not everyone took it so seriously. When Janós Plesch arrived at Frankfurt-am-Main station on November 9 in uniform, representatives of the local soviet confiscated his sword, asking him for his address so that they might return it "after the revolution." In due course it came back to him in a very neat parcel.

In spite of the cutting off of shoulder straps and confiscation of swords, not all officers went underground. F. Gedye, who later became the *Manchester Guardian* correspondent in the Rhineland, observed Frankfurt-an-der-Oder under soviet rule. The men, it is true, had given up saluting; but the officers still saluted one another punctiliously.

The revolution was conducted with considerable decorum. During one of the greater revolutionary demonstrations in Berlin past the Winged Victory, a city employee was seen carefully cleaning the mosaic which showed the entry of the kaiser into Berlin after the war of 1870.[15] An old man observing the orderly crowd remarked that he had lived through the revolution of 1848 and "I don't like these peaceful revolutions at all. We shall have to pay for it some day."

Hjalmar Schacht, who later became president of the Reichsbank, also found the revolution a strangely placid affair:

I saw the first lorries drive across the Potsdamer Platz with heavily armed Red troops. It was a curious sight. People passed by the lorries looking depressed and indifferent—they did not even glance at them. The Red revolutionaries shouted, brandished their rifles and generally threw their weight about. In among them, before and behind, the usual mid-day Potsdamer Platz traffic carried on. A very curious, significant scene expressive of Germany's disrupted condition, revolution in the lorries, apathy in the streets.[16]

Yet a revolution it was, and not everybody could remain so detached. Professor Reiff well remembers how, although he had fought at the front, he and many like him were genuinely frightened by truckloads of sailors tearing through the streets of Leipzig. Witness the following from another observer:

Schools close, children are kept indoors away from the windows. The lorries were driving up and down the street with soldiers and civilians, and songs and huge red flags were waving above and behind them. Then all of a sudden an armored car stormed through the road and men shouted: "Clear the streets! Shut the windows! Leave the balconies!" There were only a few people about in the street, and at once, frightened out of their wits, they ran inside. A second later the men in the car began to shoot into the air, into the houses, along the street. Opposite on the balcony, a woman who was still curiously looking on collapsed. The machine gun on the roof went off, tack-tack-tack. The shots were fired at the armored car, but a few went

16

astray and struck into the sandstone wall of our house, directly underneath our window and balcony. Half a dozen soldiers with rifles were just running into the house opposite. The machine gun fired again in a battering rhythm, on and on. Then suddenly it ceased. [17]

There could be no doubt that a revolution had taken place. A young officer who had entered hospital under the kaiser's rule in a small German town found on his discharge that he had stepped into a new world. He met a soldier without insignia and assumed he was a member of a penal battalion, only to learn from him that the sailors of Kiel had declared a revolution.

I left the station feeling as Alice felt in Wonderland. There were very few people abroad, and the next soldier I ran into was obviously a Russian officer. He saluted politely and I returned the salute dreamily. Then came another man in uniform. The cut of his coat indicated that he was a German officer. On his cap was a Bavarian, but no imperial cockade. He wore no shoulder straps and no sword. . . . Yes he was a Bavarian first lieutenant, just come from Munich. Bavaria was a republic since yesterday, didn't I know? Hence the missing cockade. I had better take a few superfluous things off myself, if he might be allowed to give me some advice. "But who is making this revolution?" I asked. He shrugged his shoulders. "I don't know, I'm going home." [18]

Although the Reds were not terrifying compared to the Bolsheviks, there was a strong sense of "Red terror." Socialism was not widely understood in Germany. To a young nobleman of 1918 it meant, quite seriously, "something terrible happening in Russia, involving the division of all personal property into equal parts, and making all women common property too." [19] Many Bavarians also tended to believe that the socialists proposed to redistribute wives.

As Germany seemed to be slipping into the hands of the revolutionary soviets, the troops continued to return from the front. Although discipline had disintegrated in Germany itself, it is greatly to the credit of the officers and men coming back from the front line that they should have done so in such an orderly and military fashion. The exercise was not a simple one, particularly since the Allies were hot on their heels. As Professor Reiff recalls, the French and German High Commands had agreed on how much ground the German army should cover in each march, but the French soon broke the agreement, steadily stepping up the daily *étape*. The soldiers did not greatly resent this, however. They quickened their pace, and their spirits rose as they drew closer to home:

On November 17, a day of bitter, sunless cold, Generals Plumer and Rawlinson began the two-hundred-mile march to the Rhine. Between times the Germans had asked the Armistice Commission at Spa that pursuers never approach closer than ten kilometers to pursued. Yet can one call the parties such? Let us glance a moment at the decamping Fieldgrays.

A week before, they looked to be in full dissolution, their War Lord a sorry fugitive, their country seemingly holding nothing for them but chaos. But now it is very different. Hindenburg, of massive character, has managed to pull together that host which once set out to a "fresh and joyous" war. and which was in danger of returning from it in so many anarchist bands. The routed German army is in orderly column of march once more, winding its way back, ahead of us at the rate of about twenty miles in twenty-four hours, chiefly by night marches. Two night marches, then twenty-four hours' rest, then two further nights on roads which either rang out hard or crunched with hoar frost. In this manner the Germans thought it best to make themselves scarce, when the majority of Belgian and French civilians would be asleep. By day the Fieldgrays . . . could hope to protect themselves better in the event of trouble. There was looting, there was shooting, and many a Fieldgray was murdered, and many another sought to stay behind in civilian clothes; but viewed in breadth, the regaining of the Rhine by the German Army of the Western Front, its being allowed to go home in the dark, unmolested, was a military classic. . . . Indeed, it finished off by being jolly nearly a triumph for all concerned. As the marchers continued into the Fatherland, it was gradually borne upon them that they were not a beaten host at all. They marched through towns and villages bedecked with flowers and flags and beneath evergreen arches erected in their honor. They were given food and boots. They were waved on their way. In Cologne such were the decorations that the marchers might have been excused for believing that they had won the war. [20]

The animosity ringing through this account was very much a part of the Allied view of their beaten enemy—an understandable animosity which would endure in some of the occupied zones longer than in others, but which would remain for many years. The actual "invasion of Germany" was a quiet enough affair, although the British Expeditionary Force kept scanning the woods for snipers:

Nothing untoward developed, and the first the BEF saw of civilian Germany was when white, scared faces peeped from behind curtains. First actual contact came when a small girl, hearing the clatter of hooves, came running down from the family cottage to wave a juvenile welcome. [21]

The British troops were surprised by the triumphal arches erected for returning German soldiers. They were more astounded still by "townlets whose folk had even added welcoming placards in English— and . . . illuminations." [22] But the sight which impressed itself most deeply on an occupying force that had fought and advanced over a devastated French countryside was the extraordinarily untouched appearance of the Rhineland:

The land is in perfect order. Every twig looks as if it had been put in splints. Compare the large areas of devastation in France with this fat, smiling country, bearing no visible signs of any kind of war, and the bitterness in many French hearts seems very natural. [23]

Meanwhile, as the German army reached home, it proceeded, very largely, to melt away. Professor Reiff and his brother were demobilized rapidly but officially. Many others just went home. Egon Jameson, a journalist, reached Berlin with his younger brother. They had lost their epaulets en route, but for some inexplicable reason Jameson senior still retained a mortar barrel:

The streets were empty. One saw the occasional tram. Most of the shops were shut. A few red flags hung from windows waving in the November wind. Every few minutes a lorry crammed with deadly earnest-looking people would tear past. No one paid any attention to us. A nine-year-old boy yelled after us "Imperial lackey!" "You, he means you," my brother explained. [24]

The returning troops were alleged to have brought certain habits with them, which would continue to feature largely in the social life of the new republic:

Our Brave Soldiers, after their helter-skelter retreat through the rain and mud of France, imported in their ragged uniforms the various plagues of any beaten army: lice (common and pubic), scabies, dysentery, an impressive variety and amplitude of venereal diseases, the coarse habits and languages of trenches and soldiers' brothels. Also, as after any war, homosexuality flourished as never before. No wonder, indeed: all those frightened, lonely youngsters huddling together under fire; the girls and women too, left behind, freezing, worried sick, exhausted, starved for a bit of warmth to give and to receive. [25]

19

ABOVE: *Crown Prince Willy on the road to exile.*
BELOW: *November 1918—revolutionary sailors with their rifles slung upside down.*

Soldaten des Arbeiter- und Soldatenra
durchstreifen die Strassen Berlins.

ABOVE: *Revolutionary soldiers at the Brandenburger Tor, Nov. 9, 1918.*
BELOW: *January 1918—armed workers and members of a soldiers'
soviet drive in front of the Royal Mews.*

"Berlin in revolution, two studies 1919" by Hans Baluschek.

A demonstration in Berlin's Siegesallee, January 5, 1919.

Revolution in Berlin 1918-19

"The German revolution was probably less disorderly than any other has ever been. . . . The German people might have accepted it as definitive had it been violent." [1]

WITH THE REVOLUTIONARIES' emphasis on the maintenance of law and order and their rejection of extremism as its dominant themes, the November Revolution was a strangely subdued affair. Indeed, these themes would persist to create the political mood of the Weimar Republic itself, imparting to it that fatal combination of a lack of self-confidence and an overdeveloped sense of decorum which would be the ultimate cause of its downfall.

The revolutionaries lacked "passionate intensity" from the start. Passionate intensity in Weimar Germany would always be the prerogative of the right. The kaiser's régime was to be overthrown in a strangely half-hearted way, as if neither revolutionaries nor their enemies had any appreciation of their historic role in a series of days that should have shaken the world. Witness the plan drawn up by the chairman of the parish council of Zehlendorf, a suburb of Berlin. He proposed to handle the approaching tide of revolution by means of a cheap popular lunch to be made available in an open-air restaurant on the outskirts of town. He hoped that by the time the revolutionaries reached the center they would be too full of food and drink to cause any trouble. [2]

Yet there was more to the November Revolution than small-town comic opera. For one thing, it was largely set in Berlin, which after years of war and privation had become a strikingly grim and run-down city, dreadfully shabby, unpainted, ungilded, cracked. It was an appropriate theater for the hungry, sickly protagonists of the November days. All the shops were empty except for the antique shops, now bursting with heirlooms and treasures which an impoverished upper and middle class had been obliged to sell so that it might eat.

On November 9 the military garrison of Berlin was still, in principle, loyal to the kaiser. That morning Theodor Wolff, a distinguished newspaperman, learned from his barber that all the streets in his neighborhood had been closed off by troops armed with machine guns. He was a trifle concerned about his children, who had to get back from school:

Naturally they took a keen interest at once in the hand grenades; a friendly soldier explained their purpose and the way to use them.[3]

At 12:45 that afternoon came the news that the kaiser had abdicated. Red flags were hoisted all over town, and soldiers began to fraternize with armed revolutionaries who stuck flowers in their uniforms. All the sentries and military posts melted away, and there was not a policeman to be seen. A red flag was waving over the Brandenburger Tor; and, rather more seriously, the trams had ceased to run:

The streets in the Regierungsviertel, the heart of official Berlin, between the Palace and the Reichstag, were filled by endless processions of soldiers and workers, passing without a break along the road; or rather it was a single interminable procession that marched past us going eastward. The fronts of the houses looked dead, the blinds had been pulled down in front of all the shop windows and doors; every shop and office had been deserted by its staff.[4]

Workers and soldiers marched side by side as chance brought them together. Most of the workers were middle-aged, with serious, bearded faces:

They lacked military training, but had the trade unionists' corporate spirit, and marched conscientiously, in order. Some of them were shouldering rifles which had been handed to them from some store. The soldiers' rifles were dangling across their back; they had pushed their caps askew; they were cheeky and jolly, smoking furiously and waving to the girls.[5]

Wolff was amazed to see how much red cloth the revolutionaries had managed to get hold of at a time when there was a severe fabric shortage! He was also impressed by the number of cars they had contrived to commandeer:

Army lorries passed by with the red flag. They bore soldiers and red-beribboned civilians, crouching, sitting, kneeling or standing alongside machine guns, all in some belligerent attitude and ready to fire, although there was no sign of any enemy about. There were also elegant little cars with five or six soldiers in them similarly ready to fire, going to and fro across the city on patrol duty. I said to myself that this is the thing that distinguishes modern wars and revolutions from those of the past: at the outbreak of every war and in every revolution the cars are taken at once from their owners as the very first thing and every fight for power or freedom begins with the pride and joy of the new speed merchants. . . .

The procession was endless. Here and there a few people would try to start a song, but the singing did not spread and soon died out again. From time to time there came from the ranks a cheer for the revolution or for freedom for the people. Sometimes it was answered by groups of spectators, but . . . in this respectable business street, the spirit of noisy demonstrations had not yet developed. Among the marchers I noticed a few soldiers who had taken off their tunics and hung them loosely over their shoulders like capes, and inside out at that. To increase the effect they had actually turned the sleeves inside out, so that they hung loosely, showing their lining, like empty sausage skins. This was the only touch of the picturesque in the whole procession, a picturesque bit of disorderliness to show that there was now an end to war and war discipline. [6]

The procession was moving towards the Palace, one of the two opposing political focal points of the day, the other being the Reichstag. This opposition mirrored a split in the SPD, the only political party that was relatively uncontaminated by the values of imperial Germany. In 1917 the radical left wing of the party had split off to form the Independent Socialists, or USPD, which would in turn spawn the Spartacusbund and later the German Communist party, the KPD. Essentially the opposition was between moderate Social Democrats, such as Philip Scheidemann and Friedrich Ebert, and Marxist radicals led by Karl Liebknecht and Rosa Luxemburg.

On that afternoon the two factions were each seeking power through the force of oratory. The Marxists had occupied the Palace, the royal residence at the top of Unter den Linden. The Social Democrats were in the Reichstag, the House of Deputies, which had taken on a peculiar appearance:

Outside the actual chamber, groups of soldiers and sailors were standing or lying on the enormous red carpet, with rifles stacked. In places a revolutionary could be found asleep on a bench. The hall itself was dim while the ugly, crowded chamber was brightly lit. A sort of popular assembly had formed, soldiers without insignia, rifles reversed, women, deputies, all wearing red. [7]

In the midst of this armed and motley camp, Philip Scheidemann, a tailor turned prominent Social Democrat who was hoping for a constitutional monarchy, was sitting in the Reichstag restaurant, trying to check his hunger with some watery soup. A group of soldiers and workers burst in to announce that Liebknecht was speaking from a balcony at the Palace and calling for a republic modeled upon Soviet Russia. If disaster was to be averted, Scheidemann was told, he must act at once. Leaving his soup half-eaten, he went out onto the balcony of the Reichstag and addressed the crowd. He told them that the rotten hulk of the imperial order was no more, and proceeded to proclaim a republic. Friedrich Ebert had been named chancellor, he announced, and would form a government which would include representatives of all socialist parties. He pleaded for responsible behaviour and the maintenance of law and order, informing them that the army had undertaken to

27

respect the authority of Chancellor Ebert. Scheidemann then went back and finished his soup.

In the meantime, a red flag flew over the Palace where Liebknecht continued to speak. There seems, incidentally, to have been some tacit agreement whereby neither faction would interfere with the other's oratory. Liebknecht called for: "All executive, legislative and judicial power to the workers' and soldiers' soviets." The sentiment was appropriately revolutionary, and yet even here one may detect a certain Germanic tendency toward theoretical elaboration at the expense of conciseness. Compare the German formula with the more incisive and embracing Bolshevik slogan, "All power to the soviets."

Later that day Liebknecht appeared at the Reichstag demanding that the soviets be granted their power. As he made his speech there was silence. No one wished to argue with him at a time when Scheidemann was urgently trying to persuade the USPD to collaborate with the Social Democrats.

It was in this way that the new German republic began to take shape. In place of a Hohenzollern emperor supported by his generals, Hindenburg and Ludendorff and a devoted officer caste, an ex-tailor had proclaimed an ex-saddler the new leader of Germany. Typically, the saddler was enraged by what the tailor had done. Ebert wanted not a republic but a constitutional monarchy! He went red with fury, banged his fist on the table and informed Scheidemann that he had no right to proclaim a republic. But the republic which nobody wanted had been born.

Sefton Delmer considers that the republic also died that selfsame night. Ebert had gone to the chancellor's private office in the government building on the Wilhelmstrasse, close to the spot where one day work on a certain bunker would begin. It is now a wasteland in East Berlin, inhabited only by a huge population of rabbits. It may be argued that Germany's future—bunker, rabbits and all—was to a great extent determined that night, when Ebert heard a telephone, no. 988, begin to ring. He picked it up and found himself connected via a secret line to General Groener at army headquarters in Spa. Groener announced that the kaiser had left for exile in Holland and that Hindenburg was bringing the German army home intact. He required the new government to support the officer corps in maintaining army discipline. He also required the government to resist bolshevism and offered the support of the army to that effect. The first chancellor and future president of Germany's first republic, himself a monarchist at heart, agreed. He pledged his republic's support to the preservation of the Prussian military tradition, joining with the army to combat a revolution which, as he put it, they both "hated like sin." Sefton Delmer has referred to the Weimar

Republic as the "republic with a hole in its heart." The hole was there from the start.

It may be argued that Ebert had no choice. He was caught between the army and "Red terror." Yet he was nominally a head of state, and heads of state do not normally place themselves at the disposal of their military commanders—at least not immediately, not without attempting to assert their nominal authority. Unless, that is, the army in question considers itself a state within a state, as it did in Prussia, and the head of state in question is a saddler talking to a warlord.

Scheidemann's call to the people of Berlin to respect law and order was echoed in the manifestoes of the more radical factions. On the first day of the republic they issued a proclamation:

Citizens, workers: Order and law are necessary for the effective conduct of the revolutionary movement. The population is urgently requested to keep the streets clear and not to go out after dark.[8]

It is true that the Spartacists had called a general strike, but they made exceptions. Some strikers had made life too difficult for the man in the street and the following services were to be continued: transport, food manufacture, power services, garbage collection, sewerage, medical services, and restaurants(!) but not cafés.[9] In other words, the strike was to be general in name alone. The trams soon started to run again and by evening the town was relatively quiet. There were a few pockets of right-wing resistance, but nothing serious. In the meantime on the Friedrichstrasse, one of Berlin's main pleasure centers after dark, it was more or less "business as usual":

The cafés and dance halls were so crowded that we had difficulty in finding seats. Soldiers, men in evening clothes, and girls of all shades and types formed the bulk of the crowds. Suddenly the orchestra was drowned by sounds of machine-gun fire. One of the windows near us was punctured by bullets, and fragments of glass flew in all directions. The orchestra stopped playing. Then from the street came the sound of hand grenades. Someone screamed. The crowd made for the back of the restaurant. Then the door burst open and a man reeled into the room, blood streaming from his forehead. . . . Soon the street grew quiet again, and someone jumped up onto the platform. "Meine Damen und Herren, please excuse the brief interruption. Government troops were being sniped from the housetops. However, the incident is now past. Don't let your enjoyment be interrupted any longer."[10]

In spite of such occurrences, the general consensus was that the revolution had been a calm and orderly affair with none of the unseemly hysteria which had accompanied the outbreak of war in August 1914. As a spectacle it had been something of a disappointment. The liberal Eugen Schiffer found:

Nothing exciting, nothing impressive, nothing to fire the enthusiasm. As

I got home all I could say to my wife was that I thought a revolution would be very different. The monarchy seemed to have fallen like a rotten oak in a puff of wind.[11]

In the ensuing days Berlin was a strange blend of order and turmoil. There were sporadic spasms of street fighting in the center of town, and this created traffic problems. Civilians were advised to do all their traveling by tram, since warring elements had agreed not to shoot up public transport.

A group of revolutionary sailors from Kiel had seized the main telegraph office on behalf of the provisional government. The operation succeeded in keeping the lines open but, unfortunately, there was nothing to eat except for some cases of emergency rations which could only be broached with a written government order. The hungry sailors decided to send three men to Ebert in the Reichstag. They could not find him, but Wolfgang Heine, the newly appointed minister of justice, told them that it would be quite all right to go ahead and eat. However, there was still no written order. The deputation returned to him, and this time he went back with them in person. His presence failed to convince the sailors. He had to obtain a typed order, signed by Ebert, before the revolutionaries could be persuaded to break their fast.[12]

By and large, as Count Kessler observed, there was no serious disruption to transport, main services, sewerage or the telephone system. Life went on much as before, and although many shots were fired there were surprisingly few casualties.[13] Yet there was turmoil as well as order. Not only was the tension between the Spartacusbund and the SPD growing ominously, but discipline was breaking down in the Berlin garrison, which could no longer be relied on as an effective support for the provisional government. The adjutant reported to his commanding officer:

Disorder, lack of discipline, looting, wild commandeering and house searching. . . . The troops go their own way, the barracks are like a madhouse. Sentry posts don't exist. There are soldiers' soviets in every corner and alley. . . . The true masters of Berlin are indiscipline, vice and chaos. The barracks are worst of all. Full to bursting when it is time to eat or be paid, but empty whenever the CO needs a dozen men. Day and night senseless shooting out of exhilaration and fear.[14]

Indeed, military units, half revolutionary, half criminal, went in for systematic looting of houses in the more prosperous quarters of town. Announcing their presence with a grenade suspended from the front door handle, they would move into a house, terrorize its occupants and clean it out.[15]

The government, desperate to persuade the population to resist the left-wing attempt to turn a Social Democratic revolution into a bolshevist chaos of violence and disruption resorted to public advertisement in an effort to persuade the people that they were flirting with self-destruction. They borrowed a line from a poem by the brilliant writer Walter Mehring. All over Berlin around this time one could see on the *Litfasssäulen*, or advertising columns, huge placards reading: *Berlin, dein Tanzer ist der Tod*. Berlin, your dancing partner is death.

There were now three separate political elements seeking power: the SPD, the USPD, and the Spartacusbund led by Rosa Luxemburg and Karl Liebknecht, who was sending messages of fraternal greeting to the Bolsheviks. On November 10 Liebknecht declined to join the SPD–USPD executive council, so the latter party put up Emil Barth, an ex-metalworker. At 5 P.M. in the Busch Circus there was a mass meeting of representatives from soviets all over the country to decide what form the new government should take. The Spartacusbund attempted to win them over, but instead the three thousand delegates chose Barth as their representative. In effect, they were opting for social democracy.

Looking back, Professor Reiff believes that it was at that moment that Ebert turned the country away from bolshevism. He effectively persuaded the soviets to abandon their power in favor of a democratic representative system and eventual elections. His announcement that the SPD and USPD would form a joint government was acclaimed, as the soviets gave their revolution away and denied the Spartacusbund their support. The vote, however, was followed by a long debate about the constitution of the new government; so long that a soldier called out: "If you can't make up your minds soon, we soldiers will form the government ourselves." A decision was then reached quite quickly and a provisional government formed.

Its most immediate threat took the form of a half-hearted right-wing putsch. On December 6 a member of a soldiers' soviet named Feldwebel Fischer, a dubious American-German journalist named Martens, and two young aristocrats from the Foreign Office summoned Ebert from the Reichstag and urged him to declare himself president. At the same time a squad of armed men arrested the executive council. Ebert replied that he would have to discuss the matter with his council. They were released accordingly, and the putsch petered out.

Meanwhile, Spartacist agitators were at work drumming up support in the poorer districts of Berlin. They secured permission to hold an unarmed demonstration from the chief of police, Emil Eichhorn, an unstable man of left-wing persuasions. When the army learned that the demonstrators might in fact be armed, they proceeded to take their own measures. The *Gardefusiliere*, known in Berlin as the *Maikäfer*, or Maybugs, were ordered to defend the *Regierungsviertel*. On December 6 sixteen demonstrators died in the first clashes between army and revolutionaries; twelve were seriously wounded and there were many minor casualties. No one could say who fired the first shot.

The deaths reinforced the split between SPD and the Spartacusbund, and civil war began to seem a real possibility. *Rote Fahne*, the Spartacist paper, held forth the next morning:

Workers, soldiers, comrades, fourteen (sic) coffins lie on the pavements of Berlin. Defenseless peaceful soldiers brought down by cowardly assassins. Make those guilty of this bloody crime pay for it. Throw those who are really guilty out of the government, those betrayers of ignorant soldiers, Ebert, Scheidemann and Co. Their names have become a counter revolutionary battle cry, a banner of anarchy, fratricide and betrayal of the revolution. Energy! Strength! Determination! The time has come for action. The bloody crime must be avenged, the conspiracy of Ebert and Scheidemann must be crushed with an iron fist; the revolution must be saved. Down with Ebert, Scheidemann and Co. All power to the workers' and soldiers' soviets. To work. To the barricades. To battle. Down with the blood-stained cowardly putschists. Long live the revolution![16]

In the midst of all the furor, Hindenburg's front-line troops were beginning to arrive back in Berlin, in good order, to receive a pathetically heroic welcome. Count Kessler saw a division marching down Unter den Linden. They wore steel helmets and some of them had garlands of flowers. They displayed countless black, white and red flags, the colors of the old Germany. There was not a single red banner. The officers, also decked with flowers, rode out ahead of their columns. A huge crowd was there to acclaim them; flags were flying from the houses. Kessler, an intelligent, politically aware liberal, was cut to the heart by a blend of shame, sadness and love for a brave army which was returning glorious but unlucky. The tragedy of that returning army was compounded by the behavior of Ebert, who greeted it at the Brandenburger Tor, saying: "As you return unconquered from the field of battle, I salute you."[17] With the word *unconquered*, Ebert gave yet another boost to the legend of the "Stab in the back," the founding myth of the persisting militarism which was to haunt the Weimar Republic. Whoever may have lost the Great War, it was certainly not the invincible German army. In fact, it would not be long before the Nazis and others would pin the loss on "the criminals of November," one of the chief criminals being, of course, none other than Friedrich Ebert.

A more immediate threat to a distinctly fragile new government came from the navy. In mid-November the town commandant, Otto Wels, had invited six hundred sailors from Cuxhaven to Berlin, as a reserve unit for the defense of the republic. They had been billeted in the Palace and royal mews, and had christened themselves the People's Marine Division. When revolution first broke out on the coast, they had proved both effective and reliable; but on arriving in Berlin they had taken an increasingly independent line, setting up their own administrative and disciplinary soviet, much to the disapproval of their hosts and pay-masters, the new government.

The relationship between sailors and government deteriorated steadily. It is true that they never actually sacked the Palace, as rev-olutionaries had once sacked the Tuileries, but there was a perpetual furtive stream of stolen ex-imperial treasures shipped out at night by boat (the Palace being on the river Spree). The sailors were guilty, shall we say, of a certain lack of vigilance, but at least this cut two ways. At the height of their occupation Max Bode, head of the Berlin museums, succeeded in smuggling Watteau's two greatest paintings, *L'Embar-quement pour Cythère* and *L'Enseigne de Gersaint*, out of the Palace on a hand cart.[18] Understandably, the government began to question the desirability of maintaining six hundred sailors in the Palace. It became increasingly clear that the official administration was not able to control its men.

On December 12 Hugo Simon, the finance minister, recommended the immediate and unannounced removal of the sailors from the capital — while there were still treasures left. Wels was authorized to negotiate their departure and the running down of their unit. They wanted to remain, to expand, and above all to be paid, while challenging the authority of their paymaster to give them orders. On December 21 Wels was authorized to pay them 80,000 marks after they had left the Palace and surrendered its keys — objects which were shortly to take on an important if symbolic significance. They were to move into the royal mews and would in future have a maximum strength of six hundred men.

The sailors agreed, but they handed the keys not to Wels but to the USPD man Emil Barth. The latter telephoned Wels in the presence of the sailors' representatives and told him that it would be in order to authorize payment. Wels, who did not trust Barth, replied that he should have received the keys in person. He then suggested that since Ebert was nominally commander in chief of the armed services, the keys might be surrendered to him. Although Barth maintained that he and Ebert had equal authority, the key-carrying sailors set off to look for the president. Unfortunately, they missed him because he had gone to lunch. Wels thereupon refused to pay them. Since it was just before Christmas, the question of pay was not without its urgency. Accordingly, the sailors occupied the Chancellery and its telephone exchange, cutting off all lines to the outside world — except the secret line to Groener. Ebert seems to have learned from the experience of being shut up in his own Chancellery. When Albert Speer inspected the building which he was to revamp for Hitler in 1933, he was astounded to find that all the attics of a series of government buildings had been interconnected, so that a beleaguered chancellor could escape through them and emerge on the top floor of the Adlon Hotel. Hitler did not see the need for such an escape route and had it walled up.

In the meantime other sailors crowded into Wel's office demanding their pay, although the keys were by now back in the Palace. Tension mounted and they were beginning to utter threats, when suddenly shots rang out from the street. Wels ran to the balcony, calling to the government troops to stop firing as negotiations were proceeding. By 6 P.M., however, the sailors had cordoned off the area, while government troops had machine guns trained on the occupied buildings. More troops arrived in trucks and armored cars. Confrontation was avoided, however, until 7:25 P.M. when a strange truck tried to break through the sailors' cordon. They opened fire and an armored car which had just arrived started shooting back. One sailor was killed and three badly wounded. The sailors grew furious with Wels and nearly lynched him. To appease them, he authorized the issue of their pay, but this appeared to make them angrier still. Finally they kidnapped Wels and his assistant, removing them to the royal mews and beating them up on the way. On arrival, he was further mistreated and told he was going to die.

On the whole, Ebert's troops had remained fairly loyal. He therefore ordered a unit to negotiate with the sailors, while both sides agreed to vacate the Chancellery. They did so by 10 P.M., but at one o'clock the next morning Wels was still a prisoner. Ebert decided to secure his release by force. He had reason to believe that he was still in some peril since *Rote Fahne* had blamed him for the deaths of December 6.

On December 23 Lieutenant-General Lequis, commander of the Garde-Kavallerie-Schützen Division, mobilized most of the troops in Berlin. Next morning, Christmas Eve:

Unter den Linden was a huge army camp. From all sides came companies on foot, and in lorries, led by soldiers' soviets. The men were in order of battle with steel helmets, haversacks and fixed bayonets. The Potsdam Division advanced resolutely behind its field pieces, hand grenades hung from their webbing. [19]

There was a final attempt at negotiation, which failed, and at 8 A.M. precisely battle began. The troops had set up several machine guns, while the sailors had five machine guns and a heavy field gun. This impelled the officer commanding the Garde-Kavallerie Division Colonel von Tschirschky und Bösendorff, to order up artillery, and two 105 mm pieces were set up.

The first shot hit the first storey of the Palace, made a large hole and knocked out a machine gun. Other hits were made on the ground floor, and damaged the balcony from which the kaiser had promised war to an enthusiastic crowd in August 1914. Another gun started to fire on the royal mews as sailors replied with machine guns from concealed positions. The fire fight continued for some time, with at least one peculiar interruption. C. M. Schmidt, a journalist covering the event from the security of a cellar, found the firing so noisy that he could not phone his piece through to his paper, *B-Z am Mittag*. A massive man, he ordered his assistant to take up a tattered white tablecloth and together they walked towards the mews. There they explained the need for a short cease-fire in order to ensure that the whole affair be adequately covered by the press. The sailors agreed, provided that the army would stop shooting as well. A truce was negotiated and rather later a pile of *B-Z am Mittag* was delivered to the mews.[20]

Firing resumed until eventually the sailors came out under a flag of truce. After negotiating for some time, they agreed to vacate the Palace. In the interim, a group of armed Spartacists had broken through the army cordon and tried to seize the Palace, only to be driven out at bayonet point. At the same time, other armed elements, who may or may not have been policemen, attacked the army from the rear, while enormous crowds gathered to watch the fighting.

It is alleged that an amazing sense of decorum was displayed. As the crowd came under machine-gun fire and raced for cover, it avoided taking shortcuts across the ex-kaiser's lawn, dutifully scuttling round the little gates with their injunction: "It is forbidden to walk on the grass."[21] The crowds seemed to Count Kessler to be the sailors' salvation. They inhibited the attacking troops and actively discouraged some units from moving up into the line.[22] Spartacist agitators made speeches calling for action of various kinds, and Count Kessler felt it all looked rather like Hyde Park Corner on a Sunday morning.

Amid all the fighting and demonstrating, the pre-holiday atmosphere carried on. A block away the Friedrichstrasse was full of shoppers, barrel organs played, and peddlers sold indoor fireworks and cakes. It was "business as usual" in the jewelry stores on Unter den Linden, and in all the big department stores as well. Christmas in Europe is celebrated when the first star appears on Christmas Eve, and December 24, 1918 was no exception. It was just that there was sporadic shooting going on in front of the Palace.

The army found it increasingly difficult to continue fighting. In effect both sailors and government troops just gave up. The sailors left the Palace but were allowed to remain in the mews. They agreed to be incorporated into the republican armed services, and promised not to fight the government again. The troops were withdrawn and the Berlin garrison taken off alert. Wels was released. The sailors lost nine men and had many wounded; the Spartacists lost twenty and the army two. The next morning the newspapers all agreed that the government had capitulated to forces of disorder, and it would have been better had they done nothing at all in the first place. An eyewitness to the fighting between the sailors and the government summed up the episode when he said that it arose from confusion and a failure to follow instructions: "Order and discipline are as important in a revolution as at any other time."[23]

The next day, Christmas Day, Spartacists and sailors staged a huge demonstration around the Palace. They occupied the buildings of the SPD newspaper *Vorwärts* and published their own "revolutionary" edition—on red paper. It was generally felt that if conditions in Berlin deteriorated any further the capital would soon be occupied by Allied troops.

The fire fight around the Palace had done more damage to the outside of the building than it had to the sailors. It may or may not have been true that they put cloths beneath the tripods of their machine guns to avoid scratching the floors,[24] but certainly Count Kessler, who toured the Palace a day or so later, was surprised at how little damage had been done to the public rooms. In the private apartments of the imperial couple, things were a little different. The sailors had broken open desks and stolen letters, the imperial wardrobe had vanished, and the gold knobs had been removed from all the imperial walking sticks.

But the fighting and tension notwithstanding, the year ended cheerfully enough. Berlin was still under the so-called *Tanzverbot*: dancing had been forbidden during the latter war years and all places of entertainment were obliged to close early. This had given rise to enormous numbers of clandestine nightclubs which sprang up almost immediately after the signing of the armistice and formed the basis of Berlin night life in the years to come. The *Verbot* persisted after the peace, since it was felt that public celebration would be inconsistent with Germany's defeat and mourning for her dead. But it was lifted for New Year's Eve 1918, and Berlin responded accordingly:

Demonstrations ten thousand strong. The air is charged with electricity, unparalleled political high tension. Berlin is red-hot. The old year ended in feverish excitement, and it appeared that all thoughts were for the seriousness of the hour. But the confetti came down, and men and women thirsty for life danced in the new year. Bands played in every establishment, waltzes, fox trots, one-steps. Legs flashed across the dancefloor, coat-tails flew, champagne corks popped. Hands were raised and "Happy New Year" rang out over the streets, which still echoed with the sound of demonstrations.[25]

The author of these lines went on to say that he had never seen Berlin dancing and seeking its pleasure with such hysterical urgency, as frenzied couples saw the new year in with a mixture of waltz time and rioting, confetti and red flags.

January 1919 saw the last really serious attempt at a left-wing putsch in Berlin. It was not unexpected by the government, who took a preventive measure that would, in the long run, contribute to their final undoing: they inaugurated the Weimar tradition of the private army.

Since the abortive action around the Palace, there was every reason to doubt the reliability of the Berlin garrison. It was therefore decided to recruit irregular volunteer companies who would provide the young republic with the support it needed. Thus the Freikorps was born. Its architect was Gustav Noske, an ex-NCO who had distinguished himself earlier in his handling of mutinous North Sea sailors. He undertook to raise and direct the irregulars with the observation: "Well somebody's got to be the bloodhound."

Volunteers flocked to the Freikorps; at one time there were 177 different units. They joined for a variety of reasons. Young officer cadets like Ernst von Salomon joined because they felt humiliated by Germany's defeat and collapse, and because they had not experienced the front, not had that "*Fronterlebnis*" which alone tests and forges a man. Others joined because war was the only trade they knew—those in particular, said Professor Reiff, who had been highly trained shock troops, like the irregulars after World War II, commandoes, SAS, and who now felt completely out of place in peacetime. Still others joined because of the opportunities for looting and excitement. Yet in the early weeks of 1919, when it seemed that Germany might follow the example of Soviet Russia and a whole order appeared in danger of imminent collapse, the great majority joined, as Sefton Delmer put it, "because it was the patriotic thing to do." It is a view confirmed by the experience of Dr. Karl Heck, who had served on the Western Front and was then a student at Tübingen. He and many others in his student corporation, or fraternity, joined the Freikorps, partly out of a sense of adventure, but largely because they felt their country to be in danger. As another Freikorps man observed:

We were far from regarding the working man, the man without property as our enemy. . . . On the contrary, our sympathies were more with him than they were with those who were owners of property. It was very hard for us to think of them as our enemies. But that they had turned into our enemies was beyond dispute. [26]

In many ways, however, the cure proved almost as bad as the disease. The Freikorps undoubtedly stopped the Spartacusbund in its tracks, and perhaps played an effective military role on the eastern frontiers, against Poles, Letts and others anxious to possess or repossess parts of what the Germans considered to be German territory. But it perpetuated the romance of militarism and, when disbanded, turned into a series of secret militaristic societies that practiced political assassination and generally provided a focus for right-wing military and paramilitary organizations.

Nevertheless in January 1919 some kind of paramilitary organization was all too necessary. The government was quite uncertain of the extent of its support and was very much feeling its way — witness its plan to have daily military parades in front of the Reichstag as a show of strength. The idea was abandoned, however, when it proved almost impossible to find music which the bands could play that would not be politically divisive. [27]

In a rather more positive mood, the government precipitated its confrontation with the Spartacusbund by its attempt to dismiss the newly appointed Berlin chief of police Emil Eichhorn. Theodor Wolff has described him as "a man of lower-middle class filled with the frenzy of the small man turned Jacobite." [28]   Count Kessler is possibly kinder when he describes him as a figure out of an Offenbach opera. He found it strange that Eichhorn should have sought to secure the public peace by means of issuing arms to all Spartacists upon request.

What was a Spartacist? Theodor Wolff provides an answer of sorts in his description of a typical revolutionary. The portrait has more pathos than revolutionary fervor and fits well with the sad, gray and hopeless story of the German left's attempt at bolshevism without Bolsheviks, as he observed a major demonstration:

A shabby little man in a threadbare jacket too short for him; he had buttoned it close because he was cold. His beard had a moth-eaten look; he evidently had not shaved for some time. His sharp nose sadly pointed earthwards. He hung his head as though it were too heavy a burden for his weak and skinny neck, but probably he was simply too dog-tired to hold it up. He was terribly tired, and on top of that had very likely had even less to eat than usual on this eventful day. He hardly lifted his feet as he shuffled mechanically along. A soft hat, years old and worn by the rain and the blows of fate, a hat which an old clothes dealer would scarcely have taken as a gift, was pulled over his already graying hair. The rifle hung loosely on his emaciated back, and it must have pressed uncomfortably on his projecting bones. [29]

On the night of January 5 the Spartacusbund had the strength to seize and hold all government buildings. As a result, the government had nowhere to eat — strange how frequently the theme of food crops up in Weimar history. It gladly accepted an invitation from the dubious businessman George Sklarz, who had met Noske in the street, to spend the evening with him. It was not the last time that a republican government would be grateful for a bit of shelter.

That evening the Sparticists seized the *Vorwärts* building again. The occupation was a symbolic act. *Vorwärts* had once been a radical left-wing journal, which was now considered to have betrayed the revolution. The Reds were determined to hold it at all costs. They then proceeded to occupy the whole, so-called Newspaper Quarter, a part of Berlin in and around the Kochstrasse. It was a few minutes' walk away from the government quarter and *"Stadtmitte"*, the very center of town. Now it is on the eastern side of West Berlin, up against the Berlin Wall and two minutes from Checkpoint Charlie. Ullstein and Axel Springer still have their headquarters there.

The next morning successful Spartacist news management suppressed all papers except for their own publications, all of which suggested that the Ebert government had been overthrown. They called on the people to take to the streets. The result was one of the largest and least effective demonstrations in history. As *Rote Fahne* described it:

What was seen that Monday was probably the greatest proletariat demonstration in history. From the statue of Roland to the statue of Victory, the people were massed shoulder to shoulder. The mob extended right into the Tiergarten. They were armed and carried red flags . . . an army two hundred thousand strong. Then something extraordinary happened. The crowds had been standing in the cold and fog since 9 A.M. and their leaders [the so-called Revolutionary Council of 33, including Liebknecht] *were seated, no one knew where, and were deliberating. Noon came; cold and hunger increased. The crowds grew impatient. They demanded action—words even—anything to break the suspense. But no one knew what to do, for the leaders were deliberating. . . . The fog thickened and night began to fall. The people went sadly home.* [30]

The first revolutionary action of the Council of 33 had been to confirm Eichhorn's appointment as Berlin's chief of police.

The same attitude—whether it was lack of conviction, or respect for order—characterized the action of a revolutionary sailor named Lemmser. Accompanied by three hundred armed men he had that morning called on the undersecretary, Hamburger, asking him to hand the War Ministry over to them. The sailor produced a piece of paper stating that Ebert's government had been deposed by the soviets. Hamburger pointed out that the paper was unsigned and asked him to come back with a proper authorization. Lemmser obligingly withdrew, then realizing he had made a fool of himself, went sick for a week instead of returning.

On his way out of Berlin to become the Freikorps bloodhound, Noske had had occasion to observe the demonstrators. He had seen soldiers and Spartacists fraternizing, and the spectacle convinced him that it would be unwise to try to form his Freikorps in Berlin. Instead he withdrew to Dahlem to an empty girls' school. In three days he had turned it into an army camp and was raising republican regiments from volunteers. The first was named "Reichstag," the second "Liebe"! More typically the third was called "General Grantoff's Regiment." Not many Freikorps units were to have republican names.

In the meantime the situation in the capital was confused. There was sporadic hand-to-hand fighting, and frequent clashes between the Spartacusbund and government troops—some of a farcical nature. Spartacists invaded Berlin's newest and most luxurious hotel, the Adlon, to requisition its food. They were beginning to clear the larders when government troops arrived with similar intent. Fortunately, Louis Adlon had the presence of mind to suggest that they share the spoils rather than shoot it out.[31] On another occasion the Spartacists had mounted a machine gun on the Brandenburger Tor, enabling them to shoot down Unter den Linden. This caused severe disruption of traffic in the Friedrichstrasse, and a regular cease-fire, signaled by flags, was agreed to in order to keep the traffic flowing.[32]

The fighting had its serious side, too. It was the first widespread street fighting that the capital had seen. On January 5 and 6 Count Kessler saw demonstrators, soldiers, and the occasional mortar shell exploding, as he walked through Berlin. Once he was nearly stranded in the Kaiserhof Hotel, where the ranks of red-clad page boys and waiters were on duty as usual. He wrote his diary to the sound of rifle and artillery fire: "As it appeared that the hotel was about to be surrounded, I decided to go home." The next morning he awoke to the rattle of machine-gun fire. He went out to see what could be seen and found government troops taking cover under the elevated railway, as a train went along it through the middle of the fire fight. The mood of those day is caught by the following entry:

At nine-fifteen sharp a shell dropped in front of my door. For a quarter of an hour I have been listening to machine guns and grenades in the distance. Potsdamer Platz I should say. At half past nine machine guns and rifles opened up just opposite. A noisy night. Around one o'clock a short lively fire fight on my street. Rifle and machine-gun fire. More rifle fire around two o'clock.[33]

Yet the fighting had not closed the city down. Cafés remained open, and for the street peddlers and prostitutes it was business as usual. Crowds would admittedly scatter as they came under fire, but they would soon re-form. Cafés and restaurants were full, fully lit, and singers, musicians and dancers were performing, although at any moment they might get shot up. It was as if the street fighting were taking place in another dimension. Even the trams kept on running, although they were blacked out at night and only announced their arrival by the occasional spark. There were streets, however, which looked less like streets than battlefields. The Reichstag itself was an armed camp full of bivouacking soldiers, while its old liveried servants picked their way through piles of rifles. One of them whispered to Count Kessler that it was *not at all* as it used to be. After the fighting was over and politics returned to normal, it was indeed necessary to have the Reichstag deloused.

Count Kessler was struck by the failure of the revolution to make any real impact upon Berlin's night life. A few evenings later he was sitting in a cabaret watching a Spanish dancer when a bullet flew through the room. No one paid the slightest attention. Kessler concluded that Berlin's big city atmosphere was:

... so basic that even a revolution affecting world history, such as this one, does not create any fundamental disturbance for it. The Babylonian, the bottomless, deep, chaotic and compelling qualities of Berlin only impressed themselves upon me through the revolution, for it showed that this gigantic movement was little more than a minor disturbance in the to-and-fro of Berlin, as if an elephant were to receive a cut from a penknife. It shakes itself but proceeds as if nothing had happened. [34]

Berlin had found for the first time that identity which made it, at last, one of the great capitals of Europe; an identity found in and perhaps through revolution and the indifference which its pleasure seekers displayed toward it. Yet if Berlin itself proceeded as if nothing had happened, the same cannot be said of the luckless Spartacists.

On Saturday, January 11, the main "Noskito" forces entered Berlin, two thousand of them. Their advance was not seriously opposed. The evening before an attack had been mounted upon the *Vorwärt;* building, which was stormed the next morning at dawn. It was a warren of connecting houses and was easily defended, until it came under artillery fire which its heavy machine guns were powerless to stop. After two hours of bombardment its defenders attempted to negotiate. The troops declined, demanding unconditional surrender. They then attacked with mortars and flame throwers, and at last some three hundred defenders came out with their hands up. At least seven of them were murdered on the spot after a brutal beating, the troops having received conflicting orders, one of which had been to shoot anyone found in the building.

The other Spartacist bastion, the huge red-brick police headquarters on Alexanderplatz, Berlin's greatest square, was attacked on January 12 by Lieutenant Schulze of the "Maybugs" with a scratch unit. He came under heavy machine-gun fire, but replied with artillery and soon knocked out most of the machine guns. The Spartacists surrendered almost at once and Schulze cleared the building. This time five prisoners were shot. With the fall of police headquarters the rebellion was effectively over. Victory was celebrated in its ruined hall by a Freikorps band which played a medley from Lohengrin, much to the amusement of passers-by.

The Freikorps turned Berlin into an armed camp with steel-helmeted, grenade-carrying sentries at every crossroads and artillery pieces stationed at strategic points. The city was to remain under martial law for many months. Yet, curiously, the greatest disruption was yet to come. Some days later the power workers went on strike and Berlin was paralyzed. Shops shut early; there were no telephones, no lights. Count Kessler found it a much more fundamental disruption than any armed rising. The whole city had been shut down, including the government. Fourteen hundred men had achieved peacefully, and at a stroke, more than all the shooting and demonstrations. [35]

Karl Liebknecht and Rosa Luxemburg were nearly captured on the morning of January 11, but made their way to the working-class suburb of Neuköln. Two days later they moved on again. Liebknecht wrote a last piece for *Rote Fahne*, declaring that contrary to rumor their leaders had not left the country and that their work would survive whatever might happen to them. On January 15 at 9:30, Liebknecht and Rosa Luxemburg were arrested during a house-to-house search in Wilmersdorf and brought to the Eden Hotel, the headquarters of the Garde-Kavallerie-Schützen-division.

When Liebknecht was taken from the hotel toward a car, there was scarcely anyone about. A certain Private Runge hit him twice on the head with a truncheon and Liebknecht sank to his knees, half unconscious. Officers who were standing around did nothing. Heavily armed men were to drive him to Moabit prison, but on the way, close to an unlit footpath, he was asked if he felt strong enough to walk. He was supported on both sides and surrounded by men with cocked pistols and armed grenades. After a few steps he was shot attempting to escape. Captain von Pflugk-Harttung fired the first shot.

As Rosa Luxemburg left the hotel, Private Runge was waiting for her. A certain Captain Petri had given orders that she should not reach prison alive. As she came out, Runge hit her twice on the head—the blows could be heard from inside the hotel. She fell and was bundled into a car. As it drove off, someone hit her on the head again. En route Oberleutnant Vogel shot her in the head and her body gave a twitch. The car stopped at the point where the road leaves the zoo by the Landwehr Canal, and a group of soldiers waiting there took delivery of the body. On Vogel's orders they threw it into the canal. The next day the killers had their photograph taken. [36]

These men were subsequently brought to trial, as *The Times* (London) reported:

The accused were not brought to the dock the normal way, but were introduced from the judge's room. They arrived laughing and radiant, their breasts decorated with orders. They gave the impression of going to a wedding rather than to the dock to be tried for murder. [37]

In the meantime a certain song spread with lightning speed all over Germany. It was heard in strange places, such as a dancing party for young people in Hamburg:

> *A corpse there is a swimming*
> *In the Landwehr Canal*
> *Please give her to me*
> *But do not pet her too much.* [38]

The murders were presented, passed off and condoned as acts of impulse, and it wasn't till 1962 that one of the protagonists more or less conceded in an interview that they had all been obeying orders.

The last episode in the history of Berlin in revolution was set off by the elections to the National Assembly which took place on January 19. The bourgeois Volkspartei got 16.4 million votes, the SPD 11.4. It was the last time that social democracy would have the support of the majority in the entire history of the republic. In Berlin the Reds outnumbered the rest by nearly two to one and resentment at the dissolution and demobilization of soldiers' soviets was considerable. Meanwhile the Freikorps was signing up large numbers of new recruits.

On March 3 the Berlin soviet called for a general strike. Noske declared the city to be in a state of emergency and members of the Freikorps occupied police headquarters. Heavy fighting broke out and continued for some days, during which time the sailors seem to have attacked police headquarters. Artillery and mortars were used by both sides; the fighting was on a larger scale than anything witnessed before, and even involved aircraft. It was a bitter kind of a fight. When a spokesman from the sailors left police headquarters under a flag of truce, he was shot in the back. Yet the sailors were peculiarly trusting. It was finally decided that they should be disarmed, and three hundred were lured into a paymaster's office with the promise of money. Twenty-nine were butchered by machine-gun fire and the rest were thrown into prison.

Atrocities aside, Count Kessler found the two sides enjoying a peculiar relationship. He observed a troop of left-wing soldiers marching with a band down Unter den Linden, straight past a Freikorps unit which did nothing, while in the background he could see a poster inviting all and sundry to a ball to discover who had the most beautiful pair of legs in Berlin.

As the Spartacists were pushed ever further east toward the suburb of Lichtenberg, the atmosphere grew increasingly violent. In certain parts of town Freikorps men were found lynched or with their throats cut. The Freikorps treated their own prisoners dreadfully, from spitting in their face, to lashing them across the face with whips, to putting them up against a wall.[39] The "White terror," as they were known, were the most violent element that Berlin had seen to date. Noske had announced that anyone found with a weapon in his hand would be shot on sight. It was an announcement which the Whites took literally. A climate of amazing military brutality and "overkill" now sets the style of revolution and its repression and it was the dominant mood of the right wing for years to come. For days after the collapse of resistance, the Freikorps continued to arrest and execute its enemies and others. One day outside the Eden Hotel a lieutenant shot a private because he was without papers and answered back a little rudely.[40] It was to such a level of arbitrary violence that Noske and his men had reduced the capital.

Noske, however, was in a position to assure the National Assembly that order had been restored. When charged with condoning an excessive degree of violence, the once-reluctant "bloodhound" who appears to have warmed to the task replied, "When you cut wood, the chips must fly." Philip Scheidemann said of Noske to the British ambassador: "He was a good man; he shot in case of necessity." The total number of his victims came to at least 1,200. It is small wonder one recalls that the Freikorps made use of artillery, aircraft, armor and flame throwers against the wretched Spartacists. Berlin was not released from martial law until eight months had passed, on December 6, 1919.

ABOVE: *Mess time, revolutionary sailors in the Royal Mews, 1918.*
BELOW: *A photographer finds cover during the street fighting in Berlin, 1918.*

ABOVE: *Karl Liebknecht and Rosa Luxemburg.*
BELOW: *The occupation of the Vorwärts Newspaper office, January 1919.*

"Blase" by Max Beckmann. *"Nude Cabaret" by Max Beckmann.*

BELOW: *Noske's men in action, March 1919.*

A Bavarian Freikorpsman.

3
Munich 1918-19

In many ways the Bavarian revolution was more extreme than its Prussian counterpart. Munich actually had a soviet, then a Communist government for a short time. There was fighting involving a Freikorps army of one hundred thousand. There were extremes of lunacy, idealism, sexual excess and atrocity. In short, it was all a very Bavarian affair.

Bavarians neither resemble nor like the Prussians. It has been said that if ever a Prussian were to have the temerity to climb upon a table in Munich's greatest beer hall, the Hofbräuhaus, and yell, "I'm a Prussian," he would be stoned to death within seconds with heavy one-liter beer mugs, the Münchener's favorite side arm. Unlike the "Saupreuss," Prussian swine, the Bavarians love food, wine, culture and the Catholic church. They are extremely conscious of being Bavarian, and are prepared to bring extremes of violence to the defense not only of the physical manifestations of their culture, such as the twin towers of the Frauenkirche, but also to the defense of the Bavarian idea: a small-town idea, the amplification of a typical municipal-council mentality. The Bavarian way of life—part conservative, part happy-go-lucky with Bohemian overtones—is defended with a savage and deliberately close-minded passion. In other words, it might be said that Bavaria is Germany's Deep South.

It may seem surprising that Bavaria had a revolution at all. Yet it should be remembered that Bavarians are both unstable and unpredictable. They had, after all, run Lola Montez, Louis I's famous mistress, out of Munich not so many years earlier and now, almost by chance, they had done the same thing to Louis III. As the writer Zarek put it:

(Bavarians) are an ardent, head-strong, full-blooded people for whom drinking provides the meaning and end of life. A citizen of Munich was capable of quarreling with his best friend over beer mugs, killing the said best friend with one of the said beer mugs, bitterly repenting the whole affair the

49

next morning. He was usually found by the police at prayer in the local church. [1]

On the morning of November 7, 1918, most of the population of Munich was to be found demonstrating, and cursing their "old un-witting king." They were under the influence of the orator Kurt Eisner, who has been variously described. "A dirty little fellow," Zarek calls him, but others have seen him differently. Half-Jewish, a confirmed socialist, he had been to prison for inciting poison-gas workers to strike in January 1918. He observed at that time he was risking his life: "But what does my little life matter?" On another occasion he spoke out in Switzerland against the German view of the war, acknowledging that the speech was quite likely to be his death warrant. Eisner had a great sense of family and of decency. He was small and slight, with gray hair falling over his collar; with calm, short-sighted eyes, a lined face, and small feminine hands; with a will to action and no fear of death. This was the man who led Bavaria into revolution.

That night there was riot in the streets around the royal palace. Unfortunately, there were lights on in the royal living quarters. . . . If that had not been so, the people would have thought the old king was asleep and perhaps have come back tomorrow. And tomorrow. Well, one never knows in Bavaria what tomorrow will bring. That day, however, Eisner had written an article pointing out that the king's dairy farms were incompetently run, and the king was now driven from his palace by a shout from a thousand throats: "Milk thief!" The next morning Eisner proclaimed a socialist and separatist republic. He was to be its prime minister for three short months. [2]

It was a strange kind of revolution. As another observer commented:

The victors suffered agonies of triumph. They had managed to make a revolution that had succeeded because no one opposed them. Had the fire brigade been called out at the right moment and turned the hoses on them, they would have been washed under. [3]

The socialist revolution caught most people by surprise. The Bavarian minister of war was alarmed: "My God, revolution. And here I am still in uniform." [4] From the start it was led by left-wing intellectuals presenting themselves as the workers' friend. One rather successful writer, finding himself too well dressed to appear on a public platform, wired an SOS home: "Send oldest greatcoat." [5] Many young officers were initially at a loss. They imagined they would be deposed by soldiers' soviets; but they were quite wrong. When some of their number used the traditional socialist weapon, threatening to strike they were reassured by the minister of war that they would remain in authority, with the proviso that all orders written by the commanding officer be countersigned by a member of the soldiers' soviet. This was proclaimed on November 11:

Soldiers, all officers and civil servants have resumed their positions in accordance with the wishes of an overwhelming majority of the soldiers' soviet.

Soldiers, demobilization has not yet begun. The officers have returned with the best intentions on order of the minister to secure the return home of hundreds and thousands of your comrades at the front. The officers come back to you not as your superiors but as soldiers who wish to work for the common good of our people. You are not obliged to salute them on or off duty. . . . The soldiers' soviet of Munich reminds officers at all times to remain aware of the new spirit of the Free People's State of Bavaria, to remove shoulder straps, to recognize a fait accompli *and work as hard for it as have the soldiers since their victorious revolution, in their efforts to maintain and assure order.* [6]

The revolutionary and playwright Ernst Toller observed that what was required was a "Bavarian revolution of love."

Unfortunately, though scarcely surprisingly, the Eisner-Toller line found comparatively little popular support. Although Eisner had hoped to gain 90 percent of the vote in the January elections, he had to settle for less than 2 percent. He hung on for six weeks trying to form a coalition, but abandoned the attempt. On his way to resign in favor of Auer—a more conventional social democrat and leader of the Majority Socialists—he was shot by Count Arco auf Valley, a right-wing anti-Semite of Jewish extraction who was trying to prove that his Jewish blood should not be held against him, and that he was as good an enemy of republicanism as the next officer.

The diet was in session at the time. One of Eisner's bodyguards, stained with blood, burst into the VIP's gallery, pointing his finger at Eisner's wife and stammering that her husband had been shot. Half an hour later a man in an army greatcoat walked up to Auer, whom he held responsible for the assassination, and shot him. The wound was not fatal. He fired two more shots at Auer, killing two other deputies, then ran out in the confusion. The man, who was discovered to be a butcher named Lindner and a member of a soviet, was eventually sentenced to fifteen years in prison.

The soldiers defending the chamber turned their machine guns in on it, threatening to gun down various deputies in revenge for Eisner's death. They were requested to refrain, and complied sullenly. Some deputies were hospitalized with shock. Others went home, entering by the front door and leaving at once by back windows. [7] There was tremendous tension that night and for some days a 9 P.M. curfew was imposed.

After a power struggle between the Majority Socialists under a certain Hoffmann and a group of intellectual bohemian radicals headed by Toller, Hoffman founded a government on March 7. Exactly a month later, Toller staged a coup, proclaiming the Soviet Republic of Bavaria, and obliging Hoffmann and his government to flee to Bamberg. Bavaria now had two governments.

The six days of Toller's régime was a period of high unreality. It began with a letter from Hoffmann, who wrote to inquire whether the new Soviet Republic was prepared to pay pensions to former socialist ministers. Toller's own policies were no less eccentric, with that particular eccentricity which occurs when a thinking man has power thrust suddenly upon him. He devised a new form of currency: *"Schwundgeld,"* or vanishing money. And to encourage his people to spend, he decreed that the currency would lose one-thousandth of its value every week.

The most exotic member of Toller's—indeed of any German government—was Dr. Lipp, the people's commissar for foreign affairs. Appointed for his big beard and frock coat, and for being an alleged acquaintance of the pope, Dr. Lipp was perfectly mad. He dispatched a telegram to his Holiness:

Proletariat of Upper Bavaria united. Socialists and Independent Socialists and Communists firmly as one, together with Farmer's Union. Liberal bourgeoisie totally disarmed as Prussian agents. Cowardly Hoffmann who took away the keys of my lavatory in his flight now established at Bamberg. . . . Receiving coal and food in tremendous quantities from Switzerland and Italy. We want peace for ever, Immannuel Kant, Von Ewiger Freiheit, 1795. Theses 2–5. Prussia only wants armistice to prepare for her revenge.

He subsequently declared war on Switzerland and Würtemberg for failing to provide the sixty locomotives he had demanded of them.

On the morning it was decided to pack the people's commissar off to a sanatorium, Lipp had filled the Foreign Office with red carnations. He was concerned about a small paddle found in the ex-king's bathroom, scandalized that the king might have spent hours in his bath playing with toy boats. When asked to resign he complied with sadness: "Even this will I do for the republic." [8]

The Toller régime had not enjoyed the support of the Communists, and the government was brought down when the Bamberg socialists attempted to recapture Munich. A trainload of counterrevolutionaries, arrived on April 13. Sympathetic soldiers arrested the leaders of the Soviet Republic, but they missed Toller when they came to arrest him and had to content themselves with the removal of his large collection of neck ties. They retained control of the area around the station until the Communists fought back with soldiers and workers. The station was retaken after heavy fighting, whereupon the disappointed putschists took their train back to Bamberg. Happily they had kept up steam in the engine.

It was at this point that the Communists, Eugen Leviné and Max Levien, distinctly un-Bavarian names, proclaimed a Communist Soviet Republic. Leviné, a Bolshevik of Russian extraction, was a well-schooled Marxist and a trained revolutionary. He was an intelligent and resolute man. Levien was scarcely his equal: he had been a militant patriot during the war and was now a militant pacifist. Twenty-six years old, he favored massive riding boots and a Napoleonic manner.

The Communists hoped to start a political groundswell throughout Germany. The idea of a German revolution originating from Munich would also appeal to Hitler in four years' time. However, in neither case was a groundswell forthcoming. Leviné's movement has been described as a Leninist revolution without a Lenin. Certainly there were attempts to apply Bolshevik principles of agrarian reform, which entailed going into the country and obliging peasants to give up their grain and milk. This policy had proved disastrous enough in Russia and, as Toller observed, anyone seeking to execute it in Bavaria would not have survived long enough to call on the second farm. The Communists did succeed in commandeering large quantities of food in Munich itself, but they tended to retain it for their own use rather than redistributing it. There were, however, examples of generosity. When some revolutionary soldiers had to search the pantry of an elderly historian for hoarded food, and they saw how poorly stocked it was, one of them offered to put the professor in touch with his own black market contacts.[9]

The image that the Communist government projected was of Red terror. It was indeed a time of great violence and excess. Drunken Red Guards prowled the streets in search of loot, and remarkable orgies took place in the Wittelsbach Palace, now the Communist HQ. Their army has been described as the highest paid in history, counting free liquor and free whores among its fringe benefits. It should be recalled that, as a Catholic carnival town, Munich was accustomed to going on the rampage. The Red revolution became a kind of violent carnival with a peculiar streak of carnival lunacy running through it. Ernst Toller came across a girl who had enjoyed the enforced attentions of some twenty men in their barracks. He sent her off to a hospital and on the way she asked for a rest. She was left in the care of a sentry, but when Toller returned he found that she had departed with him.[10]

The carnival was brought to an abrupt halt however. The Hoffmann government had attempted an attack on Munich only to be routed at Dachau. They now called on Noske's Freikorps to help them recapture the city. There was nothing funny about what followed.

Munich was rapidly surrounded by one hundred thousand men. The Red defending army proved to be almost totally ineffective. It was founded on principles of free will, sympathy and self-discipline, principles which, as Toller said, were quite unacceptable to veterans of the Imperial Army. They longed for the old days and deserted in droves. Matters were made no easier by the fact that the Red battle plan was drawn up by a man who later turned out to be a White agent.

As the Freikorps moved in, the Reds were told that the city was simply not defensible. The only people still enjoying themselves as the ring tightened were the children, who continued to play at revolution and arrest one another. The Whites moved into Munich on May Day, meeting only light resistance. The next day Thomas Mann's twelve-year-old son Klaus wrote in his diary:

Before lunch we played rounders and at the same time listened to the noise of the guns. The Reds and the Whites are fighting. Later we looked at the big machine gun posted near our house. There is no bread. Fanny has made a sort of cake instead. Read a fine story by Walter Scott. [11]

Dr. Karl Heck, a student at Tübingen, had served in the war and had now joined a student unit of the Freikorps with forty-three other members of his corporation. They had advanced towards Munich through Augsburg, where they had forced some Reds out of a munitions dump after a short fire fight. The march on Munich was one of his pleasantest memories. The people of Augsburg had been delighted to see the end of civil war and Red terror. They gave the soldiers little gifts and arranged dances in their honor. They caught two Red leaders, who were shot after a court-martial. The attack on Munich itself was easy; the artillery coped with any pockets of resistance. The next day, the third, Dr. Heck's unit took part in house-to-house searches. They found a lot of weapons and a wounded Red hiding under bales of cloth in a tailor's shop.

A day later there was a victory parade, and afterwards the unit had time to wander about and look up old friends. After an address by a General Haas, they left Munich by train on May 8, singing their student songs. At Tübingen they received a hero's welcome.

The unit's only casualty occurred on the journey home. One of their number, Hans Scheid, elected to travel not in the compartment but on the carriage roof. He failed to notice a low wire, which swept him off, but fortunately he only suffered minor injuries. On the whole, Dr. Heck found that the student units restrained others from excessive violence. Indeed, although he accepts that World War One Russian POWs who fought with the Reds against the Whites were massacred to a man, he encountered very little violence after the fighting ended. There was no cause for violence, he felt. The students were all close friends and comrades; they had suffered no losses; they felt no bitterness. They had had a good time.

54

Dr. Heck was lucky to have missed the worst of the White terror, for a White terror there was. In a limited sense it was provoked. The Reds had taken hostages, and when the Freikorps closed in, they panicked and shot more than twenty of them. There can be no doubt that this assassination acted as a catalyst, yet the reaction which it brought about was out of all proportion.

The Freikorps got out of hand. Its leaders insisted that there should be no shootings without court-martials, but these seldom happened, or if they did they were perfunctory affairs.

"I hereby summon a court-martial; members are myself, the chief of staff and the ordnance officer. I order the death penalty by hanging be applied at once. Agreed?"

The accused was hanged publicly within two minutes.[12]

On the matter of killing in general, one Freikorps officer said:

Gentlemen! Anyone who does not now understand that there is a lot of hard work to be done here or whose conscience bothers him had better depart. It is a great deal better to kill a few innocent people than to let one guilty man escape. . . . You know what to do: shoot, and report the prisoner attacked you or tried to escape.[13]

Another observer remembers:

Two of my men approached a woman we found in the street. She tried to bite them. A blow on the mouth brought her to reason. They laid her over a wagon tongue and hit her so often with sticks that not a white spot remained on her back.[14]

The White terror was dreadfully indiscriminate. It was used by the inhabitants of Munich to settle old scores; a denunciation was usually enough to get an enemy shot. Others were killed by mistake. A number of Munich chimney sweeps, who used to have little red flags on their carts, were shot by the Prussian Freikorps before it could be explained to them that they were sweeps and not Red Guards. Twenty-one members of a Catholic club were found congregating and arrested on suspicion. The official report continues:

The group was arrested by government troops and taken to a prison on the Karoliner Platz. Around 9 P.M. a group of armed Bavarian soldiers broke in, took them for Spartacists, and shot all twenty-one.[15]

The house-to-house searches were frequently used as pretexts for looting, although the Freikorps punished looters when it discovered them. Its main objective, however, was to purge Munich of Reds once and for all. Most of the revolutionary leaders were shot. As one Freikorps man reported:

The ring leaders were hotly pursued from the start. Landauer was captured . . . on May 1. He was subsequently killed in prison by soldiers. Mühsam, the noble anarchist, was arrested and like ex-general Toller received a long prison sentence. The commander in chief Egelhofer was found hiding under dirty laundry on May 2 and was shot the next day while attempting to escape. Leviné, arrested on May 3, was shot after a court-martial. Sontheimer had to pay with his life as well. The man responsible for killing the hostages, Seidel, tried to escape after the court-martial passed sentence. One of his escort observed correctly that a bullet was too good for him, and beat the creature to death. Six others were shot by decree on September 19, others sentenced to forced labor. It was a great clean-up. [16]

Toller was walked past a wall against which prisoners had been shot and wondered why the bullet marks were so low, only to be told that an instant death was too good for swine like him. They were gut-shot instead.

Scheusinger, a soviet leader, was taken out. First he was obliged to watch his fellow prisoners collapse under the volley.

. . . they fell backward like so many sacks. After the main volley there were a few irregular shots, and one man was still screaming with two bullets in his body. One of the squad went up to within two yards and finished him off. [17]

Scheusinger himself was just about to be shot when a reprieve arrived. Thirty seconds later and it would have been all over.

This brief period of history can be summed up with a single image—a blood-spattered wall:

The high wall on the other side was spattered with blood. When I came closer I saw spattered brains. Tiny bits of gray brains were stuck onto the wall among splotches of blood. The blood had run down the walls as if it had been splashed out of pails over a stretch of at least fifty feet. Between the streaks of blood were lighter spots where the bullets had struck the wall, so many spots that you couldn't count them. [18]

Said Noske to the commanding officer of the White army:

I am extremely pleased with the discreet and wholly successful way in which you have conducted operations in Munich; please convey my thanks to your troops. [19]

While Toller and other revolutionaries went to prison, where they conducted elaborate homosexual courts of love, Munich remained in a state of apparent peace. Everyone pretended that neither revolution nor White terror had ever happened. Yet things in Munich would never be the same. The various parties remained ready to spring at each other's throats at a moment's notice.

In the meantime the Bavarians had proved to themselves, and others, to what lengths they were prepared to go to defend their Bavarian idea. One historian even maintains that it was the threat to that idea, and the response to that threat, which was to make Bavaria the Nazi stronghold that it would become.

ABOVE: *Munich 1919—infantrymen in the city.*
BELOW: *An emergency billet.*

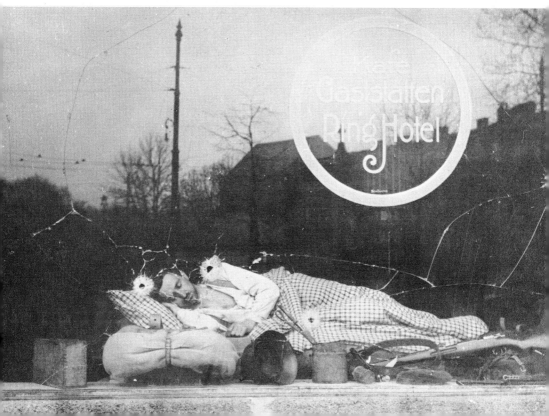

Ernst Toller   *Max Levien*
BELOW: *Members of von Epp's Bavarian Freikorps.*

ABOVE: *Starving citizens of Munich tear apart the remains of a horse.*
BELOW: *A red guard under arrest.*

A man is searched for weapons by Kapp soldiers.

60

4

The Kapp Putsch

MUNICH WAS NOT the Freikorps' last campaign by any means. They were to see action against other Reds in the Ruhr and, more important, on the eastern frontier against Poles and Latvians. The Freikorps, or Free-booters as they were known after the *Landesknechte* of the Thirty Years War, fought there brilliantly, for Germany and for the sake of the fight. In a war which saw astounding atrocities, few prisoners and much mutilation of bodies both dead and sometimes alive, their spirit, sense of comradeship and courage were outstanding.

The Freikorps initially enjoyed government support, and continued to receive unofficial aid long after they had been ordered to withdraw. The official change of heart seems to have been brought about by Allied pressure. Eventually the Freikorps were obliged to return from the Baltic provinces, and to disband. This convinced them that once again the German army had been betrayed on the home front. This sense of betrayal was magnified beyond measure by Germany's signing of the Versailles Treaty, the treaty of shame. From that moment the Freikorps had a mission: to overthrow the government that had brought disgrace upon the nation. Whenever they could, they kept their units together, even if this meant going to work on East Prussian agricultural estates as a "laboring force."

One of the most prominent leaders of the Freikorps was Captain Ehrhardt, once a corvette commander in the Imperial Navy. In January 1919 he had formed a small band to fight the Reds in Wilhelmshaven and was so successful that Noske instructed him to raise a more sub-stantial troop, which became the Ehrhardt 2nd Marine Brigade. It saw action in Brunswick and Upper Silesia, and was later ordered to Döberitz, twenty miles from Berlin, to guard the capital against Reds. A crack Freikorps unit, its attitudes were reflected in some of its pass-words for September 1919:

Black and gold (the republican colors)
Incredible
League of Nations: nonsense
Erzberger (signatory of the Versailles Treaty with little time to live
before assassination)
Grave digger
Marine Brigade: Phoenix
Poles: Smash them [1]

They were eventually ordered to disband, a command which they greeted with a parade to celebrate their first birthday. The *Deutsche Zeitung* for March 4, 1920 reported the event:

On Döberitz Field the 2nd Marine Brigade stands, fully armed, under its CO, Captain Ehrhardt. Crack troops, that held firm fighting the enemy, both without and within. Steeped in patriotism, discipline, comradeship and loyalty to their leader, the brigade has given priceless, unselfish assistance to the present government in the maintenance of law and order from Wilhelmshaven to Berlin, Brunswick, Munich and Upper Silesia. Today the government, now confident of survival, orders its dissolution.

The first birthday parade was held on March 1 before Their Excellencies von Lüttwitz and von Throta. With band playing, banners waving, storm troopers, infantry, artillery, machine-gun and mortar companies, filed past in perfect order. Then a field service was held under a blue sky, like the old days. Then sports and a get-together in the evening, all like the old days. Even the weather was Hohenzollern weather. Only a single man was missing [i.e., the kaiser]. [2]

The brigade was not to be dissolved, however. For some months Gustav Kapp, a Prussian bureaucrat and founder of the Fatherland Party, had been plotting to overthrow the government. He had first approached various generals including von Seeckt, the commander-in-chief, for support, but found them lukewarm to neutral. He finally joined forces with the hot-headed and mentally limited General von Lüttwitz, commander of the Freikorps around Berlin. He, too, failed to get any support from the regular army, so instead he turned to Ehrhardt's 2nd Marine Brigade.

In the early days of March 1920 the atmosphere in Berlin was charged. There was the feeling that something was about to explode. A week before the putsch an ugly scene took place in the Adlon Hotel. Prince Joachim, officer cadet of the house of Hohenzollern, was dining there with friends. After dinner he ordered the violinist to play "Deutschland, Deutschland über Alles." About half the room got to their feet, but two French officers dining there in uniform remained seated. The prince invited them to rise, and when they declined, he and his party began to pelt them with wine glasses. One Frenchman collapsed. The police arrived just as the *chef de cuisine* appeared in full regalia, forbidding the violinist ever to play that tune again. Joachim was arrested. [3]

Another celebration of the old values occurred a couple of days later. Gross Lichterfelde, the cadet academy, had been the one great private school in Germany. Its graduates became a caste within a caste. At HKA, as it was known, discipline was dreadfully tough. Inmates even had to go to breakfast on the march. In 1920 it was disbanded and on March 10 of that year it held its farewell parade.

Sitting in my room in the deepening twilight I suddenly heard the stirring music of "Fridericus Rex." I went to the window and below I saw the cadets marching in columns of four across the Potsdamer Platz in their blue trousers with red facings and their gold-mounted Pickelhauben [Prussian helmets]. *A company of the Guards Schutzen regiment followed them like a rear guard. At the head of the column marched the older generation of alumni, generals and colonels who had grown gray in the service, in a uniform representing the flower of the army in dissolution and of regiments doomed to disappear—Guards, Cuirassiers, Foot Guards, Death's Head Hussars, Foot Artillery, Uhlans—like a parade of ghosts. . . . The cadets marched at parade step in perfect time, with a precision of dressing so faultless that they might have been a regiment of guards. As they kept their eyes fixed straight ahead on the colors of their corps, their young faces seemed strangely expressionless and immobile as though they mastered some emotion too deep for tears. At a corner of the square, a German general mounted on a gray horse took their salute and as their eyes turned toward him it seemed as though a mighty cry went up from a thousand hearts: "Morituri te salutamus."* [4]

Two days later the Ehrhardt Brigade moved on Berlin. At 6 P.M. on March 12 Ehrhardt called his commanders together: "Gentlemen, I have promised General von Lüttwitz that tomorrow morning at 6 P.M. the brigade will be by the Brandenburger Tor. We shall recover our honor." [5] That night the brigade prepared itself and celebrated. Recovery, release, fulfillment were in the air. There was a sense of excitement and exhilaration of the kind that precedes the crossing of a Rubicon. "We are going to throw the government out," were the words on every lip, "we and our commander. Germany will be ours, will have our spirit, our will, our führer."[6]

The march to Berlin took place in almost total silence, on a warm night in early spring. "There were the fieldgray columns, ready to fight their own government as if it were a matter of course. It was the brigade, our brigade! Now it would show that it meant business. Here was the new army, so self-confident and self-contained that it set off for a military coup against its own government, as if it were conducting a

63

night exercise with blank cartridges. The quiet restrained noises of a great body of troops on the march was heard on the barracks road. Lanterns were reflected by steel helmets. ... It was a pleasure to march that night. Two thousand five hundred men on parade, two thousand five hundred men immaculate, armed to the teeth. Two thousand five hundred men with but a single goal." [7]

No one spoke, we were all preoccupied with but one thought. Each one of us savored the happiness. We march! And with us marches the spirit of a better Germany. We are the young guard that has been chosen for the deed. [8]

As the brigade swung toward Berlin, the government had a hurried conference with regular-army generals, asking them whether their army would support the legitimate government. One, Reinhardt, said it would; but von Seeckt was more concerned with the unity of the army than he was with the legitimate government. He replied:

Troops do not fire on troops. So you perhaps intend, Herr Minister, that a battle be fought before the Brandenburger Tor between troops that have fought side by side against a common enemy? When Reichswehr fires on Reichswehr, then all comradeship within the officer corps will have vanished.

Thus Ehrhardt's men entered Berlin virtually unopposed. At one moment they were faced with a small home-guard unit dressed in civilian overcoats and steel helmets—except for one man who was wearing a straw hat. After assessing the situation, the civilians prudently went home.

The brigade sang as they marched into the city:

> Hakenkreuz am Stahlhelm
> Schwarz weiss rotes Band
> Die Brigade Ehrhardt
> Werden wir genannt. [9]

> Swastika on helmet
> Black white red brassard
> The Ehrhardt Brigade
> Is what we are called.

The song was to be heard for many years—except that line three came to read: "*Sturmabteilung Hitler.*"

The brigade had the appearance of a crack force. Looking at countless pictures of Freikorps and regular army units in the course of researching this book, I soon found it easy to pick out the putschist units without reference to any written information. The men of the Ehrhardt Brigade were immaculately turned out. Their uniforms were cleaner and better pressed, the men better shaven and sprucer than any other regular or irregular military units of the age, many of whom had a sad and scruffy appearance.

Within Berlin itself they did encounter a little opposition. They were fired on by Spartacists in Berlin East, and even in the West there was a small amount of shooting. The journalist Bella Fromm was riding her horse, Strolch, through the Uhlandstrasse toward the Tiergarten at the time.

We ran into an almost solid hail of bullets at the railway bridge. . . . Strolch, whom I had bought from an officer, paid no attention. . . . He trotted on without so much as pricking his ears. My friend . . . had a harder time of it with my other horse, Totila, who bolted and couldn't be pulled up until he had put two miles between himself and the shooting. [10]

As the men moved toward the Brandenburger Tor, they were greeted by Kapp, and by General Ludendorff in civilian dress, who just happened to be out for a walk at quarter to seven on a spring morning. Fifteen minutes later they marched through the gate and down the Wilhelm-strasse. They quickly deployed, occupying government buildings and key points with very considerable efficiency.

The putschists had been expected, and various persons had done their utmost to sabotage things for them. The sheer feebleness of their actions says much for that deadly lack of purpose and conviction found in the heart of official Weimar. Thus we find an SPD deputy, one Alfringshaus, changing round the name plaques of the SPD and right-wing, monarchist, Deutschnational committee rooms in the Reichstag. "At least the vandals will smash the wrong typewriters," he said.[11] Equally ineffectual were the actions of the head of the chancellor's office. When the government, almost to a man, withdrew in haste to Dresden, he stayed behind and prepared for the vandals. "I remembered during the first revolution how bare the first official passes looked without proper stamps. So I collected all the chancellory stamps and smuggled them out." [12] In addition to such heady action, he told the switch-board girl she was to go home for a week. She wondered if it would be deducted from her summer holiday.

Collapse of morale among other minor officials who had stayed behind to be captured was total. Prostrate with fear and despair, they sat in a darkened room expecting to be shot. One member of the government, Heine, kept asserting that no one would touch him as he had been intending to resign. [13]

The official German government spent an uncomfortable few days. Dresden, their initial refuge, seemed to them uncomfortably close to Berlin. They were met there by General Maercker of the Volunteer Rifles with orders to arrest them. They explained to Maercker that the Kapp government was not legitimate and lacked the authority to order their arrest. He graciously replied that he would do his utmost to "interpret his orders in favor of the Ebert régime."

The Ebert régime, however, had prudently left for Stuttgart by car, but unfortunately they ran out of fuel and were forced to switch to a train. There were frequent document checks. One official asked to see Ebert's papers and read, "Friedrich Ebert, Reichpräsident." He handed them back without looking up. They arrived in Munich where they were obliged to change trains for Stuttgart. While they waited they had coffee in the station restaurant. Reichskanzler Bauer was worried about a suitcase sent on in advance, because he needed a clean collar, size 44.

The image of the first democratic government of Germany huddled together on a station platform, worrying about luggage, passing unnoticed, unacclaimed, having traveled incognito across the breadth of Germany, spells the doom of German democracy. On the train ride back to Berlin after the fall of Kapp, most of the government got very drunk and ended up vomiting in one another's compartments.

The Kappists had hoped for a groundswell of response right across Germany. They looked, in particular, to Munich for support, but there was none forthcoming. There was a certain amount of fighting between Reds and Freikorps in other towns, however. Ernst von Salomon and his Freikorps unit were trapped in a building in Hamburg and after a stiff fight they were obliged to surrender. Their leaders were shot or lynched, and they all had to run the gauntlet between rows of massive Red Guards. There was fighting in Dresden, too. After a bullet hit a Rubens in the Zwinger Gallery, the painter Kokoschka issued a public appeal to persons of all persuasions, asking them not to indulge in warlike activity in front of the gallery and requesting that they stick to places where human culture would not be endangered.

The Kapp government remained the master of Berlin for six days. The troops themselves were puzzled by the lack of military opposition and the extreme hostility of the population. They moved through the city, said one observer, as if in a "moral vacuum," in, but not of it. Some moved faster than others. The officers tended to drive around town in vehicles which they had commandeered at pistol point. They were more punctilious in other respects, however, taking care to salute the rare civilians who raised their hats to them.

The truth was that having conquered Berlin the conquerors had no idea what to do with it. On the first Saturday of his rule Kapp dissolved the Prussian State Legislature, and had reinstated it by the following Monday. He arrested the Prussian Cabinet, and then ordered its release. He tried to win over the students of Berlin University by abolishing all examinations. He confiscated all the matzo flour for the impending Passover. It rapidly emerged that he was a political bankrupt, and he had lost all support, whereupon he announced that he had accomplished all he had set out to do, and resigned in favor of von Lüttwitz. He then took a plane to Sweden.

It was not just his own hopelessness that was the undoing of Kapp. The putsch saw the last effective anti-right-wing action of Weimar Berlin. Shortly after the troops moved in, a general strike broke out. Unlike the partial general strike of November 1918, the workers really shut down the city and all its services—garbage, water, power, light and transport. Nothing moved. There was a slogan:

All Räder stehen still
Wenn der Arbeiter es will.

All the wheels are standing still
When it is the workers' will.

"Berlin was blacked out, watered out," observed one eyewitness. "The Adlon stood like a great empty barrack. Locked, with the reception clerk acting as a night porter." [14] There were no newspapers, so the Kappists tried to communicate with the people by means of pamphlets which they distributed. Berlin's verdict: "They promised many things."

It soon became clear to all concerned in the putsch that their position was untenable. Bitterly Ehrhardt accepted defeat and his brigade pulled out without a fight. As they marched, watched by silent crowds, a boy burst out laughing. Two men broke ranks, hit him over the head and kicked him senseless. A machine gun fired a few bursts into the crowd and the 2nd Marine Brigade withdrew to Döberitz.

The men grew visibly more cheerful as they left the capital behind them, and soon they were singing again. R. G. Waite has given us an effective English rendering of one of their numbers:

Why should we cry when a putsch goes wrong
There's another one coming before very long. [15]

Indeed, they had little reason to cry. Kapp had promised them 16,000 gold marks if they overthrew Ebert's régime. They failed, but they received their bonus anyway—from the hands of Ebert, to soothe them in their discontent.

Official circles bent over backward in their favor. Count Kessler knew the owner of the house in which Kapp had lodged when planning his putsch. The home guard was detailed to search his room for incriminating documents. They were reluctant to go through the desk in case it contained anything of that kind, and only decided to do so when they realized that it was most unlikely that they would find anything. [16]

The pattern of violence, mingled with farce and lack of conviction which ran through the early history of the republic continued. After the troops left, the strike persisted for some days and Berlin remained in a state of unrest. There was anti-army action in Berlin East and elsewhere. J. H. Morgan recalls seeing the Potsdamer Platz on a spring afternoon, five days after the troops had left. A twelve-man police-cycle patrol pedaling across the square interrupted its course among the peaceful pedestrians to gun a man down with an automatic before pedaling on. [17] The army was also in the habit at this time of shooting up streets with machine guns, more or less indiscriminately. [18]

Farce and lack of conviction are to be found too in the subsequent history of the putsch. Not only was the Ehrhardt Brigade paid its reward, but instead of being disbanded it was incorporated into the army of the republic it had attempted to overthrow. Proceedings were instigated against the ringleaders, however, with the following results:

> *Amnestied:* 412
>
> *Dead or otherwise impossible to bring to trial:* 109
>
> *Case suspended:* 176
>
> *Not caught:* 7
>
> *Condemned to three years' fortress arrest:* 1

There were other political consequences. Noske was dismissed. Anyone in the War Ministry who had shown too much republican loyalty during the putsch found his career blocked. The republican general, Reinhardt, was also dismissed, and von Seeckt became commander-in-chief of the army. Shortly afterwards, when he was asked whether the army was politically reliable, he replied, "I do not know if it is reliable, but it obeys me."

The putsch had the effect of consolidating anti-republican feelings and demonstrating the essential feebleness of a government which could only reward the men who had plotted against it. The putschists themselves came away with a slight sense of failure and the readiness to learn from their mistakes. Were they to do it all over again, things would be very different. In the words of one lieutenant, "Everything would have been all right if we had just shot more people." [19]

The Kapp Putsch had repercussions in the Ruhr when Germany heard the news that a Red army had "occupied" key towns such as Essen. During the putsch the Ruhr had gone on general strike and when it returned to work there were calls, apparently, to Communists and Independent Socialists to renew strike action, calls which their leaders disowned. The Reichswehr then withdrew from the Ruhr towns although they had encountered no opposition, leaving the Ruhr in Communist hands. The Communists were used as a pretext to justify the movement of vast numbers of troops into the so-called Neutral Zone, a band thirty miles wide on the east bank of the Rhine, which was supposed to be demilitarized. The Allies had already allowed a limited number of troops to be kept there for a period which was just about to expire. Hence the Red army proved distinctly welcome as an excuse.

It was neither an elaborate nor a well-equipped fighting force, though its members were capable of acts of considerable courage and terrorism. A terrorist remembers:

To increase the explosive power of the bomb, which was large, I had planned to place it in a closed room in the town hall. A few seconds before midnight I ran toward the town hall with the bomb. Comrade Richard Loose was with me. The others were to watch the explosion from a safe distance. Loose was to throw a hand grenade as soon as I had set the bomb; in case the fuse did not function, the grenade would detonate the bomb. As I was trying the main door to the police station, into which I had decided to throw the bomb, I lit the fuse with my cigarette. Commander Loose had released the safety catch of the grenade. Then I noticed to my horror that the door was locked. We were lost.

I was holding the ignited bomb in my hand, while Loose held the grenade. We threw them into a corner almost simultaneously. The grenade exploded. A splinter struck my face and blood began to flow. By acting quickly, Comrade Loose saved my life. When he noticed that my face was bleeding and that I was staggering, he took hold of me quickly, pulled me down the steps, and walked me round the corner. At this moment the surrounding buildings were shaken by a tremendous explosion. A number of windows were smashed, and huge blocks of stone rolled out onto the street. [20]

When the Reichswehr and the Freikorps finally attacked the Reds, they simply butchered them. They moved in on Easter Sunday. The heaviest fighting was in and around Essen, which fell on April 7. Even the army admitted that it had been brutal. People were dragged from cars and beaten to death, or shot, regardless of whether they had been Red Guards or not. Others were shot in front of their wives and children. [21] Prisoners were not taken. As a certain Major von Guichardt observed, "Most of these fellows are young men who during five years of war had no paternal discipline, and, as it is too late to train them, the best thing is to wipe them out." [22]

The Freikorps were not particularly ashamed of their role in the butchery:

Wischenhofen April 2, 1920— I have finally joined my company. . . . Yesterday at one o'clock in the afternoon we staged our first attack. If I were to tell you everything you wouldn't believe me. No quarter is given. We even shot the wounded. There is terrific, unbelievable enthusiasm. Our battalion has had two men killed, the Reds two or three hundred. Anyone we capture first gets the rifle butt then the bullet. We even shot two Red Cross nurses on sight because they were carrying pistols. We shot the ladies with pleasure. How they cried and pleaded for their lives. No chance! [23]

Dr. Karl Heck had a more peaceful time with his student company as they moved into Dortmund. He did not know the Ruhr at all and was struck by the poor quality of life in an industrial town. However, he enjoyed being with his friends:

Since the expedition, as far as we were concerned, claimed no victims, and we had to spill no blood, we found our task an easy one and in retrospect it appears bathed in a particularly fine light." [24]

On leaving the Ruhr, Heck and two friends were making their way to Kiel in uniform. They arrived in Weimar at 1 A.M. to find it still in the hands of the Reds who had just fought off the army in a bloody battle. It had been agreed that the Reds would keep a low profile in town provided the army did not try to invade, which it was now apparently doing in the shape of the unwitting student soldiers. They spent the night at an inn and were arrested by Red Guards the next morning. Interrogated by the commanding officer, a brutal sergeant-major type in a leather jacket, and a civilian in a dirty morning coat—"a typical failed academic," Heck thought—they were taken for Kapp's men. When they persuaded their questioners that they were not, they were told to leave town after surrendering their weapons, for which they got receipts. They went back to their rooms, put on ties and white collars over their army shirts, as demobilized soldiers often did, and spent the day sightseeing before moving on to Kiel. Dr. Heck is still worried about having to give up his weapon. Had he as a Red fallen into Reichswehr hands, he would have been past worrying over fifty years ago.

ABOVE: *Kapp's men enter Berlin, March 14, 1920.*
BELOW: *The putschists—typically well turned out.*

A Kapp poster—the government of "freedom, order and action" calls to German men and women, promising elections within sixty days and announcing an end to the rule of usurers, Schiebers, good-for-nothings and betrayers of the people.

Deutsche Männer und Frauen!

Euch ruft die Regierung der Freiheit, der Ordnung und der Tat!

Die neue Regierung hat sich zum Treuhänder Eurer Freiheit, Eures Rechts auf Selbstbestimmung gemacht.

Die Wahlen zum verfassungsmässigen Reichstage werden binnen 60 Tagen stattfinden.

Die neue Regierung schafft Euch die Ordnung, die allein Deutschlands Wiederaufbau ermöglicht.

Die Herrschaft der Wucherer, der Schieber, der Nichtstuer und Volksverräter hat ein Ende.

BELOW: *A barricade in the Leipzigerstrasse.*

Die deutsche Gegenrevolution am 13. 3. 1920.
Militärische Absperrungen in der Leipziger Straße in Berlin.

ABOVE: *A Kapp armored train in Berlin.*
BELOW: *Kapp en route for Sweden.*

A French soldier guarding coal.

5

The Rhine and the Ruhr 1919-24

BY 1945 MOST children in the English countryside where I grew up were used to the spectacle of POWs working in their fields or in their gardens. We had some Italians and a Ukrainian who taught us anti-German songs on the mandoline, but he was exceptional. On the whole, we felt embarrassed by the prisoners, grown men in an obvious state of some humiliation. They had once been "dirty Jerries" but could no longer seriously be thought of as the enemy. We avoided catching their eye, and were thrown into fits of terrible embarrassment when they tried to talk to us. We were embarrassed because we found them a little frightening and, in the noblest sense of the word, pathetic.

Our fathers' attitudes to their POWs in 1918 was strikingly different. The difference helps to characterize the attitude of the Allies to a beaten enemy in the years of occupation, an attitude which played its part in the shaping of the antirepublican, antipacifist attitudes which were to be so dominant throughout the Weimar period. Alec Swan remembers something of the spirit of 1918:

You must realize when thinking about the extraordinary anti-German feeling at that time that people had got a tremendous shock from the war, all that trench business. I well remember riding my bicycle past some German POWs shouting something about Der Tag. *Even we children were imbued with this hate thing. As far as Europe was concerned, our statesmen were very small-minded indeed. "Make them pay." "Squeeze them till the pips squeak." And this was before the time that Chamberlain described Czecho-slovakia as "a small distant country about which we know very little."*

This was the attitude that dominated the Allies' treatment of their beaten enemy: repression combined with ignorance. There was no thought of actually helping Germany evolve political institutions which might help it to liberate itself from its imperial past. Instead, ignorant repression had the effect of kindling resentment without ever ensuring that the beaten enemy complied properly with the conditions imposed upon her by the peace treaty. The Allies antagonized without controlling, with an unreflective hostility. The press ran stories such as the following:

The examination of thousands of letters written by Germans to the Allied and neutral countries since the extension of the postal privilege to the inhabitants of the occupied Rhine Valley reveals a total lack of appreciation on the part of the Germans of the feelings existing toward them throughout the civilized world.

The great majority of the letters contain offers to do business, and plainly indicate that Germany has a tremendous reserve of wealth with which to resume her struggle for commercial and industrial supremacy. ... The Germans assume that they will be quite welcome as customers, and that business as usual will go on, the threads being caught up again just where they were broken off in 1914. [1]

One New York firm received a letter starting: "In reply to yours of June 6, 1914." [2]

It must be said that in certain circles, German attitudes toward the Allies were no less bitter, more so indeed.

KILL THE LOT
THE LAST GREAT JUDGMENT WILL HOLD YOU BLAMELESS

Every morning I walk through the Siegesallee to gaze upon the monuments of our heroes, the monuments which commemorate the race that for five hundred years slaved to make the lands of Brandenburg what they are today; the race which, daring everything, struggled for the unity of their people, and for the elevation of this race to that position of power which was theirs before the war. Every morning in the Allee, I see the triumphant soldiers of France and Britain, striding carelessly, cigarette in mouth, and staring ironically at the statues of the Hohenzollerns. Once I went on my way through the Brandenburger Tor and along the Budapeststrasse to the Potsdamer Platz. On the way I met six English soldiers. The Germans stared at them sullenly, they just laughed in return. Workers of Germany! It is time you realized the shame that the armistice and the quasi-peace have brought on you and your country. Do you not still carry in your hearts that pride of country which you cast into the mud on the ninth of November 1918? It will be hard not to rise under the influence of National Pride. The day will come when all your comrades will think: "We should thrash these fellows."

KILL THEM! THE LAST JUDGMENT WILL HOLD YOU BLAMELESS [3]

Whatever the feeling against the Allies, there was much about their policies immediately after the armistice that astonishes. It is true that the withholding of the "postal privilege" from the occupied territories might appear a mere irritant, but to deny the occupied population radio sets [4] was certainly an additional aggravation. Without a doubt, however, the most shameful feature of Allied policy was the maintenance of the food blockade until June 1919. [5] This was despite an appalling degree of infant mortality and universal undernourishment. Starvation, which had brought wartime Germany to its knees, was used as a political weapon, among other things to compel Germany to hand over her merchant fleet. [6] An English observer in Cologne noticed the universal effect of the diet upon German children, in much worse shape than their English counterparts, who had endured severe rationing owing to the U-boat war. [7] In February 1919 the weekly ration for an adult in that city amounted to $4\frac{1}{2}$ pounds of bread, 5 ounces of meat, 2 ounces of butter, 1 ounce of fat, $2\frac{1}{2}$ ounces of coffee and 7 ounces of jam. The result was a vast proliferation of food black marketeers, or "Hamster" as they were known, who would go into the country, going from farm to farm until they found someone who would do business with them. Returning to the cities, they had to pass checkpoints at the stations. Some displayed great ingenuity in the concealment of provisions about their persons, others were caught. A man with a starving family might have spent two days in the country searching for food, only to find his booty confiscated on arrival, obliging him to return home with nothing.

The black market was essential to avoid undernourishment, but it produced an unhealthy number of hustlers and profiteers, dealing in food, cocaine or medicine. They were known as *Schieber*, and they grew rich very fast indeed. I asked Herr Wallenberg whether *Schieber* were instantly recognizable. After a little thought, he said they were. I expected him to describe a person of flashy appearance and behavior, but the answer was simple and full of pathos: "If I saw a young man of my own age who appeared healthy and clearly had enough to eat, I could be certain that he was a *Schieber*."

Yet amid all this hustling and profiteering there remained an enormously widespread and underlying, quiet, German decency. Many families lived on the official ration out of sense of honor and public duty. Helena Boucholz-Starck describes her life in an impoverished East Prussian family of noble extraction just after the war:

My parents were always highly critical of the kaiser and his clique. But they were devout churchgoers, too. "Remain the subject of Authority." We were never Hamsters. . . . It made things very difficult for my mother. We got ourselves a goat which gave a little milk, because my father nearly died of undernourishment. That was the way we lived—today we'd be called naive. There were many who lived and thought that way in Germany, and thought no evil, did no evil to anyone.

Not everyone was so decent, however. Farms suffered from large-scale, systematic robbery from organized gangs numbering up to two hundred people. They would commandeer food stocks and even compel farmers to make them butter. [8] Many fortunes were made through such actions. The effect was a growing *Schieber* class, which stood out against the backdrop of utter economic misery as persons "for whom no price is too high, no pleasure too extravagant." [9] Small wonder that the Allies, who did so little officially to prevent starvation, who encouraged profiteering by sustaining shortages, earned little thanks from the beaten German nation and merely exacerbated that nation's endemic revanchism.

Defeat, particularly as it was administered in the Treaty of Versailles, was a traumatic experience for German patriots, reinforcing the sense of collapse and betrayal inaugurated by the armistice, abdication and civil war. The treaty was considered by the Germans to be punitive to a degree, designed to humiliate and strip the Fatherland. It must be admitted that in some respects it did have a flavor of excess about it. Persons unfamiliar with its contents might be surprised to learn that Germany was expected to continue paying reparations to the Allies in compensation for the war until the 1960s. The reparations issue became an obvious rallying point for anti-Allied animosity, a part of the national disgrace to which the "November Criminals" had assented. It is important to realize that many reparations were made in kind, in the shape of tangible objects which could be seen leaving the country. There is a railway line running through the middle of Bonn, and Alec Swan remembers seeing train after train going through carrying coal to France. The populace looked on, muttering "*Ententekohlen, Ententekohlen*" (coal for the Allies) bitterly beneath its breath.

Reparations did not do much toward rebuilding a brave new world. The tiny amount the Allies actually received was out of all proportion to the tremendous pressurehead of animosity which they built up. Moreover, the Allies did nothing to assist the young German republic, providing it with neither financial support nor moral guidance: "It will be the eternal reproach to the Allied policy that it had done nothing whatever to help the better elements in Germany consolidate their position." [10] Indeed, it might be argued that Allied policy—French policy in particular—never gave those "better elements" a chance. As the eyewitness accounts and recollections that make up the rest of the chapter demonstrate, it would not be excessive to say that Allied policy could be represented as having inhibited a normal rate of economic recovery and reinforced ever powerful and antidemocratic feelings which were founded in a deadly blend of jingoistic patriotism and economic crisis.

The first impression the British had of the occupation came via the army who felt they had moved into a hostile and conquered land. It will be recalled that absence of war damage was understandably resented by troops who had seen France and Flanders. Indeed, it is probable that the spectacle of Germany after World War II, devastated by Allied bombing, did much to set the humane and constructive attitudes of the second occupation. At the age of eight I must have been one of the first civilian tourists to visit Bremen. Nothing was standing. The entire city appeared to consist of neat piles of rubble at regular intervals where there had been buildings. As I chanted "Good old RAF" for the twentieth time, my father boxed my ears in an attempt to teach me sympathy for a beaten enemy.

The first occupiers were less sympathetic and were bent, quite understandably, on savoring the fruits of victory. Overnight Germans had become cowed second-class citizens. An Englishwoman proudly offers as an image of victory the following icon of "German servility":

A large German standing hat in hand before the fair-haired English girl stamping his pass is eloquent as to some lessons taught by the occupation. [11]

Initially, at least, the occupation régime was a severe one, with considerable restrictions on freedom. The British carried out their administration largely through the civil authority, who were told what to tell their own people. Where possible, direct contact with the civilian population was avoided, although red-capped MPs did direct the traffic. Among other regulations were:

A seven o'clock curfew. All civilians to be in their houses from 7 P.M. till morning. Practically no passes were issued in early days. When the Germans objected, as they objected on principle to everything, they were told that they had kept many French Belgians to a 6 P.M. curfew for the best part of four years. (Later Cologne curfew was extended to 9 P.M. and eventually to 11 P.M.)

Permits to circulate had to be secured by all, and they were liable to be asked for many times a day. No German might leave his zone without permission.

All telephones were disconnected. Owners could only use their motorcars by special authority.

A strict censorship was put on all letters and newspapers, the local examples of which were frequently stopped on the presses.

Public meetings might only be held with military sanction.

Compulsory registration of all civilians was enforced.

Identification numbers for all houses, flats and hotels, with a list of all inmates, duly kept up to date, had to be put up on the door. This public placarding ("as for a household with the plague") was in particular resented. . . .

Billeting. The civilian population had to provide housing, light, firing, service, plates, linen.

Central European time was changed to Greenwich.

. . . The one that Jerry found most difficult to swallow was the last named. The bubonic door lists did not bite into him so deeply as the appalling change to the meridian of Greenwich, veritable refinement of English cruelty! [12]

Another regulation detested by the Germans, and by most British officers, required civilians to take their hats off to them. "It is true," wrote a *Manchester Guardian* correspondent, "that in late 1918 and early 1919 British troops might knock the hats off civilians failing to comply, but the French, who had ordered the gesture in the first place, were still knocking hats off five years later!" [13] Many men in the occupied zones preferred to go bare-headed. Germans who refused to raise their hats to French officers were pushed into the gutter or even struck with riding crops. The English, however, according to one observer at least, were soon too bored by the whole business to bother to enforce it. [14]

Matters were not helped by the large numbers of restaurants, railway compartments and swimming pools marked "For Allied Troops Only," "No Germans Allowed Here." The signs may have been intended to keep "fraternization" to a minimum, and with good reason. Morale among the British troops was very low indeed. They wanted to go home. Indeed, they were seriously influenced by Spartacist agitators, and in February 1919 actually formed some soldiers' soviets. [15] In Cologne motor transport and bakers units went on strike, forming soviets, and this meant that the date of their demobilization had to be advanced. [16] Discipline grew increasingly slack. Colonial troops—South Africans, Australians and New Zealanders in particular—impatient to get home, grew rather wild. They were in the habit of commandeering steamers and joy riding up and down the Rhine. Indiscipline in the British army was dealt with by means of special companies of the Guards who would be sent out to "collect salutes" and would return with a batallion of non-saluters. [17]

Morale was not to be perfectly restored until the falling mark made rich men of the occupying armies. Yet the army did enjoy other consolations, witness this parody of a comic opera song:

> *Wo steht es denn geschrieben*
> *Du sollst nur Deutsche lieben?*
> *Man schwärmt ja auch für Engländer,*
> *Für Schottländer, Neuseeländer.*

> Where then is it written
> That you must love only Germans?
> They're crazy too for Englishmen,
> For Scotsmen and New Zealanders.

> *Komm mit mein schönes Mädchen,*
> *Es gibt auch Schockolädchen.*

Komm mit mir in mein Himmelreich.
Dort gibt es Büchsenfleisch.
    Come on, my pretty maiden,
    There are chocolates to be had.
    Come to my heavenly kindom.
    There you'll find bully-beef.

The English in the occupied zone felt strangely detached from the country in which they were staying. Alec Swan remembers seeing Germans raising their hats to English officers or getting off the pavement to walk past a sentry on duty, and is now bewildered to find that he accepted it all as a matter of course. On one occasion he was sitting in a tram in Cologne when he absentmindedly began to whistle. The other passengers took this to be a mortal insult—the musical equivalent of lounging in public with your hands in your pockets, a moral offense for which one could still pay dearly as late as 1960. *"Konzert, Konzert,"* went up the angry murmur. However, the young Englishman declined to stop, and as a last and rather unlovely gesture called behind him as he left the tram, *"Gott straff England."*

The sense of detached superiority which he felt was a cause of some sadness to his German teacher. On one occasion they had a difference of opinion about the French seizure of the Ruhr and Swan ended the discussion by saying, "Well, you know, we in England see things rather differently from you." The very decent lady was dreadfully distressed at his attitude. "Herr Swan," she said, and rightly, "you must never say or think that."

Being an Allied person in the occupied zone gave a man enormous prestige, made him feel above the world in which he had his being. Swan had a Dutch friend who sought to improve his position by masquerading as a South African. When I asked Swan if he felt secure in occupied Germany he replied:

Well, to some extent you felt contempt for the German police as being somewhat ineffective—you know, sort of small village policeman. As an Allied person you really felt above all that. Things were somewhat different in the rest of Germany. There you had to carry your passport. They used to have terrific meetings and Frau Dette, our German teacher, used to tell us how they would go across there and be addressed by rabble rousers and right-wing agitators, till their eyes streamed with grief for their stricken country. Outside the occupied zone one did not feel less secure exactly, but one certainly felt different. One avoided getting into political discussions.

The least unpopular elements among the occupying forces were, without any doubt, the Americans. Many returned home with the equivalent of GI war brides; and when the United States occupying forces pulled out and the French took over their zone, the Germans were bitterly sorry to see the "Sammies" go.

Whatever lasting hostility Tommies and Sammies might have succeeded in arousing, paled into insignificance when compared with the impact of the French. They displayed their full potential for vanity, pettiness, and short-sighted politicking on an unprecedented scale, doing untold damage to themselves in the long run. Although the men of Weimar preached peace and reconciliation with France, it was to be some forty years before France and Germany would be able to come to any kind of soundly based political understanding. Even now, talking to intelligent, European-minded Germans of that generation — such as Herr Wallenberg, who fought in a mixed unit against the Nazis, with French soldiers under his command — I was struck by the vehemence with which he condemned France's behavior and policies in the occupied zone. He believes that they made a substantial contribution to the rise of National Socialism, and helped to foster "patriotic" — that is to say, antirepublican — attitudes. An examination of French behavior in the occupied territory may help to explain why so many people found their policies unacceptable.

The French were in the habit of arresting German civil servants who failed to cooperate with them whole-heartedly. Officers were regularly known to take their whips to persons who did not yield the pavement to them fast enough. On one occasion, in occupied Essen, they even pursued some such offenders into a theater, interrupting a performance of King Lear. [18] When the locals ignored them or cut them dead, they were driven into paroxysms of wounded vanity, making them behave more provocatively still. [19]

Alec Swan, who lived in the French zone, agrees that the French behaved vilely, but points out that they had, of course, experienced the devastation of a third of their own country and had not undergone the most agreeable of occupations themselves. In such circumstances, he argues, their behavior was perhaps excusable. But whatever degree of excusable vileness they displayed, they accompanied it with a breathtaking capacity for administrative pettiness, the special quality that marks the French *fonctionnaire*. In Mannheim, in 1922, inhabitants had to apply to the French for permission to repair or even repaint their houses. In addition to such petty regulations there was an elaborate system of press, film and book censorship, on a scale quite surpassing that found in other zones.

Control of the local press was absolute. Suspension of publication for three months could be ordered in serious cases, and in the event of the repetition of an offense, permanent suppression. Most of the big popular German publications were banned entirely. . . . In 1920 there were 42 such suspen-

*sions or suppressions or bannings. The following year the number had risen
to 55, and in 1922 to 94. In the book line, the* Index Expurgatorius *came
to include 180 volumes. Verily the Rhinelanders could not read what they
wanted to.* [20]

There were some 40 films banned too. All banning was done in the
name of France, and the impression created was that:

*Not a few of the measures must have originated from the mere desire to lord
it. For instance there was the comic one-time suppression of national colors,
even for the lapels of German coats. In the street gendarmes and others would
order these to be removed or ripped off ... tiny emblems, monarchical,
republican or provincial, would be systematically removed from the hoods
of motorcars, from motorcycles ...* [21]

In Landau a French major once prevented a furniture van painted
black, white and red from unloading until it was painted over. As one
observer commented, "Much of all this was inclined to be on the
laughable side. But the French took it all *au grand sérieux*, since one
can hardly practice *gloire* and see the humor in things at one and the
same time." [22]

Unfortunately, the beaten nation over which France was exerting its
gloire was equally short of humor. The Germans were exasperated by
the way in which the French rubbed their victory in. At Trier only
French soldiers could use the main entrance to the station; Germans
had to jostle through side entrances. In Coblenz "The locals were ordered
to the galleries of their own church and Tricolors were swung out right
and left over the altar." [23] But it must be said that on occasion the
French got as good as they gave. Tuohy recalls a waiter in a Mainz café
accidentally knocking a French officer's gloves off the table. "*Schwein-
hund*," called the Frenchman. "*Schmidt*" came the German's reply.

The French were so remarkably unpopular that one must be careful
in one's assessment of contemporary German accounts of their behavior. The sexologist Magnus Hirschfeld has much to say about the
French and their brothels. He claims that the occupying forces ordered
the civil authorities to organize brothels for them with a fixed tariff:
visite courte, 5 M; *visite d'une heure,* 15 M; *visite de la nuit entière,*
30 M. [24] In München Gladbach, where the 256th French Brigade was
stationed, the brothel had a total staff of two. They eventually complained that between them they could not be expected to handle more
than twenty clients a day, and must have evenings and Sundays off.
It appears that there was no possibility of recruiting more staff locally.
As a result, the commanding officer agreed to their demands, formalized
their working hours and divided the days of the week between the two
local regiments the 164th and 169th. Each company received five
"entry tickets" every other day.

Such arrangements notwithstanding, the greatest of all sources of anti-French feeling was their use of black and Moorish troops. The French have always claimed that this was not intended to be a provocative act. They wished to demobilize their own nationals first, and had always used their colonial forces in auxiliary roles. It seems likely that the French moved in the North African troops out of self-interest rather than to provoke: they probably had no idea of the traumatic impact the presence of the North Africans would have on the Germans. However, once they saw what was happening, they were still quite content to let the North African troops stay there. According to US commander General Allan there were some 25,000 of them in the French zone. [25]

Alec Swan remembers the North African troops as being very much a part of the feel of the French sector. He found them gray, sluggish and not very soldier-like. Their relationship with the civilian population was complicated by the fact that many of them could often speak no European tongue, and only recognized the authority of a French uniform. Thus when English officers crossed over into the French sector they could be very unpleasant indeed. When cars failed to stop fast enough at a checkpoint, sentries were known to use their rifles and bayonets as javelins and spear the tire of the offending vehicle. [26]

The North African occupation also had its lighter side, for the troops were sometimes displayed in strange and distinctly Gallic ways. Witness the following account by an American general in 1920:

A truly French event was also staged, the beauty prize. The beauty was selected from twelve Algerian and Moroccan soldiers by a committee of French ladies. The men were dolled up to the limit and each had a big number attached to his uniform. Some had their hair passed through their fezzes in some mystifying way and plastered down over the fez tops. One or more had heavy full beards and were fantastically dressed. [27]

Yet for all their "truly French" beauty, the North African troops came as a terrible shock to occupied Germany. One should remember that the generation which was to evolve and subscribe to the idea of a Master Race had just reached intellectual maturity, and the impact of a black heel upon their neck—as they might put it—cannot be overestimated. Initial hostility was compounded by the behavior, or alleged behavior, of the troops themselves. All Germany was horror-struck by the "Black Shame," an expression inspired by the thought of great hulking Algerians raping innocent blond little Gretchens. As propaganda, the image could not fail. Many Germans seemed to believe that the North Africans were practising a systematic and unpunished rape of German maidenhood. Magnus Hirschfeld writes of regular hetero and homosexual violation by black troops. Anyone attempting to stop them was severely handled and often actually killed. He cites histories such as:

Frankfurt. April 1920. A black soldier forces his way into a woman's house, assaults her, nearly strangles her, sticks a knife into the floor within his grasp, as he rapes her. He lets her go. She goes out into the street and complains to a platoon of French soldiers. They replied that her attacker had not seen a woman for two and a half years and that such things happen. One of them pointing to her fair hair remarked that black men preferred blondes. [28]

That item is followed by a whole series of case histories, including multiple rape and armed robbery, the victims ranging from seven to sixty-five years old.

There is an obvious temptation to discount such allegations as German propaganda. Most Allied civilians involved in the occupation were disinclined to believe a word of such stories. Accordingly, it is somewhat disturbing to find them, or others like them, confirmed by an impartial observer who researched the subject carefully. Tuohy became convinced that the French troops, both African and European, did indeed go in for rape, and often went unpunished. He recalls that some sixty-eight cases of rape by non-European troops were reported between January 1919 and January 1920. Moreover, he continues, "Aggrieved German women or their menfolk met only with rebuff when they brought their suffering to the notice of French justice as this was militarily dispensed." [29]

The multi-millionaire Hugo Stinnes—a rabid German nationalist, profiteer, speculator and super-*Schieber*, who thrived on inflation and the economic plight of Germany, owning some 1,535 companies when he died—had predicted as early as 1921 that French occupation of the Ruhr was a certainty. When the Germans failed to deliver a reparations consignment of telegraph poles on time the French used this as a pretext to move into the Ruhr. One observer said at the time that not since the days of the Trojan horse had wood been so misused. They invaded on a war footing, with cavalry and armor. A Frenchman recalls the taking of a city:

The occupation commenced with the first streaks of dawn. While three battalions (chasseurs and Moroccans) were railed into the heart of the town, the remainder of the infantry, supported by a cavalry division and by field batteries, surrounded the city and gradually moved toward the center. Simultaneously aviators flew overhead ready to attack if necessary, while the Rhine flotilla took the bridges and mounted machine guns on them.

I went in with the first battalion. Because the police showed opposition I ordered them to be disarmed. Some days later the mob fell upon an Algerian post and it was obliged to open fire with machine guns. About 150 Germans were killed and wounded. This brought quiet. Show the Germans force and they always bow to it. [30]

85

The French looked to the Ruhr for economic benefit. They would take, direct, what they were failing to get in reparations. Yet benefit was not forthcoming. Chancellor Cuno ordered a policy of "passive resistance" to the French. The administration of the Coal Trust, the body which ran the industry, had already moved out to the unoccupied territories, and the French were obliged to run coal mines and steel works, railways and canals themselves. The total efficacy of the German action in the short term, made the French a laughing stock. Under their direction—and assisted by copious acts of sabotage—production and transportation came to a standstill. The French retaliated in various ways. They raided banks and commandeered office equipment, typewriters in particular. They tried to impose a coal blockade upon unoccupied Germany. They arrested civil servants for noncooperation. They arrested almost the entire police force of the Ruhr and declared Essen an open city. The less real progress they made, the more bullying they became.

On a punitive expedition to Gelsenkirchen on February 17, 1923, they not only robbed banks, but cordoned off the main street and robbed passers-by as well. Eight days later in Bochum they sacked the town hall, imposed a six o'clock curfew, and knocked the hats off civilians trying to get through their cordon. This was four and a half years after the end of the war.

March saw a long record of French brutality: shootings, thrashings and terrorization. Yet by the end of that month, at huge expense, they were getting only 1 percent of the coal that they had previously enjoyed from the Ruhr. They were quite unable to make anything run. One observer wrote:

At Godesberg I noticed a truck which had been loaded with sacks of corn on the day the French first seized the line. In the meantime the corn had sprouted merrily, and now stood a foot and a half high, giving every prospect of an excellent harvest. [31]

The French were not helped in their task by persistent and highly successful acts of sabotage, a crime punishable by death. One saboteur, the ex-Freikorps man Leo Schlageter, was executed and many of his friends sent to a French penal settlement. This had the predictable result that Schlageter became first a right-wing, then a Nazi and always a German, hero-martyr. There was even a play composed about his life. It contains the line: "When I hear the word *culture* I reach for my revolver."

This was precisely the kind of provocation needed to keep militant patriotism on the boil. Indeed, it was perpetually stirred up by events such as Essen's "Bloody Sunday," March 31. Some soldiers had been sent out to stop a demonstration at the Krupp works. The officer lost his nerve and ordered his men to fire into the crowd, killing fifteen workers and wounding fifteen others. Seventy thousand people attended the funeral, where a Catholic, a Lutheran and a Communist all spoke from the same platform—living proof of the extent to which France had succeeded in uniting her enemy. Independently of each other, Ludendorff, the Bavarian monarchist von Kahr, and Otto von Bismarck all told one particular Englishman that the occupation of the Ruhr could only be considered as a godsend. [32] But not even they could see just how greatly it would contribute to the collapse of the Weimar Republic. The occupation, and passive resistance in particular, had had a disastrous effect upon the German economy. It was to be the immediate cause of the galloping inflation that broke the Germans' back, shattering any sense of security they might have left, thrusting them overnight into a world in which nothing would ever be the same again. Those who came through the inflation must have felt they would do anything to prevent history from repeating itself—even vote for Hitler.

Not content with occupying the Ruhr, the French army was also politically active in the Rhineland. Rhinelanders traditionally tended to look west to France, rather than east to Prussia, and the French attempted to develop this attitude by fostering a Rhineland separatist movement. They intrigued against the German civil authority and actively sought to bring the Rhineland to the point of civil war. It was a short-sighted and provocative policy which could only fuel German nationalism, yet the French motives are clear enough: maximum dismemberment of Germany and the creation of a French client state on the Rhine. While discussing French policy with me, a long-retired British diplomat agreed that France brought its future troubles upon itself through her treatment of Germany. He added that in one respect England was also much to blame, for it failed to provide France with adequate guarantees against future aggression from a Germany which had been allowed to keep its army more or less intact. As a result, France felt obliged to pursue a militant anti-German policy in order to ensure that her old enemy remained a broken nation. Accordingly, she fished diligently, and badly, in the troubled waters of separatism.

The French actively encouraged the raising of separatist storm troops and paramilitary organizations, which were used to confront the civil authority. In Düsseldorf there was an attempted separatist putsch, begun when putschists deliberately fired into the crowd as a provocation. In the ensuing fight between police and separatists, the police won; but they were consequently disarmed by the French.

Led by a dozen separatists, twenty French cavalrymen rode up to a policeman and disarmed him. When this had been done, the separatists turned on the defenseless man and beat him to death with clubs and lengths of lead piping. The disarmed policeman buried his face in his hands and sank to the ground. The French cavalry remained on their horses and looked on calmly. The body was left lying in the road while French and separatists moved on to the next policeman. [33]

Another Englishman, a liaison officer with the French army named B. T. Reynolds, also saw police and separatists fighting in Düsseldorf on that day. French officers encouraged the separatists, pointing targets out to them among the police. The police had to refrain from firing for fear of hitting the Frenchmen, whom they still saluted punctiliously. The French officers returned their salutes by shaking their fists at them. Mrs. Reynolds contributed to the affair by leaning out of her hotel window and crying, "Come on the Schupo" (i.e., the police). That day in Düsseldorf a Rhineland Republic was declared. The police were all either arrested, killed or deported. The French had a very good way of coping with the German police: they would encourage the separatists to fire on them, then arrest them for shooting back.

In Bonn separatists attacked the town hall. They were repelled not with guns but with fire hoses and truncheons—until the mayor proposed to the French that he issue arms to the police. Thereupon the French stormed the hall on behalf of the separatists.

German patriots had their own, equally brutal methods of dealing with separatism.

I was just finishing dinner when four young men followed the waiter into the room. At the table opposite me sat Heinz, who was now dignified by the title of President of the Autonomous Palatinate, together with other members of his dummy cabinet. . . . At the next table sat a visitor registered in the hotel as "Dr. Weiss." As the waiter left in search of a table for the young men, "Dr. Weiss" sprang to his feet, flinging his chair to the ground with a crash, and pointing a Mauser at the table where the separatist cabinet was sitting, bellowed in stentorian tones: "Hands up! Everyone stand to the wall."

In a flash the four young men had surrounded the table indicated by his revolver. The separatists sprang up and fumbled for their own weapons, but before they could draw them half a dozen shots rang out. Heinz had barely risen to his feet when a bullet passed through the back of his head. . . . Two other men of his company tottered forward to the next table and fell, blood streaming from their faces.

. . . One of the young men put a hand to the light switch. "Ladies and gentlemen," he said, "we apologize for the shock we have been obliged to give you. It was the only way of settling the score with the traitors who have betrayed our country. No one else will be touched. . . . Long live united Germany."

Five bodies lie in their blood. Four very dead and then the fifth gets up, face streaming blood. "Thank you so much. This is a nice way to treat a man who only came to Speyer this morning to sell shirts. . . . I believe I have lost two teeth." [34]

In fact, the separatists enjoyed very little popular support. Described as a series of "weedy and terrified youths in French and Belgian pay," [35] they were swept from "power" with remarkable ease. In Aachen they were lynched by a crowd after firing on it and killing a child of three. In Pirmasens, on February 13, 1924, they fired on a crowd from the town hall, and the crowd retaliated by setting the building alight, ensuring that its occupants were burned alive.

Separatism never had any real credibility, except to the French and, of course, the German nationalists, who could whistle up storms of popular sympathy by pointing at yet another way in which France sought to humiliate and destroy a Germany that had been betrayed but never beaten.

ABOVE: *Street scene in the Ruhr—the original caption read: "French soldiers molest an old man."*
BELOW: *The French move into Essen, 1923.*

ABOVE: *Five Germans shot by the French for breaking the curfew.*

BELOW: *The funeral of the Krupp workers.*

The original caption to this picture read: "Jewish Schiebers in the Grenadierstrasse."

6

Inflation

THE YEAR 1923 has a special and dreadful connotation in German history, for it was the year of the great inflation. If defeat, abdication and revolution had begun to undermine the traditional values of German culture, then the inflation finished the process so completely that in the end there were no such values left. By November 1918 there were 184.8 marks to the pound. By late November 1923 there were 18,000,000,000,000. Although the mark was eventually "restored," and the period of inflation succeeded by a time of relative prosperity for many people, life for anyone who had lived through the lunatic year of 1923 could never be the same again.

Such a cataclysmic loss of a currency's value can never be ascribed to a single cause. Once confidence goes, the process of decline is a self-feeding one. By late 1923 no one would hold German money one moment longer than it was really necessary. It was essential to convert it into something, some object, within minutes of receiving it, if one were not to see it lose all value in a world in which prices were being marked up by 20 percent every day.

If we go back beyond the immediate cause of hyperinflation—beyond a total lack of confidence in a currency that would consequently never "find its floor," however undervalued it might appear—we find that passive resistance in the Ruhr was a major factor. Effective loss of the entire Ruhr output weakened the mark disastrously, encouraging dealers to speculate against it, since the balance of payments was bound to show a vast deficit. Confidence in the currency could only begin to be restored when resistance ended late in 1923.

It has been the "patriotic" view that reparations were also a significant factor. Certainly they constituted a steady drain upon the nation's resources, a drain for which it got no return. But reparations alone would not have brought about hyperinflation. There were still other causes. Sefton Delmer believes that the true explanation lay in Germany's financing of the war. She had done so very largely on credit, and was thereafter obliged to run a gigantic deficit. There were other more immediate causes, such as a total incomprehension of the situation on the part of Havenstein, director of the Reichsbank. Failing to understand why the currency was falling, he was content to blame it upon forces beyond his control—reparations—and attempted to deal with the situation by stepping up the money supply!

The first British ambassador to the Weimar Republic, Lord d'Abernon, had no illusions about the economic plight of Germany. He observed in his diary that "German finance is dying beyond its means," [1] and no one seemed to know why. In the meantime, he noted:

Currency experts have a sad fate. During life they empty every room in which they hold forth, and death finds them in madhouses. Berlin has been deluged with these gentlemen for the last week and still survives; but the currency has gone to the devil. [2]

He saw the Reichsbank compounding its own mistakes:

In the whole course of history, no dog has run after its own tail with the speed of the Reichsbank. The discredit they throw on their own notes increases even faster than the volume of the notes in circulation. The effect is greater than the cause; the tail goes faster than the dog. [3]

By October 1923 it cost more to print a note than the note was worth. Nevertheless Havenstein mobilized all the printing resources that he could. Some of the presses of the Ullstein newspaper and publishing group were even commandeered by the mint and turned to the printing of money. Havenstein made regular announcements to the Reichstag to the effect that all was well since print capacity was increasing. By August 1923 he was able to print in a day a sum equivalent to two-thirds of the money in circulation. Needless to say, as an anti-inflationary policy, his measures failed.

In his documentary novel *Success*, Leon Feuchtwanger has suggested that inflation had less obvious and more sinister causes. Certainly it had its beneficiaries as well as its victims. Anyone living on a pension or on fixed-interest investments—the small and cautious investor—was wiped out. Savings disappeared overnight. Pensions, annuities, government stocks, debentures, the usual investments of a careful middle class, lost all value. In the meantime big business, and export business in particular, prospered. It was so easy to get a bank loan, use it to acquire assets, and repay the loan a few months later for a tiny proportion of the original. Factory owners and agriculturalists who had issued loan stock or raised gold mortgages on their properties saw themselves released from those obligations in the same way, paying them off with worthless currency on the principle that "mark equals mark." It would be rash to suggest, as Feuchtwanger hints, that the occupation of the Ruhr was planned by industrialists to create an inflation which could only be to their benefit. Yet we should remember that Stinnes, the multi-millionaire, had both predicted that occupation and ended up the owner of more than 1,500 enterprises. It should also be remembered that some businessmen had a distinctly strange view of the shareholder. He was regarded by many as a burdensome nuisance, a drag upon their enterprise. He was the enemy and they were quite happy to see him wiped out to their benefit. Inflation was their chance to smash him. Witness the behavior of a banker at a shareholders' meeting at which it was suggested he should make a greater distribution of profit: "Why should I throw away my good money for the benefit of people whom I do not know?" [4]

The ingenious businessman had many ways of turning inflation to good account. Thus employees had to pay income tax weekly. Employers paid their tax yearly upon profits which were almost impossible to assess. They would exploit the situation of a smaller businessman, obliged to offer six to eight weeks of credit to keep his customers, by insisting on payment in cash. The delay between paying for the goods and reselling them eroded any profit the small man might make, while the big supplier prospered. [5]

Whether or not the industrialists actually caused inflation, their visible prosperity made them detested by an otherwise impoverished nation. Hugo Stinnes became an almost legendary embodiment of speculation and evil. Alec Swan remembers how hungry Germans would stare at prosperous fellow countrymen in fur coats, sullenly muttering *"Fabrikbesitzer"* (factory owner) at them. The term had become an insult and an expression of envy at one and the same time.

Hyperinflation created social chaos on an extraordinary scale. As soon as one was paid, one rushed off to the shops and bought absolutely anything in exchange for paper about to become worthless. If a woman had the misfortune to have a husband working away from home and sending money through the post, the money was virtually without value by the time it arrived. Workers were paid once, then twice, then five times a week with an ever-depreciating currency. By November 1923 real wages were down 25 percent compared with 1913, and envelopes were not big enough to accommodate all the stamps needed to mail them; the excess stamps were stuck to separate sheets affixed to the letter.[6] Normal commercial transactions became virtually impossible. One luckless author received a sizable advance on a work only to find that within a week it was just enough to pay the postage on the manuscript. [7] By late 1923 it was not unusual to find 100,000 mark notes in the gutter, tossed there by contemptuous beggars at a time when $50 could buy a row of houses in Berlin's smartest street. [8]

A Berlin couple who were about to celebrate their golden wedding received an official letter advising them that the mayor, in accordance with Prussian custom, would call and present them with a donation of money.

Next morning the mayor, accompanied by several aldermen in picturesque robes, arrived at the aged couple's house, and solemnly handed over in the name of the Prussian State 1,000,000,000,000 marks or one halfpenny.[9]

The banks were flourishing, however. They found it necessary to build annexes and would regularly advertise for more staff, especially bookkeepers "good with zeros." Alec Swan knew a girl who worked in a bank in Bonn. She told him that it eventually became impossible to count out the enormous numbers of notes required for a "modest" withdrawal, and the banks had to reconcile themselves to issuing bank-notes by their weight.

By the autumn of 1923 the currency had virtually broken down. Cities and even individual businesses would print their own notes, secured by food stocks, or even the objects the money was printed on. Notes were issued on leather, porcelain, even lace, with the idea that the object itself was guarantee of the value of the "coin."[10] It was a view of the relationship between monetary and real value that took one back five hundred years. Germany had become a barter society; the Middle Ages had returned. Shoe factories would pay their workers in bonds for shoes, which were negotiable. Theaters carried signs advertising the cheapest seats for two eggs, the most expensive for a few ounces of butter which was the most negotiable of all commodities. It was so precious that the very rich, such as Stinnes, used to take a traveling butter dish with them when they put up at Berlin's smartest hotel. [11] A pound of butter attained "fantastic value." It could purchase a pair of boots, trousers made to measure, a portrait, a semester's schooling, or even love. A young girl stayed out late one night while her parents waited up anxiously. When she came in at four in the morning, her mother prevented her father from taking a strap to her by showing him the pound of butter that she had "earned."[12] Boots were also highly negotiable: "The immense paper value of a pair of boots renders it hazardous for the traveler to leave them outside the door of his bedroom at his hotel." [13]

Thieves grew more enterprising still in their search for a hedge against inflation.

Even the mailboxes are plundered for the sake of the stamps attached to the letters. Door handles and metal facings are torn from doors; telephone and telegraph wires are stolen wholesale and the lead removed from roofs.[14]

In Berlin all metal statues were removed from public places because they constituted too great a temptation to an ever-increasing number of thieves. One of the consequences of the soaring crime rate was a shortage of prison accommodation. Criminals given short sentences were released and told to reapply for admission in due course.[15]

It was always possible that one might discover an unexpected source of wealth. A Munich newspaperman was going through his attic when he came upon a set of partly gold dentures, once the property of his grandmother, long since dead. He was able to live royally upon the proceeds of the sale for several weeks.[16]

The period threw up other anomalies. Rents on old houses were fixed by law, while those on new ones were exorbitantly high. As a result in many parts of Germany housing was literally rationed. If one were fortunate enough to live in old rented property, one lived virtually free. The landlord, however, suffered dreadfully: to repair a window might cost him the equivalent of a whole month's rent. Thus yet another of the traditional modes of safe investment, renting property, proved a disaster. Hitherto well-to-do middle-class families found it necessary to take in lodgers to make ends meet. The practice was so widespread that not to do so attracted unfavorable attention suggesting that one was a profiteer. Pearl S. Buck records the case of one family where the woman of the house reluctantly confessed to her husband that they would have to have a lodger. He greeted the news not with anger, but with a sigh of relief: the neighbors had begun to talk. Real property lost its value like everything else. Pearl Buck notes the case of a couple selling their house in order to marry their daughter in some kind of style. More telling is a famous song of inflation:

> We are drinking away our grandma's
> Little capital
> And her first and second mortgage too.[17]

As noted in the famous and highly intelligent paper the *Weltbühne*, the song picked out the difference between the "old" generation of grandparents who had scraped and saved carefully in order to acquire the security of a house, and the "new generation" for whom there could be no security any more, who "raided capital" or what was left of it, and were prepared to go to any lengths to enjoy themselves. Where their parents' lives had been structured with certainties, the only certainty that they possessed was that saving was a form of madness.

Not all Germans suffered, of course. Late in 1923 Hugo Stinnes did what he could to alleviate the misery of his fellow countrymen by the magnanimous decision to double his tipping rate in view of the inflation. [18] Along with rents, rail fares were also fixed and did not go up in proportion to inflation. Consequently, travel appeared absurdly cheap. Alec Swan recalls crossing Germany in the greatest style for a handful of copper coins. Yet even this was beyond the means of most Germans. A German train in 1923 would consist of several first-class carriages occupied entirely by comfortable foreigners, and a series of run-down third-class carriages crammed to bursting with impoverished and wretched Germans.

Although the shops were full of food, no one could afford it except foreigners. Germans often had to be content with food not normally thought of as fit for human consumption. In Hamburg there were riots when it was discovered that the local canning factory was using cats and rats for its preserved meats. Sausage factories also made much use of cat and horse meat.[19] Moreover, as we shall see, some of the most famous mass murderers of the age used to preserve and sell the meat of their victims in a combination of savagery and an almost sexual obsession with food that mythologizes much of the darkness and the violence that were latent in the mood of Weimar.

If 1923 was a bad year for the Germans it was an *annus mirabilis* for foreigners. Inflation restored the sinking morale of the army of occupation; small wonder when every private found himself a rich man overnight. In Cologne an English girl took lessons from the *prima donna* of the opera for sixpence a lesson. When she insisted that in future she pay a shilling, the *prima donna* wept with delight.[20] Shopping became a way of life: "All through that autumn and winter whenever we felt hipped we went out and bought something. It was a relaxation limited at home, unlimited in the Rhineland."[21]

Germany was suddenly infested with foreigners. It has been suggested that the English actually sent their unemployed out and put them up in hotels because it was cheaper than paying out the dole.[22] Alec Swan stayed with his family in a pension in Bonn. They had moved to Germany because life was so much cheaper there. The inmates of Swan's pension were mostly foreigners of strange complexion, such as the Swede suffering from tertiary syphilis who would bombard heads of state with urgent telegrams. There was also an extremely fat German, christened Glaxo by the Swans. He was in the habit of helping himself to gigantic mounds of the spaghetti which formed the staple diet of the common table, saying apologetically, "My stomach, my stomach," with a hand upon the offending organ, as a form of explanation.

To find oneself suddenly wealthy in the midst of tremendous hardship proved rather unsettling. Inflation corrupted foreigners almost as much as the Germans. The English in Cologne could think of nothing else.

They talked with sparkling eyes and a heightened color, in the banks, the streets, the shops, the restaurants, any public place, with Germans standing around gazing at them.

Scruples were on the whole overwhelmed by the sudden onslaught of wealth and purchasing power beyond one's dreams.[23]

As Alec Swan put it:

You felt yourself superior to the others, and at the same time you realized that it was not quite justified. When we went to Bellingshausen, which was a sort of wine place near Königswinter, we would start drinking in the afternoon. I would always order champagne and my Dutch friend would shake his head in disapproval. We'd have two ice buckets: he with some Rhine wine and me with German champagne. It was really rather ridiculous for a chap of my age to drink champagne on his own.

Being as wealthy as that was an extraordinary feeling, although there were many things you couldn't get in Germany. It was impossible to buy a decent hat, for instance. But you could have any food you wanted if you could pay for it. I haven't eaten anything like as well as that in my life. I used to go to the Königshalle (that was the big café in Bonn) at eleven o'clock in the morning for a Frühschoppen *and a* Bergmann's Stückchen, *a large piece of toast with fresh shrimps and mayonnaise. For a German that would have been quite impossible.*

I paid two million marks for a glass of beer. You changed as little money as you could every day. No, one did not feel guilty, one felt it was perfectly normal, a gift from the gods. Of course there was hatred in the air, and I dare say a lot of resentment against foreigners, but we never noticed it. They were still beaten, you see, a bit under and occupied.

My mother did buy meat for three or four German families. I remember I bought an air gun, and, when I grew tired of it, I gave it to my German teacher's son, with some pellets. Some time later the woman came to me in tears saying the boy had run out of pellets, and they could not afford to buy any more.

On another occasion Swan, all of twenty-two at the time, took the head of the Leipzig book fair out for a meal and looked on incredulously as the elderly and eminent bookseller cast dignity to the winds and started to eat as if he had not had a meal in months.

Stories of money changing and currency speculation are legion. *Bureaux de change* were to be found in every shop, apartment block, hairdresser's, tobacconist's. An Englishman named Sandford Griffith remembers having to visit a number of cities in the Ruhr which had local currencies. He stopped at a dealer's to change some money, but when he produced a pound note the dealer was so overcome by such wealth that he simply waved a hand at his stock of currency and invited the astonished Englishman to help himself.[24] Foreigners acquired antiques and *objets de valeur* at rock-bottom prices. A favorite trick was to buy in the morning with a down payment, saying that one would fetch the rest of the money from the bank. By waiting until the new exchange rate had come out at noon before changing one's money into marks, an extra profit could be made on the amount that the mark had fallen since the day before.[25]

The population responded to the foreign onslaught with a double pricing system. Shops would make their prices up for foreigners. It would cost a tourist 200 marks to visit Potsdam, when it cost a German 25. Some shops simply declined to sell to foreigners at all.[26] In Berlin a *Schlemmsteuer*, or tax on gluttony, was appended to all meals taken in luxury restaurants.[27]

Foreign embassies were also major beneficiaries of inflation, giving lavish banquets for virtually nothing. Indeed the *Weltbühne* noted with great resentment the presence of foreign legations of nations so insignificant that they would never hitherto have dreamed of being represented in Germany.[28] The spectacle of foreigners of all nations, living grotesquely well and eating beyond their fill in the middle of an impoverished and starving Germany did not encourage the Germans to rally to the causes of pacificism and internationalism. The apparent reason for their inflation was there for all to see, occupying the Ruhr.

The surface manifestations of inflation were unnerving enough, but its effect upon behavior, values and morals were to reach very deep indeed, persisting for years after the stabilization of the mark, right up to the moment when Hitler came to power. The middle class—civil servants, professional men, academics—which had stood for stability, social respectability, cultural continuity, and constituted a conservative and restraining influence was wiped out. A French author met a threadbare and dignified old couple in spotless but well-worn prewar clothes in a café. They ordered two clear soups and one beer, eating as if they were famished. He struck up a conversation with the man, who spoke excellent French and had known Paris before the war. "Monsieur," the man replied, when asked his profession, "I used to be a retired professor, but we are beggars now."[29]

There was a general feeling that an old and decent society was being destroyed. If the year 1918 had removed that society's political traditions and its national pride, 1923 was disposing of its financial substructure. In response, people grew either listless or hysterical. A German woman told Pearl Buck that a whole generation simply lost its taste for life—a taste that would only be restored to them by the Nazis. Family bonds melted away. A friend of Swan, a most respectable German whose father was a civil servant on the railways, simply left home and roamed the country with a band. It was a typical 1923 case history. Young men born between 1900 and 1905 who had grown up expecting to inherit a place in the sun from their well-to-do parents suddenly found they had nothing. From imperial officer to bank clerk became a "normal" progression. Such disinherited young men naturally gravitated toward the illegal right-wing organizations and other extremist groups. Inflation had destroyed savings, self-assurance, a belief in the value of hard work, morality and sheer human decency. Young people felt that they had no prospects and no hope. All around them they could see nothing but worried faces. "When they are crying even a gay laughter seems impossible . . . and all around it was the same . . . quite different from the days of revolution when we had hoped things would be better."[30]

Traditional middle-class morality disappeared overnight. People of good family co-habited and had illegitimate children. The impossibility of making a marriage economically secure apparently led to a disappearance of marriage itself.[31] Germany in 1923 was a hundred years away from those stable middle-class values that Thomas Mann depicted in *The Magic Mountain*, set in a period scarcely ten years before. Pearl Buck wrote that "Love was old-fashioned, sex was modern. It was the Nazis who restored the 'right to love' in their propaganda."[32]

Paradoxically, the inflation that destroyed traditional German values was also largely responsible for the creation of that new, decadent and dissolute generation that put Berlin on the cosmopolitan pleasure seeker's map, and has kept it or its image there ever since. It was no coincidence that 1923 was the year that the Hotel Adlon first hired gigolos, professional male dancers, to entertain lady clients at so much per dance. It was also a period when prostitution boomed. A Frenchman accustomed enough to the spectacle of Montmartre was unable to believe his eyes when he beheld the open corruption of Berlin's Friedrichstrasse.[33] Klaus Mann remembers:

Some of them looked like fierce Amazons strutting in high boots made of green glossy leather. One of them brandished a supple cane and leered at me as I passed by. "Good evening, madame" I said. She whispered in my ear: "Want to be my slave? Costs only six billion and a cigarette. A bargain. Come along, honey."

. . . Some of those who looked most handsome and elegant were actually boys in disguise. It seemed incredible considering the sovereign grace with which they displayed their saucy coats and hats. I wondered if they might be wearing little silks under their exquisite gowns; must look funny I thought . . . a boy's body with pink lace-trimmed skirt.[34]

Commercial sex in Berlin was not well organized and was considered by connoisseurs to be inferior to that of Budapest, which had the best red-light district in Europe. But in Berlin there was no longer any clearcut distinction between the red-light district and the rest of town, between professional and amateur. The booted Amazons were streetwalkers who jostled for business in competition with school children. Hans Fallada has painted the following portrait of a shop girl:

Pepa Ledig was at twenty-two no longer a blank page. She had ripened, not in a peaceful atmosphere, but during the war, postwar and inflation. Only too soon she knew what it meant when a gentleman customer in her bootshop touched her lap significantly with his toe. Sometimes she nodded. . . .[35]

Stefan Zweig gives us another glimpse of inflationary Berlin:

Along the entire Kurfürstendamm powdered and rouged young men sauntered, and they were not all professionals; every schoolboy wanted to earn some money, and in the dimly lit bars one might see government officials and men of the world of finance tenderly courting drunken sailors without shame. . . .

At the pervert balls of Berlin, hundreds of men dressed as women, and hundreds of women as men danced under the benevolent eyes of the police. . . . Young girls bragged proudly of their perversion. To be sixteen and still under suspicion of virginity would have been considered a disgrace in any school in Berlin at the time.[36]

Another visitor was struck by what he referred to as Berlin's "pathological" mood:

Nowhere in Europe was the disease of sex so violent as in Germany. A sense of decency and hypocrisy made the rest of Europe suppress or hide its more uncommon manifestations. But the Germans, with their vitality and their lack of a sense of form, let their emotions run riot. Sex was one of the few pleasures left to them. . . .

In the East End of Berlin there was a large Diele *(dancing café) in which from 9 P.M. to 1 A.M. you could watch shopkeepers, clerks and policemen of mature age dance together. They treated one another with an affectionate mateyness; the evening brought them their only recreation among congenial people. Politically most of them were conservative; with the exception of sex they subscribed to all the conventions of their caste. In fact, they almost represented the normal element of German sex life.*

. . . There was a well-known Diele *frequented almost entirely by foreigners of both sexes. The entertainment was provided by native boys between 14 and 18. Often a boy would depart with one of the guests and return alone a couple of hours later. Most of the boys looked undernourished. . . . Many of them had to spend the rest of the night in a railway station, a public park, or under the arch of a bridge.* [37]

Inflation made Germany break with her past by wiping out the local equivalent of the Forsytes. It also reinforced the postwar generation's appetite for invention, innovation and compulsive pleasure seeking, while making them bitterly aware of their own rootlessness. It is not surprising that cocaine was very much in vogue in those years. The drug was peddled openly in restaurants by the hat-check girls, and formed an integral part of the social life of Berlin.

Inflation was also taken as evidence that the old order was morally and practically bankrupt. Capitalism had failed to guarantee the security of its citizens. It had benefited speculators, hustlers, con men and factory owners. It had spawned Hugo Stinnes, but had done nothing for the common good. The need for an alternative system appeared universally self-evident, and until one came along the thing to do was to enjoy oneself, drink away grandma's capital, or exchange one's clothes for cocaine: a dinner jacket got you four grams, a morning coat eight.[38]

Inflation and the despair that it created also acted as the catalyst of aggression. It was at this time that anti-Semitism began to appear in Berlin. An attractive German lady remembers walking through a prosperous suburb with a Jewish friend when someone called to her in the street, "Why do you go around with a Jew? Get yourself a good German man." In one sense she found it understandable. The ordinary German was very slow to adjust to the special situation of inflation, and in 1923 anyone who was not very quick on their feet soon went under. Jews were better at economic survival in such situations than were other Germans—so much so, she says, that by the end of inflation they had become terribly conspicuous. All the expensive restaurants, all the best theater seats, appeared to be filled by Jews who had survived or even improved their position.

One can imagine that Germans who had lost their own status might have resented the spectacle. One old conservative I spoke to added a second reason for the rise of anti-Semitism in a Prussian society which had traditionally been quite free of it. The arguments advanced are his own, and tell us something of his prejudices. He believes that the Weimar Republic was too liberal with regard to immigration from the East, admitting thousands of Jews from Galicia and the old pale of settlement, persons who, in his words, were "Asiatics, not Jews." They found themselves in a strange anonymous town, free of all the ethical restraints imposed by life in a small community where their families had lived for several generations. They tended therefore to abandon all morality as they stepped out of their own homes, morality being strictly a family affair. They would sail as close to the wind as the law would allow, for they had no good will, no neighborly esteem to lose. The gentleman in question is convinced that their mode of doing business during the inflation did a great deal to create or aggravate more general-ized anti-Semitic feelings.

Yet precisely these immigrants were to prove a mainstay of the republic. An old Berlin Jew who had spent some time in prewar Ausch-witz told me that it was just these Eastern Jews who offered the most active and effective resistance to National Socialism. They were activists where native Berliners, Jew and Gentile alike, were more inclined to remain on the sidelines.

Certainly the period saw a rise in pro-National Socialist feelings. The first Nazi that Professor Reiff knew personally was a schoolboy in his last year. The young man's father, a small civil servant, had just lost everything through inflation, and as a result his son joined the party. Pearl Buck records the views of an antimonarchical businessman worried by inflation, who said of the Nazis: "They are still young men and act foolishly, but they will grow up. If they will only drop Ludendorff and his kind, maybe someday I'll give them a chance."[39]

For many people, who felt that they had lost all zest for a life rendered colorless by war and poverty, who could see that they lived in a world in which *Schieber* won and decent folk lost, a new ideology combining patriotism and socialist anticapitalism seemed to be the only viable alternative to a totally unacceptable state of financial chaos and capitalist *laissez-faire*. The shock of inflation had made people mistrustful of the past, immensely suspicious of the present, and pathetically ready to have hopes for the future. It was perfectly clear to them that new solutions were needed, equally clear that until such solutions should appear they could put their trust in nothing except the validity of their own sensations.

The mood of the inflationary period is summed up by Stefan Zweig. It is a mood that endured well beyond inflation itself to become the mood of the Weimar age, a blend of pleasure seeking, sexual and political extremism, and a yearning for strange gods.

It was an epoch of high ecstasy and ugly scheming, a singular mixture of unrest and fanaticism. Every extravagant idea that was not subject to regulation reaped a golden harvest: theosophy, occultism, yogism and Paracelcism. Anything that gave hope of newer and greater thrills, anything in the way of narcotics, morphine, cocaine, heroin found a tremendous market; on the stage incest and parricide, in politics communism and fascism constituted the most favored themes.[40]

It was indeed a time for the revaluation of all (devalued) values.

The mood of 1923 persisted long after inflation ended, which is why the manner of its ending is offered here as a postscript, for nothing was restored but the currency.

Restoration of confidence was only possible when passive resistance in the Ruhr ended in the autumn of 1923. At the same time, the Reichsbank appointed Hjalmar Schacht to deal with inflation. He was an extremely able man with a clear grasp of essentials. He realized that his main problem was to restore confidence both within and without Germany, and to try to prevent people from spending money as soon as it came into their hands. He established a new currency, based on the notional sum total of Germany's agricultural wealth, the *Roggen-Mark* (rye mark). This had the effect of restoring psychological confidence in the currency. He combined the move with a gigantic bear trap laid by the Reichsbank to catch the speculators who would regularly build up huge short positions in marks, in the almost certain expectation that the mark would continue to fall against the dollar: i.e., they sold marks they hadn't got, knowing that they could buy them for a fraction of their present value when the time came to meet the demand. When the mark stopped falling, thanks to the Reichsbank's engineering, they had to rush to close their positions, and were forced to buy marks which had actually begun to go up. Many speculators lost the entire fortunes which they had built up over the year.

Schacht's measures sufficed to stop the rot, but in the period between the ordnance declaring the new currency and the appearance of the first notes, there was an interim of pure chaos in which, as Lord d'Abernon noted, "four kinds of paper money and five kinds of stable value currency were in use. On November 20, 1923, 1 dollar = 4.2 gold marks = 4.2 trillion paper marks. But by December the currency was stable." The last November issue of the weekly *Berliner Illustrirter Zeitung* cost a billion marks, the first December issue 20 pfennigs. Confidence seemed to have been restored overnight. Germany could breathe again.

There were those, however, who could not accept that the old certainties were lost, as this sad little postscript will prove. In the old days the highest denomination printed had been the brown thousand-mark note which had a prestigious, almost magic significance. Many people among the older generation found it impossible to accept that its value was now gone forever. The notes were seen as the symbol of the golden age of stability before inflation, and it was the touching hope of many that one day they would be restored to full value. In the meantime they were hoarded and even collected. They could be bought in the Munich flea market for five marks a million. That there was still a demand for them at all is proof of the belief that one day the Reichsbank would honor its pledge and exchange paper for gold. Weimar's electoral system of proportional representation encouraged the proliferation of small political parties, of which there were many. But without a doubt, the strangest and saddest political party of them all was the "Party for the Revaluation of the Thousand-Mark Note."

ABOVE: *The Grenadierstrasse, the ghetto of Berlin, on a Sunday morning in 1923.*

BELOW: *Queueing for food in Berlin, 1923.*

ABOVE: *A Berlin shop during inflation—the sign reads "No sales to foreigners."*
BELOW: *Selling potatoes under police escort.*

ABOVE: *A meat market set up in an apartment hallway.*
BELOW: *Collecting the payroll.*

ABOVE: *Police clear a Berlin street after looting, 1923.*
BELOW: *A Berlin beggar, 1923.*

Himmler stands at a barricade, November 9, 1923.

1

The Hitler Putsch

Ridicule does not kill in Germany. Otherwise Adolf Hitler, who staged in
1923 the most ridiculous revolt ever known, would have died of it.[1]

HITLER, THE NATIONAL Socialist Party (NSDAP) and his SA men (Stormtroopers) had been agitating in Munich since the early 1920s. Indeed,
late in 1921 the Bavarian minister of the interior had invited all party
leaders to a meeting. He proposed to deport Hitler, suggesting that he
was making an intolerable nuisance of himself, behaving as if he were
dictator of Munich. All leaders agreed with the suggestion except, with
a typical stroke of Weimar irony, the SPD leader Erhard Auer, who felt
it would be undemocratic. Hitler was an essentially comical figure, he
argued, and the good sense of the workers would ensure that he would
soon be returned to the anonymity from which he had but recently
emerged. The socialist persuaded the rest of the meeting to see things his
way and nothing was done.[2]

The young Hitler was in many ways quite unlike the plumpish, well
dressed, slightly somnolent Reichschancellor of the thirties. He was a
rather untidy and not always well-mannered runt. When he was first
introduced to Bavarian high society, which looked to him as a possible
hedge against creeping communism, he had to be shown how to use
various knives and forks, how to tackle an artichoke. Quite typically
though, he turned his ignorance into a strength. His aristocratic
hostesses were utterly charmed by the simple way in which he asked
them to show him what to do. They found him open, unaffected, powerful, and were only too willing to teach him to be less uncouth.

The Hitler of the twenties had a deadly sweet tooth. Putzi Hanfstängl
recalls seeing him heap sugar into a glass of the sweetest wine he could
get. Hanfstängl was long to remain Hitler's clown intellectual, to be
summoned at all hours to play him Wagner on the piano. He was an
ex-Harvard man, being half-American, and in the years to come was
the only party man who could talk intelligently to the foreign press.
Hanfstängl claimed to have been the one to teach Hitler the call of *Sieg*
Heil, which was allegedly based on the very different call of "Harvard!

Harvard! Rah! Rah! Rah!"[3] Eventually, he crossed the path of Joseph Goebbels once too often, and the minister for propaganda finally had him thrown out of Germany in most dubious circumstances in 1936. In due course Hanfstängl turned up at Alec Swan's flat in England to ask for some assistance. He told Swan that he had sought the advice of Goering before consenting to leave, only to be given this immortal counsel: "When *der Goebbels* says you have to go, you really have to."

According to Hanfstängl, the young Hitler was a person of the 'most curious and mixed artistic tastes. He was utterly obsessed by Caravaggio's painting of *Leda and the Swan*. In later years any Nazi painter treating the subject would be certain of a gold medal. He was also much taken with the lady wrestlers of Luna Park.[4]

Kurt Ludecke, another early admirer, shows him in two contrasting and characteristic states. First the runt:

He clung to his shapeless trenchcoat and clumsy shoes. His hair still fell over his eyes at every vehement gesture during his speeches. He continued to eat in a hurry, some messy stuff or other, while he ran from place to place. If you succeeded in making him stand still long enough to confer on important matters, he would take out of his pocket a piece of greasy sausage and a slice of bread and bolt them while he talked. The only improvement I was able to persuade him to make was to give up his ugly and uncomfortable hard collars for more suitable soft ones.[5]

Next we are shown the visionary. Ludecke and Hitler were alone overlooking the Danube. Hitler started to speak:

"Long ago there was no Poestlingberg here; all was level. No heights, no valleys, but only the unbroken earth, worked smooth by primal tides as they flowed and ebbed over the world. Then the fires burst up from the earth's center; the ice marched down from the poles; and the earthquakes convulsed with birth pangs shaping the face of the land. And after long cycles of cataclysmic change, some titanic force, elemental yet governed by supreme laws, thrust up this peak from the plain; some irresistible underground movement carved it out of deeper bedrock and lifted it high here to dominate everything. . . . Who knows what set that force in motion? The crucial strain could have come from the heavy overload of some distant mountain range. Or perhaps the natural outlet of the fire deep in the earth's core was choked, until its pent-up energy blew this mountain sky-high like a stopper from a flask. Who knows? We believe these things are ruled by law; but the law itself partly eludes us. A pity, for the process of nature probably symbolizes mankind's little life. . . ."

He was just a smallish man sitting there in a neat, cheap blue-serge suit, his head bare, his eyes shining, and I realized he was piercing back through the mists of time.[6]

His voice, the Hitler Youth leader Baldur von Schirach has said, was "low and husky, resonant, like a cello. A Lower Bavarian, not an

Austrian accent, which sounded foreign and hence commanded attention."[7] Sefton Delmer, who met Hitler some years later, told me that only a trained expert on German dialects could have told that he was an Austrian and not a Bavarian. Delmer, who got to know him better than any other foreign correspondent (and probably better than any foreigner), found him "a very ordinary man." He did not in any sense "smell of sulphur." Delmer had met Lord Beaverbrook and Hitler at approximately the same time. Beaverbrook, he said, was obviously a winner and man of power. Hitler, by comparison, in the twenties at least, seemed nothing of the sort.

Zarek and other members of a Munich theater company used to frequent a restaurant called Old Vienna, also patronized by young Nazis. The Nazis would behave quite soberly until Goering appeared in his captain's uniform with his *Pour le Mèrite* or "Blue Max." Then they would get noisy and obstreperous, staring meaningfully at the "cosmopolitan" faces at the theatrical table. On one occasion a hungry Zarek came hurrying through the swing doors of the restaurant, grazing someone's foot. The someone shouted and Zarek surprised him by yelling back. It was Hitler.

I had no impression of confronting a man of strong personality. . . . This person who accidentally crossed my way appeared to me a very mediocre individual, remarkable only for his marked nervousness. . . . What cold, heartless eyes he had! Later I often heard intelligent people speak enthusiastically about Hitler's fascinating blue eyes. I only remember their dull inexpressiveness and a certain immobility of the pupils such as is often observed in hysterical people.[8]

Hitler's landlady used to complain about him bitterly: "Just listen now how our tenant behaves himself. It's Herr Hitler—you must have heard of him. He's furious, no one knows why, and when he's furious he beats his dogs."[9]

But the little man was also an orator, as we know, and as economic misery mounted through the course of 1923 his beer-hall speeches became increasingly inflammatory. Carl Zuckmayer described the effect of his oratory:

For people like us he was a howling dervish. But he knew how to whip up those crowds jammed closely in a dense cloud of cigarette smoke and Wurst vapors—not by argument but by the fanaticism of his manner, the roaring and screeching, interlarded with middle-class oratory, and especially the hypnotic power of his repetitions delivered in a certain infectious rhythm. This was a technique he had developed himself, and it had a frightening primitive force.

He would draw up a catalogue of existing evils and imaginary abuses, and after listing them in higher and higher crescendo he screamed: "And whose fault is it?"—following up with the sharply metrical reply: "It's all / the fault / of the Jews!"

The beer mugs would swiftly take up the beat, crashing down on the wooden tables and thousands of voices, shrill and female or beer-bellied basses, repeated the imbecile line for quarter of an hour. Anger that a mug of beer cost four hundred million marks added impetus to the pounding.[10]

Munich in the early 1920s was a center of antirepublican action. Ruth Fischer, a leading member of the Communist Party, attributed this to the trauma of civil war. Had it not been for those weeks in 1919, she says, Munich would never have been the birthplace of the Hitler movement.[11] Things had appeared to return to normal after the April and May days of 1919, and yet, Leon Feuchtwanger suggests, both Reds and Whites were quietly waiting to get to grips with each other again. Memories were longer than they appeared. The Munich that Feuchtwanger depicts is an astoundingly violent place in which there is collusion between the Bavarian establishment, who are on the whole monarchist, and the NSDAP. It was a city in which it was perfectly normal for liberal attornies to be nearly beaten to death in the street simply because they were representing republican, and hence anti-Bavarian, defendants in court.

This was the climate that Hitler sought to exploit, to make Munich the starting point for a march on Berlin, in emulation of Mussolini's march on Rome. He hoped to overthrow the federal government and unite all antirepublican forces behind him, for unlike the other, basically monarchistic parties of the right, the NSDAP was the first radical party to appeal to all Germany across all class barriers, thereby uniting an otherwise fragmented opposition.

The "background to the background" of the Hitler undertaking remains something of a mystery. It looks as if Hitler received encouragement from the Bavarian establishment, who in turn were in touch with industrialists in the Ruhr. According to Feuchtwanger, this powerful support was withdrawn from Hitler at the last moment, because the Ruhr industrialists had already got what they wanted from inflation, and there was nothing to be gained from a putsch. Although this may have a ring of conspiracy theory about it, the fact remains that Hitler, throughout the putsch's early stages, acted with a confidence that suggests he had a great deal of support in high places pledged to him. Just what this support may have been we shall probably never know.

Hitler proposed to carry out the putsch by means of his own SA men, together with Freikorps units, and various and numerous unofficial armies. The principal Bavarian paramilitary organization, Bayern und Reich, had in 1923 over 56,000 members, constituting six infantry regiments, ten signals troops and twelve artillery batteries. Hitler hoped to win over such organizations, and indeed looked to the army itself to help him in his triumphant march upon Prussia and Berlin. Symbolically the business was to start on Armistice Day.

On November 8 there were some 4,000 putschist troops in Munich, as opposed to 2,600 government men. Initially, the government units were disorganized and at quarter strength, but they had considerable reserves to call on in the country. It was essential to win them over in a matter of hours if the putsch were to succeed.

Hitler's units were, on the whole, very green. Few of them were war veterans. They were, moreover, poorly armed. Most of the automatic weapons taken from them subsequently were good only for the scrap heap. They were short of ammunition and, to make matters worse, the two thousand rifles delivered to them from a secret Reichswehr store had arrived without firing pins. Hitler did not discover this until after the putsch had failed.[12]

On the evening of November 8 Kahr, who had temporarily been given emergency powers as "dictator" of Munich, was to address a meeting in the Bürgerbräu Keller on the aims of his régime. A unit of armed police were to have protected him, but to avoid a public display of nervousness the 45-man squad had been concealed in a cavalry barracks a quarter of a mile away. His sole immediate protection was 12 policemen in the hall and some 150 police outside on crowd control.

The cellar was soon full, and the doors closed early. At 7.15 P.M. Ludendorff, the greatest troubled-water fisherman of the age, was significantly absent. Two days before he had cleared his bank accounts, knowing that the putschists planned to freeze all accounts on November 10.

Hitler's troops had received an alert, but had taken the warning for a training exercise since someone had sent out white instead of red notices.

Shortly after 8, Hitler arrived at the cellar. He suggested to the police that they clear the streets, which they obligingly did, thereby assisting the deployment of his own men. Even more obligingly, they then went home.

At 8.30 SA men surrounded the cellar. Hitler entered, accompanied by an armed escort, together with the industrialist Max Aman, Rudolf Hess and Putzi Hanfstängl. He had to struggle through the crowd. An eyewitness, Admiral von Hintze, observed that he wore a badly fitting and ill-cut morning coat. Another eyewitness described him as behaving like a maniac. Hitler, however, considered that he was modelling himself upon Napoleon. He thrust his way to the front, jumped onto a table and fired his Browning into the air. "Poor little waiter," thought von Hintze.

A machine gun manned by SA men made its appearance at the back of the hall. Hitler had effectively captured the entire Bavarian government: a triumvirate consisting of Kahr; General von Lossow, commander in chief of the Bavarian army; and one, Seisser. He declared them under arrest, withdrew with them into private conference, and returned fifteen minutes later with the announcement that the federal government was overthrown and that the triumvirate had agreed to side with him. Just as Kahr was announcing that he was prepared to serve as regent until the monarchy was restored, Ludendorff arrived in uniform.

Hitler then moved on to settle a disagreement between putschists and Reichswehr at the engineers' barracks, leaving Ludendorf in charge. He permitted the triumvirate to go home. His action has been described as foolish and unthinking, and events would appear to bear the judgment out. Yet the fact that the triumvirate was allowed to leave at all and the speed with which they agreed to side with Hitler both point to the possibility of the events at the cellar being a combination of elaborate farce and doublecross. Hitler would appear to "arrest" the triumvirate, who had already agreed to come in with him. They were allowed to go home because they were, or were thought to be, Hitler's accomplices.

In the meantime Hess arrested key hostages, members of the government and senior police officers. Elsewhere, some loyal police observed putschist elements assembling and decided they ought to report in—by tram. The putschists marched off, leaving the police waiting at the tram stop. They proceeded to occupy various key points, with nobody wishing to oppose them. They seized army headquarters and the infantry school, but failed to occupy the state police headquarters after a confrontation with loyal state troopers.

Ludendorff and Hitler trusted General von Lossow to keep the word he had allegedly given them. Whether or not he ever intended to side with them we cannot say, but certainly immediately upon his release he informed his generals that he did not feel bound by a word given at pistol point. He then proceeded to mobilize the army against Hitler. That night few soldiers or police knew which side they were meant to be on. It was not until 4 A.M. on November 9 that the triumvirate firmly committed themselves to opposing Hitler. An hour later the putschists learned of their treachery. But, as was to prove the case so often up to May 1945, it was found that Hitler had no plans ready for anything other than total success.

That morning there were desultory attempts to occupy key bridges and crossroads, but by noon government troops were deployed throughout the city in overwhelming force. The population was vociferous in its support of the putschists, but there were those who were beginning to have their doubts. One man left in the middle of the morning's proceedings because he was a teacher and it was time for his class.[13]

Around army headquarters there was a little shooting—two dead, two wounded—whereupon the putschists surrendered and were allowed to go home. The main body, however, faced with failure, decided to march: not on Berlin, but through Munich. One company of the Oberland Freikorps was having lunch and got left behind, but the rest formed three forces in columns of four, side by side. They constituted something halfway between a demonstration and a military force. Two thousand of them set off through Munich. On the Odeonsplatz they came up against a small body of state troopers. The main government force was concentrated nearby. The police tried to stop the putschists with truncheons and rifles held for crowd control, and there was some hand-to-hand fighting. Lieutenant Michael Freiherr von Godin was in charge of No. 2 Company:

My men worked with rifle butt and truncheon. I myself had taken a rifle to defend myself without resorting to my pistol and parried two bayonet thrusts, overpowering the men behind them with rifle at the high port. Suddenly a Hitler man who stood a pace away to my left fired a pistol at my head. The shot missed and killed Sgt. Hollweg behind me. For a fraction of a second my company stood frozen. Then, before I could give an order, my people opened fire, a volley in effect. At the same time the Hitler people started to fire and for twenty or thirty seconds a real fire fight was on.[14]

Hitler's World War I reflexes were good enough to make him hit the cobblestones immediately—so hard that he dislocated a shoulder. Ludendorff, on the other hand, cautiously enough dressed in civilian clothes, simply continued his march right through the line of firing policemen into the arms of a certain Lieutenant Demmelmayer. The rest of the demonstration broke up in confusion, leaving fourteen dead. Goering suffered a severe wound in the groin, the eventual cause of an addiction to morphine which he would not shake off until compelled to do so by his Allied captors in 1945. The government lost four men. Hitler, nearly trapped in a sealed-off Munich, was driven to Putzi Hanfstängl's house at Uffing. Forty-eight hours later he was arrested. As Lord d'Abernon commented, "Hitler's courage was unequal to the occasion."

Carl Zuckmayer had observed the dispersal of the brown shirts, which took ten minutes,

The people in the streets were motivated more by curiosity than by any revolutionary mood. I heard cursing, but nobody seemed to know who the curses were for. Whenever that was in doubt in Bavaria, the Prussians would

do for targets. . . . In the course of that rainy day, in spite of the pools of blood near the Preysing Palace, the whole affair turned into an entertainment. Everybody went out onto the streets, not to demonstrate or take sides, but simply to be there when something was going on.[15]

Yet for all these detached observations, Munich was very sad to see the putsch fail. The triumvirate was less than popular, and for some time afterward General von Lossow resided in barracks for safety's sake. It was during this period that a grateful butcher decided to present the three men with generous quantities of *Weisswurst*, the greatest of all Bavarian delicacies, an essential feature of Bavarian culture, and for some time quite impossible to find. The three men were in a quandary, for they felt there to be a very real possibility that the splendid objects were poisoned. Finally von Lossow, with a typically Bavarian blend of guts, greed and recklessness, ploughed right in and pronounced them safe. It is a revealing anecdote. To the Bavarian mind it is not comic, but heroic. The heroism with which a general asserts his essential Bavarian-ness, by tucking into a possibly poisoned *Weisswurst* sums up the national character: "A *Weisswurst* is a *Weisswurst* and might be poisoned, but I am Bavarian and nothing will come between me and the first *Weisswurst* I have seen in months." So it goes.

It is no paradox to assert that the only successful aspect of Hitler's putsch was his trial. It was a trial in name only, in reality an antirepublican celebration. Among the accused were Ludendorff, Hitler, and Pöhner, an appeal judge. When Ludendorff appeared in court, the army guard presented arms and the entire court rose to its feet. Because he had prudently worn civilian dress during the putsch, he was pronounced innocent. (Indeed, one ex-Nazi has maintained that had he worn uniform, the putsch would have succeeded.)[16] When he drove away, his car was covered with flowers, surrounded by cheering crowds, and had a swastika on the hood. He was to remain head of all paramilitary organizations, "the supreme head of the secret Reichswehr."

Pöhner, when charged with treason, replied as follows:

What kind of a state was created in November 1918? This deception of the people was carried out by Jews, deserters and hired traitors. This government is no God-sent authority in the Christian sense. These fellows of different race are foreign rulers. The so-called Reichspräsident *was not elected by the people, but set upon the throne by a clique.*[17]

When one recalls that the speaker was a member of the republic's judiciary, it is small wonder that Weimar justice was somewhat idiosyncratic.

The *Bayrische Kurier* for April 2, 1924, commented on the trial:

A trial in name only, in essence a nationalistic propaganda meeting; a trial

*in which the accused were not cross-examined, in which jurisprudence
yielded throughout to party political considerations; a trial in fact conducted
for much of the time entirely by the accused and the defense; witnesses,
representatives of the state authorities and foreign sovereign states were
exposed, without protection, to all possible forms of abuse.*[18]

Hitler's own speech occupied an important place. It makes a point
which is central to the understanding of right-wing and Nazi attitudes
to what would disparagingly be known as the Weimar *"System."*
System means parliamentary democracy and the rule of law. In essence,
Hitler conceded that he was guilty in the eyes of the law. But he appealed
to a principle infinitely higher than that of mere law and political
institutions, some transcendent historic ideal; and, in the light of that
ideal, he was a thousand times innocent. As a mode of argument it was
deadly attractive to a people who had produced the greatest idealist
philosophers of modern times, and whose experience of democratic
institutions was not yet five years old. The call to rally to a principle
beyond mere law, beyond politics itself, was to be answered by the
German nation, and would lead it to many strange places in the next
twenty years. It also sounded the death knell of Weimar.

If the trial was a farce, then the sentence passed on Hitler was a
disaster. He was given four years' *Festungshaft*, fortress arrest. This was
less a prison sentence than a compliment quite literally without prece-
dent, an accolade even. In the rigidly stratified society of Wilhelmine
Germany, fortress arrest was a sentence reserved for "naughty boys" of
good family—students or officers who had killed their man in a duel. It
was taken as a joke and a compliment. Tales were told of students
under fortress arrest borrowing money from their jailers to spend a
weekend in Berlin.[19] It was reserved strictly for the upper classes and
persons who were *"satisfaktionsfähig"*—whom you could challenge to a
duel. It was his association with Ludendorff that earned Hitler—a
Bohemian civilian, non student, ex-lance-corporal—this most harmless
and patrician of sentences which conferred a monstrous prestige upon
him. No wonder his guards in Festung Landsberg used to salute him
with his own *Hitler Gruss*!

But the immediate future looked bad for Hitler and for his movement.
The NSDAP was dissolved, and Hitler himself became something of a
forgotten man. In conservative circles, the events now usually described
as the Hitler Putsch were known as the Ludendorff Putsch. Certain
right-wing Germans today prefer to talk of the November Rising. Just
how forgotten Hitler was is demonstrated by a fascinating slip in *The
Times* (London) on October 2, 1928. Reporting some street fighting in
Berlin between KPD and NSDAP, it refers to their leader as Herr *Max*
Hitler! Truly a forgotten man.

There was, however, at least one far-reaching consequence of the putsch. Betrayed by von Lossow, and in a sense by Ludendorff too, Hitler turned against the officer caste forever. He would never trust them again. This mistrust may have led to the creation of the SS as a state within a state, a praetorian guard. It may also have prompted the Führer's eventual decision to assume supreme command of the German army, which he sought to control down to divisional level.

A scene outside the Burgerbraukeller, Hitler's headquarters in Munich, on the day of the putsch.

120

Hitler's stormtroopers on the march on the evening of November 9, 1923.

Hitler's stormtroopers arrive at Nazi headquarters.

Hitler in Festung Landsberg in 1924. Rudolf Hess is amongst those

photographed with him (second from right).

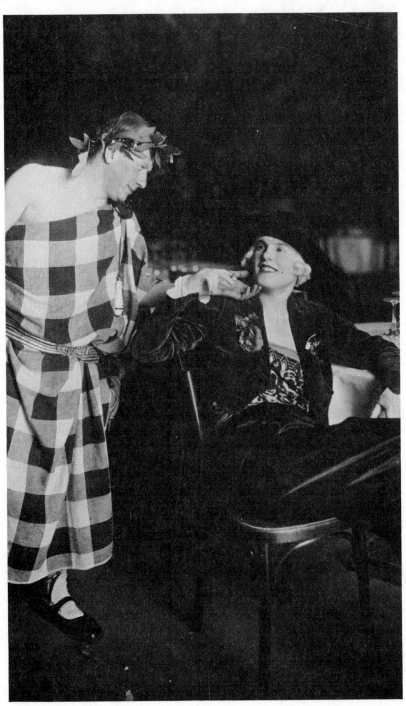

A fancy dress ball, 1927.

Berlin

Berlin was worth much more than a mass—Zuckmayer.

When I arrived in Berlin for the first time in the mid-twenties I got out at the Zoo Station and the first thing I saw there were two enormous cinemas, the Ufa Palast and the Gloria Palast with neon lights. It was the middle of the night, and I'd never seen anything like it before. There was snow on the ground and the blend of snow, neon and huge hulking buildings was unearthly. You felt you had arrived somewhere totally strange.

That was Alec Swan's first impression of Berlin: he knew London and Paris but had never seen neon lighting before. Christopher Isherwood also first found modern street lighting in Berlin: "The bright part of Berlin was terribly bright, but the dark side was very dark indeed, a kind of sinister jungle." Along with the lighting the other characteristic peculiar to Berlin for him was the all-pervading smell of sweet Balkan tobacco.

The Berliners were immensely proud of Berlin by night, seeing its light in rather different terms than Isherwood:

The best thing in that part of town was the wonderful light which flickered over the boulevard. In the twenties there was much less bad and cheap lighting. There were candelabras on the Kurfürstendamm. The tree tops filtered the light and the glimmering reflections of the advertisements gave the boulevard an intimate feel, which made every woman's face come alive. The streets did not thunder, they played music, a love song to the women of Berlin. In the twenties Berlin was a gallant city.[1]

That at least was the Berliners' view. To Bavarian eyes Berlin was a nightmare, cold, harsh, remote, a city of the north. People jostled you in the streets without the apologetic "*Hoppla, Herr Nachbarr*" with which such encounters were accompanied in Munich. One ate copiously but badly, and the waiters had no time to have a serious talk about the menu with you.

The suggestion that the streets played music, a "love song," conflicts with Alec Swan's impression. He was very impressed by the traffic lights. Again he had not seen anything like them before, strung out across the middle of the streets, and he remarked that "the Berliners were terrible drivers and always used to jump the lights, and one would regularly hear a succession of bangs as two taxis collided at a crossing."

At night then Berlin conveyed a tremendous sense of animation. Modern lighting, traffic lights, modern traffic. By day it was rather different, appearing an oppressive, gray, crude and unlovely place. Its old architecture was massive and without distinction, while its new buildings appeared frighteningly new, the anticipation of some steel, glass and concrete metropolis of the future. But night or day, the place was a very strange one. The first impressions of a traveler can catch more of the feel of a city than the affectionate recollections of its most devoted citizens. Swan noticed lights, snow and neon; Isherwood light, darkness and Balkan tobacco. A Frenchman in 1926 found it drab and gray by day, ablaze with light and animation by night. But he also noticed something else, something which would come to play an increasingly important role in the life of the city in years to come. On his first afternoon in the city he saw three paramilitary processions—with uniform caps, military music and police escorts—marching in columns of four. Two were Communist, one Reichsbanner (a privately raised paramilitary force for the defense of the republic). The very fact that the republic needed its own private army is one of the saddest of all the sad ironies of Weimar Germany.

The first impression of still another observer, a reaction that perhaps conveys the unique atmosphere of Berlin most strongly, has no neon, no private armies, no traffic lights, yet it is perfect:

Don't leave Berlin till you've seen a gasometer. . . . A Berlin gasometer seen with the moon behind it is quite a remarkable sight. They are huge round buildings of brick, with tall slender towers rising above them, and dozens of barred windows in tiers. They are evil-looking, sinister things. . . .

The first time you see one—particularly if it is at night—you wonder if it is a prison for those condemned of cold and pitiless sins, or perhaps the palace of the King of the Robots. Or the control tower for all the levers and wheels and switches that make Berlin start and stop. Or the temple of the new spirit of civilization that rushes and shouts through the streets of this metropolis on steel-winged feet. Or a theater where all the actors are machines, and the audience huge silent men in gleaming dress shirts. Or a sports palace where men fight with steel boxing gloves.

If all the barred windows suddenly sprang open and wild inhuman heads lolled out at you and shrieked, you would not be surprised.

But it's a gasometer.[2]

Such visual strangeness was matched by cultural disorientation. To arrive in Berlin from Western Europe was to arrive in a different world. The newspapers carried different stories, the faces even, and the food: all was different. Berlin is a city that has always looked east to Russia and even south to the Balkans as well as west. In the twenties it was full of Russians, White Russian cabarets and clip joints, restaurants and bookshops. Three Russian-language dailies were sold on the streets. Russian influence on the arts was immense, particularly Soviet theater and cinema. Berlin was a city, moreover, where one encountered languages —central European and Balkan—that to the Western European generally had no reality beyond the multilingual phrasebook. Then as now Berlin was a city in which one felt a long way from home.

What made Alec Swan feel so far from home was the strange and elusive crudeness that Berlin projected. It was not exactly provincial: no capital city with a hundred theaters could be called that. Rather it was very young, lacking the sophistication of Paris or London. It was, after all, the only big city in Germany, the only one indeed between Paris and Moscow on one axis, Vienna and nothing on the other. Sefton Delmer found it in many ways rather like Chicago, with the same blend of exciting modernism together with that surprising parochialism that you find in a big city isolated from other centers; modern Moscow is another example. For Swan, it was a city that played according to unaccustomed rules, with a strange undercurrent of vice and violence.

Unfamiliarity extended well beyond the more obvious and exotic manifestations of vice such as the spectacle of elderly and mustachioed shopkeepers dancing cheek to cheek. It came through in more subtle ways, Alec Swan: "When a girl wanted to pick you up, not a tart, just an ordinary girl in a shop, she used quite simply to bump into you, quite hard." The mode of approach, frequently exercised could make one feel one was in a world quite different from any other. It was as if even this most delicate of actions was tinged with a blend of crudity, exuberance and a touch of violence. When a girl went back to one's rooms with one, "Shall we drink coffee *first*?" was a standard opening gambit.

It was this blatancy, crudity and a certain naiveté—the coffee, and why not a cake or two as well?—which made up the unique atmosphere of the town. It was an atmosphere which, at least in retrospect, seems to have found very little response in Christopher Isherwood, who told me that he had little feel for Berlin as such. His books could have been inspired by any other large German-language city. Besides, he added rather sadly, not only was Berlin a subject which he had long since exhausted, it was a city in which he had very frequently been bored.

Yet it contained enough for most palates. A large, sprawling city, it had effectively two main centers. First there was the area, now in West Berlin, around the Kurfürstendamm; this was a young part of town on its way up. Then there was the center, occupied by government buildings, bounded by the newspaper quarter, Potsdamer Platz, Unter den Linden, Wilhelmstrasse, Friedrichstrasse, and then on to the Palace and the Cathedral. This section lay much further to the east, and is now either underdeveloped or in East Berlin. Proceeding east, immediately after the Palace and the Cathedral, was the center of the Berliner's Berlin: Alexanderplatz. Beyond that and on all sides, Isherwood's dark side of the city began.

From the moment that Germany lost its war—and profiteers and hustlers began to win its peace—a tremendous contrast grew up between the bright lights of Berlin West and the dark, sinister and always impoverished working-class quarters of Berlin North and East. The contrast impressed itself deeply on Knickerbocker, a brilliant American journalist, who knew his own big cities well enough but was nevertheless amazed at the extremes of poverty and luxury that Berlin had to offer.

The Russian writer Ilya Ehrenburg has given us two descriptions of the city—one in 1920, the other in 1928—which combine to bring out some of its stranger and more characteristic qualities:

In Berlin in 1920 everything seemed unreal.... The elevators worked but apartments were cold and freezing.... I was amazed to see pink and blue shirtfronts on display in shop windows. People used them in place of shirts as they had grown too expensive; the fronts were a proof if not of prosperity then at least of decency. In the Café Josty they served unspeakable ersatz coffee in metal coffeepots with a little glove on the handle to prevent you from burning your fingers. They made patisserie *out of rotten potatoes. The Berliners still smoked cigars as before, calling them "Cuban" or "Brazilian," but they were made from cabbage leaves soaked in nicotine.*[3]

A few years later it was no longer the pretence of appearances in the midst of poverty that struck him. Complacency and the craving for at least the illusion of an ordered world had now taken refuge in technology and Americanization:

One man thinks about how to seat airline passengers more economically, another invents a lighter which lights up easily.... I called on Maximilian Harden.... He, it seems, was not created to invent lighters. We spoke of the Russian Revolution and the streets of Berlin. He said, "I fear this even pace of life, the lack of the unexpected...." In the public lavatories of Berlin there is a sign: "No later than two hours after having sexual intercourse proceed to the nearest clinic." Berlin is the apostle of Americanism and lighters are the object of a particular cult here.[4]

Yet there was a part of Berlin that had nothing to do with the maintenance of appearance, or the security offered by high-speed lighters—the Berliners' part. Berliners had, and still have, a tremendous awareness of their own identity as a race apart, rather like New Yorkers. Berlin is unique—distinct and different from the rest of Germany. Berliners do not think of themselves as Prussians in the way that inhabitants of Munich consider themselves Bavarians. Prussia proper was for farm workers, civil servants, officers and landowners. There is Prussia, the Mark of Brandenburg and, quite different, the city of Berlin.

The Berliner is characterized by his dialect, which is unique and contains sounds and forms heard nowhere else. He speaks quickly, in a kind of sardonic, dry, self-mocking way that prevents any sloppy expression of feeling. This makes for rapid, witty and wry repartee, which is quite free of any so-called "Germanic" heaviness. The famous *"Berliner Schnauze,"* or Berlin wit, is in many ways reminiscent of Cockney, though it is less sentimental and has more bite. Berliners pride themselves on being *"schlagfertig,"* a revealing word. Literally meaning "ready to strike," it actually signifies that you have a witty reply on the tip of your tongue, ready for any situation.

Yet the picture of quick-witted and *schlagfertig* citizens is not quite complete. Although they pride themselves upon their style and wit, the wit itself can be astoundingly coarse and crude. I asked Sefton Delmer about the Berlin sense of humor, and he replied that peoples who pride themselves in public on a sense of humor seldom possess one: the Berliners often display more spirit of invention than actual humor.

Alec Swan remembers arriving in Berlin one day with a French cameraman: "We went up to one of those typical German whores with gold lace-up boots. The cameraman asked her, *'Können sie französisch sprechen?'* *'Nay, aber ich kann französisch lecken.'*" Later that day he went to the UFA (Universum Film Gesellschaft) studios where he encountered a similar kind of crudeness:

I remember one of the German cameramen between takes, removing a cigar, putting it up his backside and giving the general appearance that he was trying to be funny. The others recognized what he was up to and nodded in serious approval. "Grosses Stoff, grosses Stoff," they said.

Yet along with this crudity were, and are, certain admirable qualities. Not the least of these is a cynical refusal to be taken in by rhetoric and charlatanism. Berlin never returned a Nazi majority in free elections. Moreover, the Berliner retains tremendous pride and self-awareness. Walter Kiaulehn's definitive study of Berlin, which contains much that every Berliner would know anyway, has been in print and on sale in Berlin bookshops for over twenty years. Its title is significant: *Berlin Schicksal einer Weltstadt* (Berlin, Fate of a World City). It was in the twenties that Berlin became a "world city." No longer a provincial/

imperial capital, it had become "international," or so Berliners maintained. Sefton Delmer is ironic about the claim:

They like to think of themselves as a world city; it was rather a Middle Western idea, the American idea of a successful city. It was really very provincial and has been overglamorized and misrepresented by nostalgia.

But the term meant rather more than provincial self-congratulation. It marked the emergence of a new kind of city, of a new kind of Germany even, one that was no longer parochial. As Professor Reiff put it:

Until [the twenties], even in Switzerland, you could immediately tell a German couple as they checked into a hotel. They had a small-town look to them which made them unmistakably provincial wherever they went. But in the twenties all that changed. They became much more internationally minded, much more part of a world culture which could be reached through films and records. The Berliners spoke of a Weltstadt *because they could feel their city changing.*

Another observer found that Berlin had become increasingly international, as opposed to Prussian, because "it attracted the rootless, those who did not place provinces before the Reich. [5]

There was a kind of Berlin intelligentsia whose implicit collective enterprise was to make a civilized and humanitarian new Germany out of a patchwork of provinces. It was an ambition shared by Gentile and Jew alike. Yet even this internationalism had peculiarly German manifestations. H. Ostwald, author of two studies of vice and sexual mores in Berlin, comments on a particularly unsavory aspect of his capital: the organized prostitution of young amateurs for the benefit of tourists. "People have learned to take such things calmly and sensibly. Berlin has now become international in all respects."[6] *International* becomes a term like *modern* which can be used to excuse anything. "I suppose it's international."

A combination of crudity and exuberance made Berlin one of the great pleasure centers of the world. The climate helped too:

The air was always bright, as if it were peppered, like New York late in autumn: you needed little sleep and never seemed tired. Nowhere else did you fail in such good form, nowhere else could you be knocked on the chin time and again without being counted out.[7]

Another of the great virtues of Berlin air is that it seemed to cure hangovers before they happened. Alec Swan would be amazed to find himself sitting up all night yet able to get to work the next morning, apparently without ill effects. Small wonder that one of the highlights of a Berlin evening should have been its breakfasts. Carl Zuckmayer remembers:

Anyone who has lived in Berlin, especially in the theatrical world, knows why the word breakfast *comes to me so readily. The image calls to mind that lucid, shimmering early morning after a wakeful, wild, drunken opening night, or the mornings in the overcrowded train, when you were still half-dazed from nocturnal adventures and on your way to another rehearsal, trying to catch a bit of sleep standing up.*[8]

Berlin social life in the twenties was a strangely accurate mirror image of Weimar itself. Just as Weimar lacked a positive political and social center, had a hole in its heart, so it was with Berlin society. Prewar Berlin had been built around court life, and with the disappearance of the court Berlin lost its social center. If there was still any equivalent to London's society, Paris's *gratin*, or the social register, it played no perceptible part in the life of the new Berlin. Instead, private entertainment took on a strange tone of insecurity, rootless unease.

After midnight went chez Vollmoeller on the Pariser Platz to see Josephine Baker. He had assembled a strange collection of guests again. No one knew anybody — only his extremely charming lover, Fraulein Landshoff (dressed as a man again) stood out. Déclassé atmosphere. He is, or thinks he is, a déclassé poet and likes to surround himself with déclassé women in all stages of undress; one never knows who they are, whether they are "girl friends," whores or ladies; you see young men who could be publishers or ballet masters, newly "discovered" actresses. . . . I left at three; all in all a sorrowful, almost tragic atmosphere.[9]

The strange undercurrent of moral ambiguity and aimlessness was absolutely characteristic of Weimar Berlin. Sometimes it declared itself with more exuberance:

There was a new Kurfürstendamm society whose parties were more elaborate and select than those of the good old sharks of 1920 and who felt themselves entitled to an ever crasser display of snobbish cynicism. At one such affair I attended in February 1924 the walls were festooned with maxims such as: "Love is the foolish overestimation of the minimal difference between one sexual object and another." The girls hired to serve drinks went about almost naked except for transparent panties embroidered with a silk fig leaf. They were not like the "bunnies" in modern American nightclubs, there just for the looks, but could be freely handled — that had been included in their pay.[10]

In place of more conventional private entertaining, social life had come to gravitate around the big embassies, the only centers which retained any kind of formal prestige. In a limited sense they filled the gap left by court life. Equally the great hotels — the Britol, the Eden, the Adlon — took on a disproportionate significance. Alec Swan remembers that the Adlon felt remarkably like the Savoy Hotel, London. Modern, with impeccable service, it attracted top journalists and show-business people, the UFA stars who were effectively the new aristocracy of

Berlin. It had an "international" atmosphere:

You could order a pink gin there: anywhere else in Berlin they wouldn't know what you were talking about. The restaurant, the food, the service were terrific. They used to weigh caviar out for you at your table with a pair of scales. I remember Norman Ebbutt, the Times *correspondent, at the Adlon bar drinking pink gin. He had a little silver teapot for the water and measured out the appropriate portions very deliberately.*

J. H. Morgan gives us a slightly different angle on the grand hotel. With its clientele of *Schieber* and hustlers, along with the crowds of male prostitutes that could be found there of an evening, he felt that the hotel should change its emblem: a vulture seemed to him a more appropriate symbol than the eagle it then used.[11]

In the hotels and embassies film stars set the tone of high Berlin society. A typical manifestation in later years was the motoring beauty contest, involving cars, flowers, furs, jewels and dogs. Frau Louis Adlon won the first one with a white Mercedes and twenty-eight Royal Pekinese.[12]

The essential rootlessness of Berlin society is to be seen in the role of the subscription ball, which, together with entertainments offered by the embassies, formed the backbone of reputable Berlin social life. The two tennis clubs, Blue White and Red White, the Rowing Club, the cinema industry all gave annual balls. But the most prestigious, glamorous and important of the lot was the Press Ball. I asked Professor Reiff what for him had made Berlin golden in its "golden twenties," and he replied unhesitatingly: the annual Press Ball. Held in the Grosses Marmorsaal opposite the Eden Hotel, it was the great social occasion of the year. There were six thousand or more guests, and tickets could only be obtained through the personal recommendation of a member of the Press Club. A meeting place for *"tout Berlin,"* it had a strange blend of the intimate and the formal. In 1924 a woman lit a cigarette in the dancing hall. The press commented unfavorably upon her action the next day, but, presumably to spare her feelings, turned her into a man as they reported her action.[13]

Everybody attended the ball, from press barons such as the Ullstein brothers to the mayor of Berlin and the chancellor himself, together with his government. The prestige connected with the Press Ball indicates better than anything that shift away from a conventional establishment which is so characteristic of the social and political life of Weimar. The void left by an old aristocracy and civil service had been filled by a motley crowd of intellectuals, journalists and film stars. The occasion became a symbol of Weimar society, and the last Press Ball of the republic, held on January 28, 1933, was to symbolize its end.

The second great public occasion of Weimar Berlin, the six-day bicycle race, the *Sechstagerennen*, was encumbered with no such obvious significance. Held at the Sportpalast, it was the capital's greatest spectacle and an essential feature of Berlin culture.

The atmosphere of the games of ancient Rome hangs over the Sechstage-rennen. *Imagine a huge arena: tiers of seats at the sides slope up toward the roof; far below a wooden track, narrow and tilted. Imagine a dozen little fellows on bright shining bicycles, a dozen strung out in a line . . . round and round under the lamps. . . . A flash, and two go by, vanishing into the gloom beyond the lights. A flash, and two more sprint after them. . . .*

They race in teams of two. One member or the other of every team is always on the track. They stumble off their bicycles, sink half-asleep into the arms of their second, stagger away to be massaged, to have food and drink forced down their throats, to be washed and showered, to sleep. Then onto the saddle again, and round and round the track.

The public is there at all hours. People drift in and out by day and night. At two o'clock in the morning there is an immense crowd. Men in dress clothes and women in furs and diamonds shout encouragement to the racing auto-matons under the lights. Men in caps and women in shawls shriek under the roof.

Every fifteen minutes there is a prize. Aching limbs are whipped up to new endeavor. The crowd roars: Amazing prizes—suits of clothes, motorcycles, bottles of cognac. . . .

Everybody goes to see them. People look in after theater or the cabaret. Actors, actresses, financiers, gangsters, crowds of the mysterious people of Berlin who live at night and disappear in the daylight. Enthusiasts stay beside the arena the entire six days. . . .

It is the ordained sport of the Weltstadt; *the terrific test of endurance amidst the steel and stone of the arena; amidst the echoes, the shouting, the black shadows; with the snow piled up a meter high on the pavements outside, and the ice five millimeters thick on the windowpanes.*

One wonders why the vanquished are not put to death.[14]

The sport took a grip, says Herr Wallenberg, because the bicycle was such an important part of the working man's life. Moreover, it provided cheap and readily available entertainment. The *"Prominenz,"* film stars and politicians, made a point of showing themselves, rather as today's public figures go to football games. Even ex-Crown Prince Willy courted popularity in this manner. Every so often the audience would hear a special announcement: "500 marks offered by an old *Sechstage* friend from Oels," as he was known.[15]

When I asked Sefton Delmer what the attraction was, he told me, "the atmosphere, *the smell*; as far as I was concerned it was very romantic and it was quite comic." Indeed, the racing had tremendous atmosphere: its own characters, customs, even its own mythology, providing a meeting place for *Prominenz* and what might now be termed popular culture. One of its heroes was the cripple Krücke, a massive fellow who with two fingers in his mouth would lead the entire Sportpalast as he took them through the "Sportpalast Waltz" (set to the melody of Translateur's "Praterleben"). Krücke was "King of the Hayloft" (the upper gallery). He would often let a can down on a string to the expensive seats below in a request for beer money. Supported by a chorus of henchmen, he would haul it up and if he found the sum insufficient it would be lowered again. Alternatively, he would invite stars like Richard Tauber to sing to the audience, and the stars would almost invariably oblige.

As for the mythology, there is a famous anecdote concerning Bertholt Brecht. He had adopted a passion for proletarian and "American" culture, which focused on, among other subjects, boxing and other sports. Brecht believed that this was where the poetry of the future was to be found. Indeed when asked to judge a serious poetry competition run by a distinguished literary journal, he awarded the prize to an unsubmitted piece of doggerel about the American cyclist Reggie Mac-Namara. "He, he the Iron Man" was its appalling English title.

Press Balls and sporting events, even those that last for six days without interruption, are relatively harmless affairs, although they may reveal more about a city than appears at first sight. There was nothing subtle, however, about the revelations of Berlin's night life proper. It made a profound impression on sensitive visitors.

Nothing brought you so much face to face with the pathological distortion of Germany's postwar mentality as the weird night life of Berlin. Its grotesqueness destroyed for many of us younger men all the illusions about sex that some people retain throughout their whole lives. One year in Berlin revealed more of the perversions in which man's lower nature can indulge than a normal lifetime spent anywhere else.

People who had gone through their adolescence during the miserable war years, or in the stifling provincialism of Central Europe, regarded Berlin as an intoxicating paradise. It had no traditions to speak of; its yesterday had been irrevocably destroyed; the standard of living had sunk unspeakably low. To replace the pleasures of a lost past, Berlin was providing a riot of new sensations.[16]

And again:

The happenings in the night life of Berlin were as pathological as is the behavior of a man who finds satisfaction in beating his wife or kicking his children; as are the feet of Chinese girls tightly bound at birth to prevent growth; or as a woman's body in a Victorian corset.[17]

This quality is reflected in some of the peculiarities of prostitution in

Berlin. It has already been mentioned that, of an evening, the Adlon, Berlin's smartest hotel, used to swarm with male prostitutes.[18] In his novel *Fabian* Erich Kästner, who sought to capture the mood and atmosphere of Weimar Berlin, depicts a male brothel for female customers.[19] Male homosexual prostitutes were issued with police cards, documents which were essential to the successful exercise of that profession. This practice was indicative of a strange and in itself fairly pathological blend of administrative thoroughness and tolerance, for prostitution was carefully regulated in Berlin. Prostitutes were obliged to enter their names on an official list, whereupon they were permitted to walk the streets. Anyone picked up working unofficially was liable to six weeks in the workhouse.

Once on the list, prostitutes were classified as follows: Class 1 (A) persons up to 24 years old and those in trade less than a year, (B) syphilitics of less than three years' standing, and (C) prostitutes in need of special supervision. Class 1 had medical examinations twice a week. Class 2 embraced prostitutes from 25 to 34, who had a weekly check. Class 3, persons aged 34 and over, had to have a check once in three weeks. Although one can see the wisdom behind the planning, this careful organization of vice is dreadfully reminiscent of Peachum's organization and "protection" of the London beggars in *The Threepenny Opera*.

More innocent pleasures were also controlled by the civic authority. During the war, it will be recalled, dancing in public places had been forbidden, resulting in the mushrooming of secret nightclubs. In March 1919 establishments that had had dancing evenings before the war were allowed to reopen until ten at night, but dancing in bars and other cafés remained forbidden. Berliners wanted to dance, however, and the number of illicit establishments grew almost nightly. A contemporary Berliner's expression of the "philosophy" of modern dancing accounts for the craze in a rather peculiar manner:

The new dances create a hand-picked, trained and thoroughbred human type. They are more than entertainment: they are in the final analysis aesthetically developing, educational and, since they confer a new style upon courtship, make for erotic health, and place before the troubled and heavy fantasies of the bourgeois pictures which have something of the grace and cheerful amorousness of rococo art.[20]

Readiness to justify eroticism by aesthetics is found in descriptions of another feature of Berlin night life—the "*Nacktttanz*," or nude dance. These initially took place in private houses turned into clandestine nightclubs for that purpose. One evening Paul. E. Marcus accepted a tout's invitation to a *Nackttanz*. He was led to a private flat where he was met by the host, Oberleutnant A. D. Seveloh. A waiter in a worn tail coat took charge of him and led him into a room cleared as if for dancing, with three or four tables occupied by gentlemen of respectable appearance. He ordered a bottle of wine at an exorbitant price. Soon the lights went out, a door opened slowly and someone put on a record. Behind a gauze screen a naked woman stood on a small platform. She walked slowly round permitting inspection from all quarters, although she never actually danced.

Such private performances were often raided. On one occasion the police found twenty spectators and the dancers in evening dress. There had been a last minute tip-off. However, under one of the sofas the police found a suitcase full of underwear. On the long way back to the police station one of the dancers, "Black Lola," complained of the cold. A policeman handed her the case, and she finished dressing gratefully in a doorway.[21]

It was also possible to engage naked dancers for private performance. Hans Fallada's novel *Iron Gustav* portrays a scene in early 1919 in which a young *Schieber* engages a girl who dances naked to Chopin in his home: gradually his mistress, unbearably excited, strips off, and slowly the two ladies gyrate together.

The girl Paul Marcus saw at a *Nackttanz* was born Cäcilie Schmidt. Her enterprising officer husband made her into Celly de Rheydt, and she became the star of a whole series of public performances, which filled one of Berlin's largest variety theaters. These performances were naked ballets with artistic pretensions, the apotheosis of vulgarity. Claiming to emphasize the aesthetic qualities of the nude she even portrayed "a nun after Calderon's well-known depiction of *The Renunciation*, which was set in church and involved the nun Immaculata who had broken her vow of chastity and was to be driven from the church, past a statue of the Virgin—played by one of the younger dancers."[22]

Nude dancing and nude cabaret soon became a standard feature of Berlin night life. Contemporary observers who knew their Montmartre found it much cruder. By 1926 nudity for nudity's sake without any real pretence of style was the order; the Parisian settings had at least some scenic talent behind them. The mania for naked dancing was satirized frequently, notably by a cabaret song sung by one of the great stars, Trude Hersterberg:

> *Trag du als Iphigenie*
> *Dessous jedoch rect wenige*
> *Zieh dich aus, Petronella, zieh dich aus.*
>> As Iphigenia you should wear
>> Only a little underwear.
>> Get undressed, Petronella, get undressed.

Berlin abounded in places in which Petronella complied regularly.

BONBONNIÈRE, FRIEDRICHSTRASSE

There is a large cabaret, well decorated, comfortable enough, with a pretty good floor and a pretty good band.

All sorts of entertainers give performances, none of them particularly good, but the main attraction is that on stage at the Bonbonnière, nothing above the waist is de rigueur, and the usual handful of feathers or inadequate cloud of chiffon does its best for modesty from girdle to heel.

After the girls have done their tricks, they put on a few clothes and mingle with the public. Then, for a consideration of a small sum, one can dance with them in the cabaret proper. It is not particularly interesting, but the tourist who has never seen such things will probably be entertained.[23]

The author of those lines may have found the cabaret acts harmless, but one wonders how good his German was, for the acts could be talentlessly obscene. One cabaret was famed for the perversity of its *conférencière*. She would address the gentlemen of the audience, whom she called "*Bubi*," sonny, asking them if they knew what plant eroticism was. After explaining that it consisted in sexual relations between people and plants, she would then turn to her pianist: "Gustav, do you still have your violet?" To which he would reply "No, it's a tulip now." Then she would expatiate on the joys of rolling around in a bed of flowers, and finally take her public to task for its lack of sensuality, humor and perversity: "*Nicht genügend pervers!*" — "Not perverse enough!"[24]

Another characteristic Berlin institution was, and is, Resi. "*Einmal in Berlin, einmal in Resi*" went a famous song of the time. With its use of technology to assist the mingling of the sexes by means of coy, sentimental notes and telephone conversations which usually led to contacts more basic, there was something archetypically German about it. It should be said that at Resi amateurs tended to outnumber professionals, and there were more out-of-towners than Berliners:

RESI, NEUMANNSTRASSE

This place sports a glass roof, painted with flowers, fruits and birds. There are also fountains and revolving balls like globular mirrors, which split open when the lights go down and disclose dazzling reflections of sparkling waters.

But the chief attraction is the table telephones. The tables are numbered, and on every one is a small telephone. If you see a lonely little thing at table 25 and you are feeling in a romantic mood, you ring up that table, and in your most inviting German say: "Darf ich das Vergnügen haben gnädiges Fräulein?" ["May I have the pleasure, gracious fräulein?"] Whereupon she will probably make a dash at you, and you will have the pleasure for the rest of the evening.[25]

Alec Swan remembers another spot.

One of the most interesting Berlin places was Alter Zirkus, an old circus with, among other attractions, a swimming pool and a shooting gallery. It was a good place to kill time in after dinner. An American journalist I shared a flat with was there one evening, tight, throwing bottles at the girls in the pool. He hit one on the head and rapidly grew very unpopular. He was a chap who never seemed to go to bed, and when everything else closed he would resort to the Romanisches Café to see the morning in.

The pathological quality that some observers found in Berlin's pleasure seeking is, of course, to be seen in the depth and breadth of its homosexuality. At a time when the "love that dares not speak its name" had to keep very quiet indeed in the rest of Europe, Berlin was open city for homosexuals. It is this perhaps which accounts, albeit indirectly, for the prominence that Berlin has acquired in the mythology of the twentieth century. Postwar Germany was, even by today's standards, amazingly open about homosexuality. It is true that there had been a strong homosexual tradition in the Prussian army, as any cadet to go through Gross Lichterfelde soon found out. The tradition was allegedly founded by Frederick the Great who is said to have celebrated the victory of Rossbach by writing a poem to the joys of homosexual intercourse.

Certainly Prussian soldiers prostituted themselves, and because they were soldiers were much sought after.[26] In intellectual circles "neo-Grecian" friendship was an integral part of the culture pattern, and intense intellectual sympathy between men led easily to the physical expression of that sympathy. Yet the homosexuality of Berlin was infinitely more flagrant, less specialized, more widespread. It became a form of fashionable behavior.

Contemporaries sought to explain its proliferation by the plight of sex-starved soldiers at the front and of women at home. The revolutionary sailors were also held to be to blame. Yet something more than sexual deprivation and matelots is needed to explain why homosexuality for both sexes. became so fashionable. To talk about "pathological Berlin" is not quite good enough either. Of course, all these factors helped. The young people in quest of sensation in Berlin's twenties certainly believed that everything on the sexual front was permitted. There was also a sentimental undertone to sex which supported it with friendship and feeling; and homosexual relations of an enduring nature frequently draw on emotions of that order. Yet even more important perhaps was the Weimar idea of making a complete break with the staid and bankrupt past of one's parents' generation, and therefore freeing oneself of all traditional prejudice and taboo, in order to be "modern".

"We, thank God, are Different *from the Others [title of a documentary film about homosexuality]" announced a snob élite, not without pride. The motto of an erotic aristocracy which broke, in its fashion, with uniformity.*

The thirst for some kind of intoxication born from a passionate rejection of the surrender, the demand for unheard of pleasures competed, neck and neck, with an all-consuming passion for chocolate.[27]

All Weimar Germany is there: a strange combination of *a prioristic* sexual emancipation ranking *pari passu* with an obsession with food.

Yet while one may understand how homosexuality became fashionable for an "erotic aristocracy," some of its other manifestations defy comprehension. Holländer sketches the background of a very different kind of homosexual, a working-class middle-aged man, living in Berlin, and married with four children. Such men would frequent the Topkeller, a working-class homosexual nightclub, after dining *en famille*.

Anyone who has not seen the gemütlich *fifty-year-olds, salt of the earth, with rounded bellies and threadbare evening clothes (from mother's chest), wiping the foam of Pilsener from their citizenly mustaches, asking another mustache in evening dress for a dance, to glide across the room in a polka, can have no conception of this daredevil transgression raised on home cooking: a mixture of fancy-dress-ball sexual pathology and "Families may brew their own coffee on the premises."*[28]

Homosexual love and courtship were considered perfectly appropriate subjects for both stage and cinema. Count Kessler describes a play in which a young man receives and caresses a sixteen-year-old boy, sitting on his lap, in a "boudoir." He concludes proudly that by now the Berlin public has come to accept the spectacle of sexual relations between persons of the same sex with the greatest of ease—like the Greeks.[29]

Inevitably, German homosexuality was highly organized. It had its own associations, with local branches in every large town, its own newspapers and newsletters. It was, in this respect, directly comparable with other activities that bring people together, such as model making, war games or horticulture. It constituted an "interest." There were also, of course, homosexual nightclubs. One of the best known was El Dorado, coyly described here.

EL DORADO, LUTHERSTRASSE

This cabaret is being included more as a warning for the unwary tourist than anything else.

If you go in, go alone and on no account allow your wife or sister to accompany you; *and go with no other expectation than that of seeing how the other half lives.*

Nothing will happen to you; you won't be murdered, robbed or even annoyed. You will find a fairly gay cabaret in progress and . . . a visit won't cost you more than the price of a glass of beer.

But leave your womenfolk in the comparative holiness of the Kleine Scala next door.[30]

139

The ladies' equivalent to El Dorado was Silhouette, one of Berlin's most fashionable night spots.

A man was not admitted unless introduced by one of the habituées. *Most of the women, sitting on hard wooden benches along the walls, wore men's clothes with collar and tie; but the younger girls with them wore dresses with accentuated femininity. . . . You could see women well known in German literature, society, the theater and politics. They took little notice of the few male intruders. On the whole the atmosphere was quiet. There was no suggestion of vice about the place. It was a usual phenomenon in German life.*[31]

There were other more exclusive places such as Die Grotte and Entre Nous, which did not normally admit men at all. Alec Swan takes up the story:

One night I had had enough of clubs and wanted to go home, but one of the girls insisted on going on: "Alec, Alec, vicieuse," *she whispered with a fascinated urgency. So we went to one of these places and I had to wait outside until the girl eventually called me in. The first person I saw was a drunken Danish gentleman. Someone had spilled a champagne bucket down him and he was running gleefully across the dance floor, trousers hitched high. Everyone wanted to visit these places because they were "vicieuse" and they would get selfconsciously excited about them. At El Dorado it really was possible to mistake some of the* habitués *for beautiful women until you found yourself standing beside one in the pissoir.*

A German policeman once took a British army officer to such a place. The officer suggested that it was against the law. "Yes," came the reply, "but we cannot go against public opinion."[32]

Yet for all its sexual pathology, its dancing fifty-year-olds and its lesbian politicians, the best-known pleasure house of Berlin was totally harmless and utterly characteristic of Berlin life. Haus Vaterland on the Potsdamer Platz was an enormous agglomeration of restaurants.

What a jolly place! What a youthful, carefree, won't-go-home-till-morning, romantic, wonderful place! The merry illuminated bonnet it wears for a roof whirls round and round like the rings of Saturn. It has orchestras to pipe and fiddle all the different sorts of music people play from Seville to Stamboul. It has cowboys and Turks, Spanish dancing girls and buxom maidens from Bavaria. It has silver walls, and marble staircases, fountains — and even mountains and trains. It is the jolliest place in Berlin.[33]

Haus Vaterland consisted of a series of cafés: a "typical" Berlin café, a Bavarian café, a Viennese café, a Wild West bar, a Spanish inn, Old Heidelberg, a Turkish café, all with a painstakingly authentic décor, "atmosphere" and brilliant scenic effects. It was not to everybody's taste. Sefton Delmer told me with some emphasis that nothing would have made him set foot in the place. Yet it was the center of a certain kind of normal, Germanic pleasure; with its emphasis on *ersatz* travel and *ersatz* authenticity, even to the point of including a "typical" Berlin café. Haus Vaterland captures the very essence of old Berlin.

Today the Potsdamer Platz is on the very edge of the western sector. I paid a last visit to it to see Haus Vaterland, which was just about to come down. It was an empty shell of a building, dangerous to walk through as I picked my way across the girders. On the top of the shell a tree was growing.

What remained of Haus Vaterland was finally pulled down in the spring of 1976. Perhaps as it crumbled, somewhere in the background you could hear the ghost of an old Berlin twenties hit:

> *Das gibts nur einmal*
> *Das kehrt nich wieder*
> *Das ist zu schön um wahr zu sein!*
>> It happens only once
>> It will not come again
>> It is too beautiful to be true.

ABOVE: *The Gloria Palast cinema, 1930.*
BELOW: *The Kurfurstendamm.*

ABOVE: *A subscription ball in 1929.*
BELOW: *The start of the six day bicycle race in Berlin, 1929.*

Celly de Rheydt.   *Black market dealers in Alexanderplatz.*

BELOW: *A soup kitchen in Berlin, 1925.*

The Sylvester Jazz Band, 1927.

Two dancers.

Film, Theater and Cabaret

THE GERMAN FILM industry in the 1920s was one of the most advanced in Europe if not in the world. Alec Swan, who worked with the famous UFA found their work greatly superior to the French and English industries, with respect to the talent and skill of the production people. The management was also more artistically minded. UFA was the first company in the world to build proper sound stages for talkies, while other studios made do with inadequately sound-proofed silent stages—a small point, but one which was absolutely typical of the German industry in those years.

The histories of German cinema and theater in the twenties require specialist books to do justice to the subjects, and have indeed been favored with a series of distinguished studies. Within the scope of this "chronicle" we can do no more than name a few names, pick out certain highspots and perhaps offer a little unfamiliar material. We cannot cover the field either in breadth or in depth. However as an introduction to a survey of the films of the period it is worth simply noting some of the big names which the German industry of that time introduced.

It introduced the documentary film as a serious art form. Although we shall see that many documentaries had a typically "pathological" coloring, we should also recall more serious works, such as the magnificent series of mountaineering films, *The White Hell of Pitz Palu*, for example, in which Leni Reifenstahl served her apprenticeship in film. The sheer skill displayed by the production teams on these pictures defies belief. There were cameramen on *Pitz Palu* who were capable of hand holding a 35 mm camera while going downhill on skis! There were other distinguished documentaries of a different kind: essays on Berlin, *Berlin: Symphony of a Big City*; or the low key and realistic *People on Sunday*, made by Billy Wilder and Robert Siodmak.

"Expressionists" (i.e., antirealistic, neo-Gothic) cinema produced masterpieces such as *The Cabinet of Doctor Caligari, The Golem, The*

147

Student of Prague. Fritz Lang made *Siegfried*, with one of the best dragons ever to appear in any Wagnerian or para-Wagnerian work. He also made *Metropolis*, whose superb sets and crowd scenes nearly caused UFA to go bankrupt. Another of his pictures, *Frau im Mond*, was a strange anticipation of space-opera. Lang's best efforts were variously concerned with crime. The *Dr. Mabuse* pictures were something in the style of *Fu-Manchu* films and novels, but his biggest success, and one of the greatest crime pictures of all time, was *M*, a film based on the life and deeds of the famous Düsseldorf murderer, Piter Kürten.

G. W. Pabst was more of a Weimar liberal than Lang. He made the film of Brecht's *Threepenny Opera*, and also *Kameradschaft*. The sentimental story of French and German miners cooperating during a pit disaster, it had some of the most convincing sets—of a coal mine—ever to be built for the screen. Other pictures revealed more of the era's mood. *Alraune*, starring the ubiquitous and dreadful Brigitte Helm, was based on Hans Ewers's best-selling novel about a modern *femme fatale*, the offspring of a whore and a condemned murderer, who destroyed all men who loved her. It is the celebration of a particularly German erotic myth of woman. German woman is either the warm, blond Heidelberg landlady's daughter who falls in love with a student prince, a direct descendant of Goethe's Gretchen; or else she is the dark destroyer, dominant, a cold force of evil, who breaks men on her wheel—debased versions to be found in their hundreds on the Tauentzienstrasse, with lace-up boots and whip. The dark destroyer was to find her most perfect realization in *The Blue Angel*.

The staple of early German cinema was the so-called "enlightenment film," a documentary which sought to shock, stimulate and also—and this should not be forgotten—to inform. Ilya Ehrenburg believed that these films also had the function of distracting Germany's attention from its defeat. Other observers, however, felt that films about homosexuality, rape, abortion, and syphilis—featuring a doctor in a white coat—"had their finger on the pulse of the age, and its problems."[1]

There were other films, notably UFA features, which were unequivocally sensational. Ilya Ehrenberg wandered onto an UFA lot one day to find the following in progress:

Her father was trying to immure the heroine, her lover was whipping her. She jumped out of a seven-storey window and the hero hanged himself. The director told me that the picture would have an alternative, happy ending for export.[2]

Berlin cinemas played an endless succession of such films as can be seen from this selection of titles:

Sinful Blood; The Sinner; The White Sinner; The Fair Sinner; The Sins of the Father, the Sins of the Mother or, *She Goes the Same Way; The Fruit of*

Sin; The Hall of the Seven Sins; Slaves of the Senses; The Prostitute's Daughter; Lu the Cocotte; Cocottes in the Saddle; Goddess Whore and Woman; Love for a Night—"A criminal film, sensational, erotic, sadistic . . ."[3]

For all its success, however, and partly because of *Metropolis*, by 1927 UFA was virtually bankrupt. It was bought up by Alfred Hugenberg. An ex-Krupp manager, he had grown to be one of Germany's greatest media barons, controlling some 150 newspapers, a publishing house, Germany's leading wire service and now UFA. An ultra-conservative, Hugenberg was also a leading member of Stahlhelm, a paramilitary organization and veteran's association which had been founded on Christmas Day 1918 by a distiller, Franz Seldte, "to end the *Schweinerei* of revolution. . . . The Stahlhelm sees in the restoration of Germany's military power the only way to freedom and world peace."[4] Only persons who had been under fire were accepted for membership.

Much has been made of UFA's "falling" into such antirepublican hands, yet it is easy to exaggerate the consequences. UFA had always made right-wing films: among them, *Fridericus Rex*, which was so successful that it produced countless progeny. *Siegfried* itself has been said to foreshadow the Nazi pomp of Nuremburg and the Third Reich architecture of Albert Speer. Besides, UFA's production policies did not change appreciably after the takeover, and surprisingly its largely Jewish production staff cooperated in reasonable harmony with the new Stahlhelm elements. Alec Swan, who worked with UFA shortly after the takeover, recalls that "the Stahlhelm atmosphere was very much in the background, and the company was a strange mixture of Prussian corps students with scarred faces, Hungarians and Russian Jews."

They made a very mixed bag of films. There was a series starring the English Lilian Harvey and Willy Fritsch—supposedly real-life lovers for the sake of publicity—with titles like *I and the Empress, Hungarian Rhapsody, The Congress Dances*. In *Three from the Filling Station* three young men, including Hans Albers, bought a filling station and had adventures. Then there were the "*Prunkfilme*," great extravagant productions like *The Arabian Nights*. In retrospect Alec Swan does not feel that there was any undue emphasis on right-wing values, any excessive taking of the patriotic line, or rather that Hugenberg's coming had not changed the emphasis visibly. He did, however, detect the beginning of an anti-Semitic mood. The first signs in the industry came from Argentinian Germans who accused the Jews of UFA of producing extravagant *Prunkfilme* which did nothing at the box office.

Hugenberg or not, German films of the period were infinitely better than anything else being produced in Europe. Alec Swan remembers them as being vastly superior to the English domestic product—more imaginative, technically more advanced, and also "a great deal more sinister." Some of the violence, the pathological quality of Weimar life, had infiltrated the local "dream factory" to produce works like *M* or *Alraune*. Yet the industry has been charged with providing the public with easy escapism, when it should have been reminding them of harsh reality. The accusation is all part of that readiness that republican Germans of the Weimar generation display to look for scapegoats, to accuse both others and themselves of the sins of omission which made Hitler's rise to power possible. The industry which produced *The Congress Dances* is also held responsible. Whether or not the accusation is a valid one is difficult to say. Certainly anyone in the entertainment industry accused of failing to employ his money to "raise the level of the public's consciousness" would be predictably annoyed. Moreover, it must be conceded that *Kühle Wampe*, Brecht's own attempt at an alternative proletariat cinema, aimed at consciousness raising, has not stood the test of time.

On the level of myth and even perhaps artistic achievement, *The Blue Angel* was Weimar Germany's most important film. Based on a story by Heinrich Mann, and worked on by Carl Zuckmayer, among others, it tells the story of the sexual humiliation of a small-town schoolmaster and pillar of society by cabaret singer Lola Lola. Significance-hunters have seen in it an allegory of the new, young and decadent Germany overthrowing an older generation by exploration of the Germanic obsession with sexual humiliation at the hands of unfeeling beauty—a theme that was to find its finest expression in Alban Berg's unfinished masterpiece *Lulu*. But *The Blue Angel* is important for other reasons: its setting, music and atmosphere. Together with *The Threepenny Opera*, it recreates for us one of the most important moods of artistic Weimar and the subject of much unsatisfied nostalgia—the mood of the cabaret.

The Blue Angel was made by Joseph von Sternberg, once an Austrian, now an American. He spoke German with an American accent, but spoke it well. Alec Swan attended the reception UFA gave for him on his arrival. He was deeply taken with his surroundings and his welcome, and when called on for a speech simply said, "I thought it was to Berlin that I was coming, but I have surfaced in heaven" (*"Ich bin im Himmel aufgetaucht"*). The story of the casting is part of film history. Emil Jannings, one of UFA's greatest stars, was to play the schoolmaster. He was a genius at portraying the progressive stages of humiliation: in *Der Letzte Mann*, for example, in which he starred as the proud hotel porter obliged to end his days as a lavatory attendant. Jannings was a *habitué* of the Adlon bar, where the bartender would silently hand him his brimming glass of Pilsener as he arrived.[5] He was also reputed to have read Spengler's monumental *Decline of the West* at a six-day bicycle race, since it was the only place he could find any peace.

Casting Lola Lola was harder. Every actress in Berlin was after the part, and even Leni Riefenstahl wanted it. Indeed when she heard that she had failed, she collapsed into hysterics of disappointment. Von Sternberg knew what he wanted and couldn't find it. A Russian emigrée, Alexandra Bodryeva, was asked to audition for the part, although she had never acted in her life. She was so unnerved by the prison-like atmosphere of the UFA studios at Neubabelsberg that, with a distinct touch of paranoia, she promptly had herself smuggled out on the floor of a taxi and would hear no more about it.

Another girl, a cabaret artist, asked her composer Friedrich Holländer to accompany her as she went through a repertoire of songs he had written for her. Holländer wrote:

Von Sternberg was wearing a poison-green winter coat, carrying a walking stick, wearing upturned mustaches which gave him a flirtatiously pessimistic appearance. . . . I felt at once that you could only be his friend if you had known him three hundred years. Then you'd be a good one. I was right.

But three hundred years earlier we all went into Hall 5 where there was a small stage with a piano on it.[6]

The result of that audition was that the girl failed to get the part, but Holländer was asked to write the music. An immensely gifted composer with a range from cabaret to light opera, he set to work with a will. One day he had an inspired idea for the melody of one of Lola Lola's main numbers, and in order to "sell" the music to von Sternberg he rapidly penned off some words to give the impression of a finished song. Stuck for the last line, he wrote more or less the first thing that came into his head and scanned.

> *Ich bin von Kopf bis Fuss*
> *Auf Liebe eingestellt*
> *Das ist doch mein' Welt*
> *Und sonst gar nichts*—"And nothing else."

The greatest, longest lasting hit of the age, *Falling in Love Again*, was born.

Maria Magdalena von Losch, the daughter of a beautiful army widow, living at 19 Unter den Linden, had enjoyed a modest acting career. Sporting a cigarette holder and a monocle, she had played parts such as the vamp in *Duel on the Lido*.[7] She was a gawky child who had left school early to study the violin in Weimar. At sixteen she returned to the capital to play in a cinema orchestra. She got a small part in a Reinhardt play, which involved sitting at a table and playing bridge. The couturier gave her a magnificent dress, but as she had to spend most of her time onstage with her back to the audience she feared that its effect would be lost. Never herself at a loss on such occasions, she cut the back out of the dress in order to expose her own back to the public.[8] She made repeated efforts to get into films, but UFA kept turning her down. Essentially a cabaret artist, she appeared with the great Margo Lion, whose material she subsequently made ample use of in shows such as *Es liegt in der Luft*.

One day von Sternberg saw her in the Berliner Theater, and asked her to audition for his film. She was reluctant to do so, recalling her previous vain attempts to break into movies, and though she made the screen test felt it had been a disaster. She was camera shy and thought herself awkward and graceless. Yet von Sternberg knew what he was doing. Indeed to many discerning eyes who had seen her work in cabaret and the theater, her latent star quality was apparent. Alec Swan well recalls seeing her in some revue and feeling convinced that one day she would become a big star. Von Sternberg detected that quality all right, perhaps even before she did. She certainly did not expect to get the most important part there had been in German cinema for years, and could not believe her ears when later that evening Friedrich Holländer found her in Silhouette to congratulate her. That evening the Marlene Dietrich legend was born.

When Sergei Dhiagileff came to Berlin, he was amazed by what he found. He had "conquered" every other city he had played, but Berlin was too much for him. Theatrical life there was so extraordinarily rich that on a short visit he never knew which play to see first. There was, for him, no other city in the world to equal it: "Faced by Berlin I'm like a schoolboy in love with a *grande dame*, and I cannot find the key to her heart."[9]

With over one hundred theaters catering to a tremendous range of tastes and its innumerable cabarets, Berlin theatrical life had a unique breadth and depth. For someone like Alec Swan, the range and talent of Berlin theater was quite overwhelming. He came across "modern" staging, acting, lighting techniques for the first time, saw bare uncluttered and formalistic sets, saw theater in the round. It was as if he had found a theatrical world light years ahead of anything he had ever experienced.

Gerda Redlich is an Austrian who has worked in and around theater for most of her life, and worked with all the great German producers of the twenties. I asked her why she thought Berlin theater was so rich:

There was tremendous talent in Berlin at that time—acting, producing, the technicians—but it had much more to do with the public. The British public are just not theater-minded. In those days in Germany everyone went to the theater, it was part of their life. In the Berlin of my youth in the middle classes it was the done thing to go, to talk about theater, music, books, in quite ordinary homes. It seems to me that a lot of perfectly intelligent English people live very well without the arts. Well, I couldn't and there were many in Germany like me. One lived with theater as an essential part of one's life.

Of course, it was not just Berlin. The sheer richness of provincial theater is inconceivable to us today. In the past every one of the principalities and kingdoms that had come together to form Germany had possessed a court theater. A town such as Nuremberg, not even a provincial capital, contained in 1928 two theaters and an opera house —all flourishing concerns.

After the war, theater had rapidly got going again, although there were problems. Ernst Aufricht, later to have his own theater and put on the greatest success of the age, received his first acting engagement with a traveling company late in 1918 entirely because he was the proud possessor of a decent civilian suit.

He graduated to a Dresden company, which had its share of eccentrics. Not the least of these was Lothar Mehnert, a pederast who used to play the cold villains of classical German theater. One day he pursued a schoolboy down the main street of Dresden, ogling him though his gold-rimmed monocle. The boy, growing increasingly alarmed, eventually made his escape by leaping onto a passing tram. The actor stood in the middle of the street brandishing an immaculately rolled umbrella, shouting after him in a nasal voice known to the entire town, "Coward, coward." Mehnert used to sit up all night sniffing cocaine and drinking red wine. In the morning he would take massive doses of veronal to sleep. He died of angina at fifty, looking like an old man. Another Dresden company was run by a woman in her sixties. She required young male actors to sleep with her if they were to keep their jobs. The experience proved too horrible for A.W., one day to become a star. He confided to an actress friend that if it went on much longer he would never be able to sleep with a woman again; and so it turned out.

The most famous and greatest Berlin producer of the early twenties was Max Reinhardt. Many people felt that he had done his most exciting work before the war, and that his extravagant style, magnificent crowd scenes and sensational lighting effects were out of touch with the spirit of the twenties. Nevertheless, Reinhardt dominated the official theater life of the age. His most ambitious enterprise was the opening on November 28, 1919, of the Grosses Schauspielhaus—even by Berlin standards a gigantic undertaking. He bought a circus, once the Zirkus Schumann, the property of a Danish family, and commissioned the architect Poelzig to turn it into a gigantic theater. Poelzig worked on the project with Gerda Redlich's father, who came to Berlin from Vienna to do so. The result was a three-thousand-seat theater of a totally revolutionary kind. There was a raised floor which formed the acting area, providing the possibility for theater in the round or a proscenium arch with or without an apron. The arena could be filled in with seats, which was seldom done since essentially Reinhardt wanted a theater for massive spectacles.

The great problem that the architects had to solve was the acoustics:

The client wants a big new dome to replace the old one over the stage and orchestra. We have tried to give the dome a form which will eliminate the poor acoustics that are inevitable with a smooth-surfaced dome. This is why the dome is stepped with hanging pegs to break up the sound waves and prevent echo.[10]

The result was surprisingly good. "You could *whisper*," said Gerda Redlich. You could also hear perfectly well in the cheap seats. But according to Albert Dreyfuss—now head of the theater section of the Märkisches Museum and then a Communist theater technician—there was a blank spot, oddly enough in the stalls: rows 4–7.

People were divided about the appearance of the place. Gerda Redlich found it "terribly ugly. . . . I couldn't stand it. It looked like a stalactite cave, but Mr. Poelzig and Mr. Redlich thought it was marvelous." Reinhardt had hoped to create a new type of people's theater, with a scale and exuberance to match the spirit of those years of revolution. He put on *The Oresteia*, *Hamlet* and a play written by the revolutionary Ernst Toller about a revolt by the Luddite lace makers of Nottingham. He hoped eventually to secure the support and patronage of the trade unions, to create a new kind of theater with a new kind of public—but he failed.

In the foyer one wandered about during the intermissions as if under fantastic lotus stems, lit up from within, red and green. Architecturally a people's theater was born, with Bengal lights for snobs prepared to pay. Unfortunately, a program suited to the house was not forthcoming. They resorted to the normal classical repertoire. . . . The Greek plays still filled the house, but plays of our own time appropriate to Reinhardt's Playhouse of the Three Thousand were not written. . . . A general mistrust of the "Arena" developed, and the circus by the Spree became a place for pseudo-intellectual snobs.[11]

After six years' struggle Reinhardt gave up and sold his theater to Eric Charell, who mounted musical extravaganzas and put on musical comedies such as *The Merry Widow* and the world-famous *White Horse Inn*.

But despite this commercial failure, Reinhardt remains one of the great Weimar directors, indeed one of the great directors of the century. Gerda Redlich worked both with Reinhardt and Stanislavsky, and knew that in both cases she had had the privilege of working for genius. She is revealing about Reinhardt:

154

He was so much better doing theatrical "chamber music." I don't know why he went in for those big productions. It was not that I felt they were out of tune with the age, but he was so marvelous doing intimate theater: Wedekind, Brückner and Ibsen. He had such subtlety, such a gentle finesse.

Reinhardt was marvelous, too, at telling you exactly the gesture, the pitch he wanted. He could tell an actor almost anything and get him to do it right. He would just take him by the hand and tell him, gently and quietly. He was also marvelous with his students. All he would do was say to you very quietly: "But you promised me you would be an actress."

No, he wasn't frightening to work for. You see we had tremendous respect. You would not say a word too many, and would never waste his time. No, I didn't feel overdirected. I might do now, but then I was young and wanted to learn.

He was very small and very modest. At rehearsals he used to sit forward on his hands. He really was modest, using modesty without any irony. He didn't even know that he was sitting like that when he was watching. He was no poseur. That man was completely genuine. He was theater, of course, but such a simple man. He never posed.

For his contemporaries, Reinhardt's genius declared itself in his handling of spectacles:

When Shakespeare wrote "Enter with drums and colors," Reinhardt seized his opportunity. He would work on such a scene for a fortnight, till at last the crowd lived as an entity, and at the same time as a collection of individuals.[12]

Reinhardt looked for a people's theater which would bridge the gap between a classical repertoire and a popular audience, but he failed. Erwin Piscator sought for people's theater of a very different kind. It had its roots in working-class theater, in prewar plays and actors who sought to use their art to create a militant and aware proletariat. The development of this kind of theater was closely bound up with the growth of the trade union movement, worker's educational societies which used worker's theater as the highlight of political meetings; in fact, the first play ever written for German-language worker's theater had been written by Friedrich Engels in 1847.

Piscator, a Bavarian, first ran a Proletariat Theater in Berlin which performed left-wing plays in various halls. A year or so later he directed at the Volksbühne (People's Stage). Working-class theater was an important feature of Berlin life, in the sense that the working class actually went to the plays put on for them. (One can think of more recent and comparable experiments in London, where this has not proved the case.) As Gerda Redlich recalls:

Oh, yes, the workers did go. Piscator's publicity penetrated the factories, and there were very cheap tickets for the whole season. But, of course, the

155

bourgeoisie went too. It was very mixed. But the Volksbühne had a completely different public. Workers wouldn't go to Reinhardt. He was too precious.

Your generation is so cynical when it comes to ideas like playing to a working class audience, the sentimental attraction of "art for the people." You haven't lived through those days. You have no idea how idealistic we were, you don't know the excitement of the idea of Soviet Russia for young people then. I was a blazing Communist. We all used to go and wave red flags at demonstrations. That's what you do at eighteen.

There was a different electricity when you worked in front of a working-class audience. Even before the audience came in, the atmosphere was different. Less refined. The feel of the company, the relationship to the director were different. The plays were different, too. There were discussions with the audience, and plays could actually be whistled down, which was unheard of elsewhere.

Piscator's production style was very propagandistic, with banners, and slogans projected onto the wall. He was very different from Reinhardt, in his manner as well as in the style of his plays. "Where Reinhardt was very gentle and quiet Piscator *screamed.* He knew what he wanted and if he didn't get it he *screamed*—which Reinhardt would never do." He inaugurated a new style of theater, one which would be elaborated by Brecht. He sought to "raise the level of political awareness" of his public, rather than to allow them to escape to a never-never land. He was the first Western producer to make extensive and often very expensive use of machinery—cycloramas, projected slides, film even. His sets were bare, antinaturalistic, with gaunt scaffolding forming complicated patterns round the acting area. In 1927 he asked the architect Walter Gropius to design him a "total theater," with some two thousand seats. In the meantime he rented another theater and put on plays such as *Schweik, Rasputin,* and *Konjunktur,* a play about exploitation of minerals in the Balkans. All the pieces involved massive theater technology. *Schweik* had two treadmills weighing five tons each, *Rasputin* a 25-foot-high hemisphere weighing a ton. For audiences who knew little or nothing of Soviet theater, the impact of this strange blend of technology and agitprop, film and live theater was electrifying. Yet, Gerda Redlich found that as a performer, it was all too easy to be smothered by the hardware. She especially disliked being transported across stage on conveyor belts.

Piscator's techniques, his use of slogans and nonrealistic settings in the interests of left-wing propaganda smacks of plays put on by troupes of strolling ideologues playing to factory audiences in Cuba and Red China—the kind of work that fills some with enthusiastic admiration and most with a deadly boredom. Yet it can work, as anyone who saw Joan Littlewood's *Oh, What A Lovely War!*—a very Piscatorial treatment of World War I—will agree. In Gerda Redlich's view, Joan Littlewood has been the only director in the West to absorb the lessons of Piscator on the level of pure, effective theater. Yet it may be said that Piscator's greatest contribution to his art came much later, when he worked at the Dramatic Workshop in New York, where students such as Brando, Steiger, Tony Curtis, Shelley Winters, Harry Belafonte, Arthur Miller and Tennessee Williams were exposed to his influence. He also played his part in developing the ideas of Bertholt Brecht.

Brecht came from Augsburg, and he chose to emphasize his Bavarian coarseness in his speech, personal habits, and that strange parody of working-class appearance which he assumed: leather jacket and cap, dirty white shirt and a black cigar, which he used to chew instead of smoke. He had a remarkable talent for always appearing with precisely two days' growth of beard, never more, never less. Gerda Redlich did not care for him:

He stank. I couldn't stand it. He stank. That cigar, that chin, that shirt he never changed. Brecht was always making trouble for everyone including his wife. How one could live with this man? She was so nice, and she was clean.

Count Kessler found him strikingly decadent in appearance: his face almost that of a criminal type, swarthy with black hair, and eyes that were unusually watchful. Yet in conversation he would thaw, almost to the point of being naive.

Whatever his affectations, he was a person of immense talent, even to Gerda Redlich, although she feels that his genius has been over-estimated in the West. He impressed as a playwright and poet, but also as a singer of his own songs. Zuckmayer recalls an early meeting:

I didn't know his songs and ballads. And you didn't really know them until you heard him singing them while playing the guitar. He was expert at the instrument and loved complicated chords. . . . His singing was raw and abrasive, often with the crudity of a street singer or music-hall minstrel. An unmistakable Augsburg intonation underlay it. Sometimes he sang with something approaching beauty; his voice floated along with emotional vibratos, enunciating every syllable with great clarity.[13]

One critic characterized the mood of his work, as follows: "It is brutally sensual and melancholically delicate. There is vulgarity in it, and abysses of sadness, savage wit and plaintive lyricism."[14] He saw Brecht as "a poet who would seek to portray decay and with this portrayal spreads light. Who would seek to be cynical and with this cynicism moves our hearts. *Who is young and has already seen all the depths.*"[15]

Gerda Redlich, who admits her prejudice, saw him differently. She loves his plays, but could not stand the assumed ugliness of his singing in "a nasal voice, very ugly." She also found him dreadfully vain, *"eingebildet"*: "No one could tell him anything. He knew he was a genius, even if we didn't. He knew it." She also disliked the spartan and deliberate ugliness of his early productions:

Brecht had this idea of stringing hessian across the stage and projecting slogans on it. I found it so ugly I called it "hanging out the washing." You acted either in front of the washing or behind it. Then the washing was taken away for a bit. Then it was put back and another slogan projected, and you played the next scene in front. It was so primitive and ugly; you looked at nothing but ugliness.

Ugliness or not, it was Brecht who helped to create the greatest theatrical triumph of the age and the one piece to assume a place in the repertoire of world theater. *The Threepenny Opera* or *Beggar's Opera*, originally entitled *Gesindel (The Vagabonds)*, was commissioned by Ernst Aufricht, who owned the Theater am Schiffbauerdamm, now the home of the Berliner Ensemble. Although in later years much has been made of the piece's ideological commitment, it seemed at the time to Aufricht —and to Brecht—"a merry literary operetta with occasional flashes of social criticism."[16] Serious comment *was* offered by lines such as "Eating first and moralizing later," and it must be said that an operetta involving the story of Peachum organizing the beggars of London cut deep in a Berlin where unemployment was rising daily. Gerda Redlich certainly felt that the piece had plenty of bite and "relevance." Yet it was *not* an exercise in ideology, no matter what has been said about it since.

Kurt Weill was commissioned to write the music, and it is arguable that this particular collaboration brought out the best that either Brecht or Weill would ever achieve, notwithstanding *Mahagonny, Mother Courage* and "September Song." As with *The Blue Angel*, the influence of cabaret asserted itself strongly. There was an attempt to get away from straight operetta and theater by employing artists with cabaret experience. Rosa Valetti played Mrs. Peachum with her frightening face, vulgar voice and low sense of Berlin repartee.[17] Police chief Tiger Brown was played by the huge, shapeless cabaret star Kurt Gerron. His daughter Lucy was played by a ballad singer, Kate Kühl. The music, with its syncopated rhythms and hint of declamatory ballad, comes closer to cabaret than operetta—much closer. Richard Stroud, who produced the work some forty-five years later, felt that the music had been written for actors to perform rather than for singers to sing. Yet the first cast found it dreadfully difficult. The ideas were too clearly stated, the diction too thin and not as theatrical and stagey as they were used to. They felt lost and unhappy in a totally unfamiliar idiom.

One morning Weill arrived at rehearsal promising to produce the score the next day, and in the meantime he asked Aufricht to give his wife a part in the production as a whore. Aufricht remembered:

I was unimpressed. I didn't know her work, hadn't heard of her. "All right," I said all the same, for she looked as if she had talent, moved well and was attractive. "Weill is going to write a song for me," she said as she left. "She's not afraid to ask," I thought. I also felt that such a pretty wife did not suit Weill at all.[18]

The wife in question was Lotte Lenya; the song, one of her greatest, "The Song of Pirate Jenny."

The production had its problems. In particular, the leading lady was unhappy. Polly Peachum was to be played by Carola Neher, who, in future years, would be second only to Lenya in the interpretation of Brecht/Weill plays. But at the time of this production she had returned for the first run-through from St. Moritz, where her husband had just died of TB. She wore mourning and complained that her part was too small. Brecht intervened, called the curtain down and began to write. The exhausted cast sat around waiting. By 5 A.M. they had had enough; they demanded to do the last act and go home. Brecht kept passing speeches to Neher, who was in the process of appreciating them, when Aufricht suggested they call it a day. She hurled the script to the ground, said "Play it yourself," and walked out. It was one week before opening. After auditioning a series of terrible stand-ins, they found Roma Bahn who learned the part fast and well.

The dress rehearsal presented a new problem. Harald Paulsen, who played Macheath or Mack the Knife, a sinister character, was more used to operetta. He strolled on in an immensely dapper made-to-measure black suit of 1900 cut, narrow trousers with understraps, patent leather shoes with white spats, a thin sword stick and bowler hat. The costume was rounded off with a huge light-blue silk bowtie, to match the color of his eyes. He would never perform without it, and could not see why it should send the rest of the company into frenzy. He refused to dispense with it. Catastrophe loomed, but Brecht had an idea: "Let him go on, looking so sweet and charming. Weill and I will bring him on to a street song which will tell of his crimes and he'll look even more sinister with that silk tie." And that is how the greatest of all *The Threepenny Opera* songs, "Mack the Knife," was born.

The night before they opened Peachum, played by Erich Ponto, appeared in the office with his bags packed. He objected to cuts in the seventh scene and was catching the next train to Dresden. He was eventually persuaded to unpack "for the sake of Aufricht's wife and children." Next came a dreadful row over the set, with the designer, Brecht and Weill all swearing that they would never set foot in Aufricht's theater again. They soon relented.

They opened on time, with the famous fugue-like overture, a popular parody of modern musical harmonies which left the audience aghast.

Kurt Gerron was then to come on with a barrel organ singing "Mack the Knife," but the barrel organ was silent; they had forgotten to set it and the orchestra only came in on the second verse. Macheath strutted across the stage and the scene ended with Lenya the whore saying, "That was Mack the Knife." The curtain went down to amazement but no applause.

The next two scenes were played to a hostile silence. There were no laughs, and Aufricht began to shake. Then Macheath and Tiger Brown began to sing of the good old days in the army, "Soldaten wohnen auf den Kanonen" ("I must be barmy, I joined the Army"), and that was the breakthrough. They brought the house down. But there was one last hitch. During the first interval Aufricht went behind and could not believe his ears. The quiet, withdrawn Weill was yelling his head off. He was going to take his wife away immediately; she would not go on again. It appears that they had left her name off the cast list. He brandished the program in fury. Fortunately she had just had a tremendous ovation with her tango ballad, "In einer Zeit. . . ," so she soothed her husband, and the show went on. The program was later corrected and reprinted.

It is hard enough to reach for the atmosphere of theater fifty years ago; it is infinitely harder to reconstruct anything as essentially ephemeral and context-bound as cabaret. Yet cabaret was in many ways the supreme form of Weimar Berlin. Not only did it inspire works like *The Blue Angel* and *The Threepenny Opera*, it had a kind of ironic quality and informal looseness and cheekiness, a sense of political awareness that combined to make it capture the spirit of its age better than more serious forms. Moreover, it lacked the burdensome attributes of high culture. Functioning in parallel to legitimate theater, musical comedy and Moulin Rouge-type nude shows, the term *cabaret* covered a very wide range: from strip clubs to places where there was more poetry read than flesh exposed.

The cabaret in which Sally Bowles, played by Liza Minelli, performed in *Cabaret* (1972) was not a "literary" cabaret. It was closer to the conventional nightclub, with one notable exception—the MC or *conférencier*. A *conférencier* was more than the linkman between the acts, "he was much more a commentator upon the age and its conscience."[19] He would talk to the audience, comment on current events and personalities. The words of a good *conférencier* would have real political cut. Later on in the republic there was a *conférencier* of genius, Werner Fink, who risked his life in the interests of his jokes. He would raise his hand to the Hitler salute, and say "That's how deep we're in the shit," and if there were Nazis in the audience he would ask them politely if they would like him to proceed a little more slowly. Fink was the anchorman at Katakombe in the Bellevuestrasse, appropriately named as the last and, according to Sefton Delmer, the most important cabaret of them all. Fink would deliver his lines fast, stammering almost, in a modest and withdrawn style, and would tease the Nazis mercilessly. "No, I'm not Jewish," he would say, "I only look intelligent." Miraculously, his act survived Hitler's takeover; and more miraculously still, Fink survived the war. It is a terrible testament to the traumas which collective guilt inflicted upon an entire generation that when a young historian met him some years ago, Fink, one of the great names in the sad story of the attempt to fight Nazis with humor and satire, would do no more than remind him, "I was against the régime from the start."

Jushny was another famous *conférencier*. Working in a Russian cabaret called The Blue Bird, he employed an amazing blend of Russian and pidgin German to create an extraordinarily witty and engaging act. One evening he and his cabaret appeared in a Kurfürsten-damm theater. He observed a gentleman with a great gray bush of hair, having the time of his life in one of the front boxes. Jushny tossed him a huge ball from the stage, and the gentleman duly tossed it back. The two men, enthralled, continued to play a solemn game of catch for some minutes. Jushny's partner was Albert Einstein.[20]

Gerda Redlich worked a lot in cabaret. She took over from Holländer's wife, Bladine Erbinger, in one of her most famous numbers, Klabund's "Ich baumle mit der Beene." Erich Kästner, a wonderfully sour poet and novelist whose *Fabian* tells us more of the spirit of Weimar than any chronicle, wrote poems for her which she would perform at Katakombe. Himself a characteristic figure of the age, Kästner used to chain smoke, always buying a brand with a plain back to the packet on which he would compose his poems in tiny handwriting whilst sitting in a café on the Kurfürstendamm.

Redlich enjoyed working in cabaret, but much preferred the theater. Cabaret work was more demanding because of the intimate contact with the audience:

In cabaret you could see your audience, sitting and drinking at the tables. It was a good atmosphere. A literary cabaret would have a conférencier, introducing each number with a lot of satire. There would be a series of songs, sketches, poetry and some very, very good dancing. It was always topical and political, the literary cabaret. The nearest thing you would know would be that television show That Was The Week That Was *with David Frost as* conférencier. *(The difference was that the TV men were simply actors speaking lines written for them, while a good* conférencier *would improvise; cabaret people would often write their own material.) There were also people's cabarets, with popular Berlin characters such as Clare Waldorff working in*

161

dialect. She was as common as they make them, but acquired terrific snob value and became very famous.

Behind the performers was a tremendous bank of writing and composing talent. Holländer wrote music; and the two greatest Weimar satirists, Kurt Tucholsky and Walter Mehring, were among the innumerable writers who provided performers with words: words to satirize soldiers, profiteers, reactionaries and all other aspects of Germany which the new generation hoped to sweep away.

Almost a cabaret star was Anita Berber, a wild and beautiful stripper, and one of the personalities of the age. Her urgent dancing seemed to contemporaries to express the feverish urgency of their time. She was to be seen at boxing matches, six-day bicycle races, and in nightclubs keeping dubious company. She loved men but probably preferred women, and was fond of brandy, morphine and cocaine.

> *What interests the audience:*
> *Hunger, misery, suffering millions,*
> *Thousands rotting away in jail?*
> *Does that interest the audience?*
> *Alas, the naked bottom of Anita Berber:*
> *That interests the audience.*[21]

Anita Berber died at the age of twenty-nine. She was myth as much as, if not more than, artist—rather like the image of Isadora Duncan, filtered through the movies, a German version of the beautiful and the damned. As one commentator put it, "She personified the feverish twenties in Berlin, in public, as no one else."[22]

Margo Lion was different. She was tall and thin to the point of being ugly. Gerda Redlich recalls seeing her use her angular body as only a performer can; she was much like Hermione Gingold in this respect. Her voice had terrific range and she would play with it to great comic effect. Trude Hersterberg was another slightly older performer, who had her own cabaret for some time, The Wild Stage. Friedrich Holländer said that if ever there was a reincarnation of Yvette Guilbert, it was Trude Hesterberg. Her voice was throaty and animated, while Margo Lion sang as she looked with a splendid and exaggerated delivery. "Sex Appeal" was a number in which she longed to be "sexy like Lola Lola." She wanted sex, 7, 8, 9, and even 10 appeal as well.

Alas, the names remain no more than names. Reading the songs written for them can give no idea of the animation, the personality with which they brought those songs to life. The rare recordings they made are sad listening: a recording studio is no place to recreate the atmosphere of songs sung to live audiences; one gets the feeling that the performers are on best behavior. The songs themselves have very simple accompaniments, piano only, or small groups. Hersterberg's material seems to have consisted of songs with verse after verse of narration, usually with a chorus, and a distinct music-hall ring to the delivery. They are much closer to that idiom than they are to the jazz-influenced dance music of the 1920s, which fills today's listeners with *ersatz* nostalgia. The cabaret material is usually a parodistic, exaggerated and overemphasized version of conventional music-hall idiom. The songs are thin and clear, designed for a small audience that wants to hear the words. They are often full of *double entendre* and are antimilitary, parodies of working-class songs or tales of criminal life.

The massive talent behind the writing and the sheer style of the performing explains why Brecht and Weill used a cabaret idiom for their work. Yet that work both contained and surpassed it. It employed the idiom yet added enormously in verbal and musical inventiveness. In retrospect, the cabaret songs have charm, wit and a very specialized nostalgia to commend them, but they lack the special appeal of more popular "cheap dance music." To find that quality one has to go to films such as *Bombs over Monte Carlo*, which abound in jazzy material of that kind. Better still one should turn to Brecht and Weill. They combine the idioms of jazz and cabaret, work on a broad canvas, and add both resonance and genius to create the greatest work in a very considerable tradition. To listen to their songs and music is to hear the very best that Berlin had to offer. The cabaret songs were excellent of their kind, yet they lacked the overwhelming impact of works that sign an era, works like the music of Bessie Smith, Duke Ellington or Scott Joplin. Brecht/Weill delivered that kind of impact, and that is the all-important difference.

The Grosses Schauspielhaus.

Max Reinhardt rehearsing at his theater school.

164

A photomontage showing Erwin Piscator and his theater at Nollendorfplatz.

"The Threepenny Opera"—Harald Paulsen as Macheath with Roma
Bahn as Polly Peachum and Rosa Valetti as Frau Peachum.

Trude Hesterberg in Weill's "Mahagonny."

Zeppelins over Berlin.

10
The Spirit of Weimar
-a Collage

BERLIN IN THE 1920s was a very special place, for its cabarets, its theaters, for its musical, literary and artistic life. Because of the pale and colorless quality of official Weimar politics, and because the traditional upper and middle classes had lost so much ground, all moral authority, and indeed all talent flowed through exclusively cultural channels. It was as if all energy was absorbed by culture and pleasure seeking, bike races and bordellos. Moreover, the contrast between Berlin West as an isolated and localized pleasure center and the profound poverty and human misery which surrounded it, from the revolution to the slump, gave the city its particular edge and atmosphere. It had a bite to it, a sense of irony and frenzy, which was fostered by the carefree and cynical character of the Berliners themselves; this created a mood which made people behave "as if there were no tomorrow."

In the dying years of the republic, from 1928 onward, as conventional politics and politicians grew daily more impotent and the stock market erected a statue to "The Unknown Solvent," the edge grew keener still. There was an increasing sense of imminent collapse and the suspicion that there might be something nasty in the woodshed. The spirit of "mature Weimar" is a strange combination of moods: extraordinary enlightenment and liberalism; extraordinary weakness; a great capacity for creative technology; a sinister willingness to search for and worship strange gods; and occasional flashes of perverted violence and vileness that are almost beyond description.

A German study of the twenties has a chapter entitled "*Technik Technik über alles.*" It was indeed a period which saw very considerable achievements in both technology and pure science. Einstein worked and taught in Berlin, and the next generation of scientists included names such as Werner von Braun. Between 1919 and 1929 German scientists won seven Nobel prizes.

The German motor industry put names such as Mercedes, Opel,

169

BMW firmly on the map. In 1928 Fritz von Opel's rocket-powered car clocked 195 km (117 mph) on the Avus, Berlin's motor-racing track. Germany was indeed motor mad:

The most dangerous side of the motor "craze" continues to be the subject of public discussion. The Deutsche Tageszeitung *refers in indignant terms to an advertisement for a motorcycle which, it is claimed, with a little practice it can be ridden even up bad streets and round curves with the hands off the handlebars.*[1]

The period saw experimental high-speed trains such as the Flying Hamburger which clocked 151 mph. Radio broadcasting started on a large scale, and on March 8–9, 1929, between 11.30 P.M. and 1.30 A.M. the first TV broadcast went out.

Yet, for the general public, the greatest achievement was undoubtedly the perfection of the Graf Zeppelin, which became the symbol of Germany's technological achievements, "a monster of supreme beauty, the idol and fetish of a nation easily given to idolatry."[2] The Zeppelin was 260 yards long—twice the length of a soccer pitch—and the height of a twelve-storey building. Its quarters were designed in the style of a luxury ocean liner. The envelope was full of hydrogen-filled balloon cells set in two rows running the length of the craft, with a narrow catwalk in between them. Flying in the Zeppelin was quite unlike ordinary powered flight. At takeoff the ground crew lifted it up and literally threw it into the air. It would float quietly and vertically upward. Only when it reached the desired height were the engines started, but even then the only sound to be heard was a remote hum. Flight was slow, but virtually silent.

The Zeppelin was the sole asset of a company called Zeppelin Ltd., and its skipper, Dr. Eckener, "the Columbus of the air," was its managing director. In 1929 it undertook a trip to New York with sixteen passengers. According to *The Times* (London) the fare, one way, was £600, which was more than twice the price of a cheap motorcar. A passenger from Lucerne describes the trip:

No one on board suffered from air sickness, although the airship on the second half of the voyage plunged on more than fifty occasions towards the sea and recovered her altitude only with difficulty. . . . Little preparation had been made [for the passengers] on board. There was a lack of food and wine, and in case of accident only one parachute was available.[3]

He came back on *The Mauretania*.

The airship was not, in fact, the safest of vehicles. A modern hot-air balloonist and scientist considers the design to have been ludicrously dangerous. Safety depended to a great extent on the amazing intuitive abilities of skipper Eckener. He had a remarkable "nose" for danger, and would take major navigational decisions on "sniffing the air."[4] Accord-

170

ing to Captain Ernst Lehmann, Eckener's second in command, sometimes a lot depended on his "sense of smell":

On one of our flights we hit very bad weather in the Rhone Valley. Suddenly Dr. Eckener came dashing into our control gondola and simultaneously pulled at all five strings, each of which releases sand ballast. I could not believe my eyes, for one should never normally pull at more than one string, so that the ship may gain height gradually. Dr. Eckener's unorthodox action made our dirigible shoot almost perpendicularly upward. The passengers—this happened during dinner—were thrown out of their seats, and the dishes from the table crashed onto the floor. But how right was our Doctor! We would have flown straight into a mountain had he not instantly sensed the danger and released sand ballast in quantity.

Yet for all its obvious disadvantages the Zeppelin won a place in the German heart and imagination. Alec Swan remembers a Danish girl who was being courted assiduously by a Zeppelin lover. He suggested to his incredulous fiancée, in all seriousness, that they spend their honeymoon aboard that splendid dirigible!

One of the most important practical achievements of Weimar Germany was, of course, the Bauhaus movement led by the architect Walter Gropius. Its consequences for the history of design and architecture do not require emphasis here, nor is this the appropriate place to repeat its story. More interesting for an account of the spirit of Weimar is a certain fundamental strangeness, crankiness even, in its conception. It was very much a part of the series of countercultures, communes and "alternative societies" which riddled Weimar, and which show just how urgently the new generation wished to dissociate itself from its conventional cultural heritage and turn its back on the world of traditional and official values.

The Bauhaus was, initially at least, very much part of this quest for differently organized social forms. It sought for a creative association with an "organic" basis, one that tried to deny the division of labor and the separation of labor and capital. These divisions seemed to all those in search of alternatives to modern industrial society to be the distinctive features of a modern world which they abhorred—a world which was capitalized, divided, industrialized, despiritualized. William Morris would have agreed with them, as would many young people who sought to recover the sense of community and unified values which they considered to have been characteristics of the Middle Ages, and which they hoped to find again through National Socialism.

The Bauhaus was named after the medieval institution of the *Bauhütte*. First a builder's shelter, the term had come to mean a vertically structured group which included everyone working on a particular building: masons, builders, joiners, painters, sculptors, architects. The emphasis on the "vertical" structuring of an organic whole recalls the attitudes of persons who would greet the fascist notion of the corporate state with sincere idealistic excitement. Members of a *Bauhütte* would belong to different guilds, but would bring their skills together to form the collective working upon a particular project.

The early members of the Bauhaus had other, and more crankish, characteristics. Many of them followed strange gods. The Mazdaznan religion had an important influence upon the movement, and the students' canteen was run according to its principles of ritual feeding. There were also Luddites who wished to revive medieval craftsmanship and design furniture expressing the spirituality to be achieved through a meatless diet. Of course, the achievement of the most influential design school of the century transcends such crankiness, yet it is important to the feel of the era, if not to the history of style, to appreciate that in its essential attitudes and conceptions the Bauhaus was a part of the strange forces which directed people's energies away from an existing, inherited culture, encouraging them to reach toward the most radical alternatives. In art, design and politics the radical alternative acquired a dreadful attraction for the Weimar generation, an attraction which was responsible for the creation of exciting new works, modes of design and ultimately of feeling, but which would also hasten the republic's end.

The Bauhaus and what it stood for, its style and attitudes, were profoundly antipathetic to conservative circles. When Marcel Breuer wrote to a Krupp subsidiary asking for a few lengths of steel tubing to make the prototype of what was to become the famous Breuer chair, he was informed that he was dealing with a serious enterprise, which would not release its materials for so frivolous a purpose as the construction of tubular steel furniture. Later the Nazis condemned the Bauhaus style of architecture out of hand. One of the reasons given was that one of the Bauhaus's hallmarks, the flat roof, was un-German, oriental and hence Jewish. Indeed, the Bauhaus style with its radical design conceptions—which appeared to fly in the face of all German tradition in the interests of decadent innovation—was associated with communism, avant-garde art, moral decadence, Jewishness and revolution. This extraordinary amalgam of qualities, genetic characteristics and aesthetic attributes combined everything that conservatives and Nazis alike loathed. They labeled that loathing with the splendid and all-embracing term *"Kultur-Bolshewismus,"* an expression which covered all aspects of the modern movement, from abstract painting to atonal music, and took in the new permissive morality as well.

The quest for an alternative society reflected in some of the stranger aspects of the Bauhaus had started long before the war with the youth

movement, the Wandervögel. When originated it had been an immensely serious spiritual brotherhood, which sought, as an élite, for the re-
generation from within of a German nation whose sense of organic
wholeness had been eroded by the divisive forces of materialism. The
movement involved a lot of tramping around the countryside, and in
the interests of a sense of brotherhood there was much singing of old
folk songs around campfires. It was an attempt to revert to the values
of an imaginary Middle Ages, and to restore the pure Teutonic spirit. It
offered an alternative to unenlightened self-interest, the base values,
the lack of ethical and ethnic sense which seemed to so many critics of
early twentieth-century society, throughout Europe, to characterize the
modern age. The generation of 1914 believed, really believed, in their
spiritual values; and that generation of Wandervögel went to war with
books of poetry in their haversacks. The tradition continued into the
Weimar period in a different form. Wandering from youth hostel to
youth hostel, with a guitar and some friends, was a way of escaping
from the misery of an impoverished and hungry city life. Thousands of
young Germans simply went on the road, a cross between hikers, boy
scouts, tramps and seekers after truth. Much of the high seriousness of
the youth movement persisted:

*They did not greet each other in the ordinary way. When one of them
shook hands with another member, they both clasped their fingers in an iron
pressure, and at the same time looked firmly and seriously into each other's
eyes, as if they were giving at that moment the solemn promise of eternal
holy friendship. If the other person was not a member, the look was searching
as if to discover if he were worthy of such an intimacy.*[5]

Wandervögel had provided a whole regiment of Freikorps, wearing
the Wandervögel colors of red, green and gold on their sleeves and
their emblem, the swastika, upon their helmets. When the young
Prussian officer G. R. Halkett first heard of the Nazi movement, he
assumed it to be a political offshoot of the Wandervögel. They had much
in common: the swastika; the greeting of *"Heil"*; a belief in the guild
system and the abolition of usury; a belief in higher breeding; Aryan
values; and the quest for a peculiarly German form of socialism as an
alternative to the rule of big business.

The innumerable *Siedlungen* (communes) which dotted Weimar
Germany were largely peopled by old members of the youth movement
and its sympathizers. They were evidence of the enduring need felt by
that generation to escape tradition and form a new kind of society, a
new kind of community. Many of them had much in common with the
ideals of the early Bauhaus, for example the Loheland School of
Gymnastics, Crafts and Husbandry. Situated in the Rhoen, a lonely,
barren hilly country, it taught weaving, dyeing and a special form of

gymnastics and dance—to both sexes. Gymnastics were performed naked in order that body movements might be observed more closely. The serious affirmation of a serious reason for nakedness is very characteristic. Gymnastics were considered a necessary basis for both weaving and husbandry. The régime also involved sun worship and mystic vegetarianism.

Such communities were not hotbeds of immorality. Nothing could be further from the stewpots of Berlin. The mood of high seriousness running through them precluded the trivialization of sex. Traditional morality was, of course, rejected, but sex was accepted only as part of a serious relationship. Promiscuity and sexual athleticism were rejected as strongly as they would have been in any puritanical society.[6] The *Siedlungen* formed a loosely knit movement of like-minded young people trying to create a new kind of Germany, founded on certain values and beliefs: they were anticapitalist, backward-looking to the Middle Ages, intent on cultivating a healthy mind in a sun-bronzed body and putting patriotic idealism before self-interest. They were also on the lookout for a leader who would bring about the spiritual reawakening of their country, a fact, Halkett observes, reflected in the surprising number of *Siedlungen* where attempts were made to give birth to a Messiah![7]

Any resemblance between the attitudes outlined above and the values, if not practices, of National Socialism is not a coincidental one. It is hard to understand the passionate idealism with which so many Germans greeted that movement in the 1930s, the great capacity for idealistic sacrifice which a whole generation displayed, unless one realizes that for many young people National Socialism was the actualization of their dreams of an alternative society, dreams which already played such an important part in the Weimar period. Quite recently the wife of a leading Nazi observed in private conversation that for her generation National Socialism seemed to be Germany's last chance to "turn history into myth," to recreate through modern planning and technology the modern version of an organic medieval community. Small wonder, as Halkett wryly observed, that Nazi Germany became one enormous *Siedlung*.[8]

Nudism was another manifestation of Weimar culture's attempt to revaluate all values. The naked gymnasts of Loheland were anything but an isolated phenomenon. In fact "*Nacktkultur*" was perhaps the most widespread of all manifestations of the spirit of a new Germany. It had nothing to do with the titillation of strip shows, nothing indeed to do with sex at all. It was central to the cult of the body, sun worship, sport and that naturalness and freedom of physical movement permitted for the first time in women's fashions of the twenties—short skirts, bobbed hair and the disappearance of the corset. Though this was an international movement Germany was perhaps more extreme in its celebration of those values than was the rest of Europe. Nudists, inevitably, formed societies. In the summer they would swim together, and were known to skate naked on the ice in winter. When one such group, which went in for naked get-togethers in members' houses, was charged with immorality, it uttered an impassioned plea for adult morality: "We are sufficiently mature morally to remove our clothes without shyness or embarrassment when the circumstances require it."[9] Circumstances appear to have required it frequently. The headmaster of a mixed Berlin secondary school, for example, permitted nude dancing and gymnastics in his establishment "for reasons of health."[10]

One of the most characteristic of Weimar institutions, combining crankiness and high technology, was the weekly "naked day" at the Luna Park swimming pool in Berlin. The pool boasted an artificial wave machine, which sent Atlantic rollers down the bath at regular and frequent intervals. On "Naked day" German families, spanning three generations, could be seen sitting or swimming, naked as the day they were born. The peculiar atmosphere of the place was compounded by the fact that its waiters were fully and formally dressed.

Alec Swan remembers an English journalist, Douglas Reed, returning from a nudist colony which he had visited in the line of duty. He had kept his trousers on, only to be approached and reproached by a naked lady of generous proportions who derided him for "hiding the lovely body that God has given you." Nudism has spread since those days, and flourishes in Berlin today—to the extent that there are even nude discothèques. Yet in the twenties it was a unique and peculiarly German phenomenon, or "aberration" as Sefton Delmer called it, quite unknown elsewhere. To many observers it appeared to characterize the nation's capacity for pushing practice to the extremes of theory—in this case theories about the liberation of the body—in a manner that could be excessively dogmatic and sometimes downright embarrassing.

One may understand nudism of the "health and efficiency" sort but it also had other manifestations which defy belief. Alec Swan writes:

I remember a party where a lot of English film people had come over for a conference and we all went on to somebody's house to dance. People started to strip, and finally everyone ended up naked, all playfully slapping one another's bottoms. This kind of thing really happened, however hard it may be to believe. People would just take off their clothes and indulge in hearty and utterly harmless bottom-smacking. Just dancing about fairly drunk and smacking bottoms; there was no question of an orgy or anything like that. It was just the end of a fairly ordinary UFA party. That sort of thing could not have happened in Paris; it would not, at any rate, have had the peculiarly gross quality that made it a Berlin evening.

175

Yet nudity was by no means always so gross. Count Kessler took the sculptor Maillol to Frankfurt, where he was amazed and dazzled by the nude sunbathers:

I told him that this was only part of a new feeling for life, a new conception of life which had triumphed in Germany since the war. People really wanted to live, to enjoy light, sun, happiness and their own bodies.[11]

Significantly, Maillol was equally excited by the new German architecture. Kessler associated it with the spirit that informed the nudist movement, finding it the expression of that spirit through building.

The quasi-mystical crankiness that pervaded Germany at this time had more than curiosity value to it. It suggested an increasing imbalance between rational and irrational forces, an imbalance which was potentially dangerous:

One might define politics . . . as an eternal struggle between reason and the miraculous. In times of crisis reason comes under pressure, her weapons, once so keen, are suddenly blunted, she is assailed by doubts, she either flees or is imprisoned. This is what makes a Great Time. When a people is well fed, its brain free of pressures, the advantages of reason can be perceived once again, the times grow small, boring and cheerful. God grant us a Small Time.[12]

A highly perceptive observer of the period sees the irrational element undermining all the good intentions of the new republican type:

His intelligence responded to the modern spirit. He tried hard to emerge, and help the nation emerge, from the misty atmosphere of Teutonism. But his character and instincts were centuries behind his mind. He could no more escape the hereditary tendency to fanaticism and intolerance than he could prevent himself from romanticizing the "New Realism."

So it was that a mystic, ritualistic element crept into all the rationalist movements fostered by the Social Democrats, actually paving the way for the return to paganism now being consummated under the Third Reich. The Nazis were not the first to revive the ancient sun worshippers' festival on the eve of the summer solstice, that was the chief event in the calendar of the sun-bathing and nudist clubs to which most of the leading spirits among the Social Democrats belonged. . . . Gradually, too, a fetish was made of the crudity of life in the youth hostels, and this led the young German to hark back more and more to the primitive habits of his ancestors.[13]

The spirit of the new Germany was thus imbued with the doctrinaire quest for new values:

Nearly all the Social Democrats that I knew had adopted one or other of the reforms that always cling to the skirts of a progressive movement. Some were vegetarians or ate only raw food; others went in for rational dress and regarded high heels and corsets as marks of spiritual decadence; others made a fetish of personal hygiene, washing their hands so continually that one might be excused for imagining they were trying to wash away Germany's war guilt; and a great number practiced free love, not frivolously, but in the solemn conviction that they were thereby hastening the millennium and lifting mankind to a higher plane. But whatever the fad, any deviation from it was taken as seriously as a major heresy. These new games had to be played according to the rules and anyone who took them lightly was snubbed accordingly.[14]

The strange and characteristic combination of progressive thinking and primitivism emerges with great clarity in the Weimar generation's quest for strange gods. Alternative religions flourished as never before. Ludendorff even was involved in a pagan cult which sought for the values of a pre-Christian Germany, and the swastika itself, of course, is an age-old occult emblem. It was a time when people were so anxious to believe in something that they were ready to believe in anything, with a deadly gullibility that is its own evidence of the rootlessness, the lack of center that typified the time. Writing in 1932, Rudolf Olden made a study of the contemporary cult of the irrational, specifically linking it to the political climate of his age. This analysis seems fairly obvious in retrospect; it took rather more insight in the early 1930s.

If things were not as they are, if the intellectual and the rational were not always sacrificed to the miraculous, if those under its spell did not accept it so willingly as a way of expressing their feelings, I would not need to point to instances from other walks of life where the political trends of the day impose the supremacy of the irrational upon anyone who would be a thinking man. In the short history of the German republic there has been such a dramatic swing from the rational to the irrational that even a blind man could see it. Of course no political party is altogether free of the irrational. . . . But never perhaps has a nation turned its back upon the rational so decisively and unmistakably to opt openly for the miraculous as we have today.

The irrational has combined with the impact of personality to bring about the conspicuous success of the National Socialist party. This is not the place to criticize that party's program. It suffices that the program was drawn up long after the movement started, and was abandoned long before its victory. . . . It was the "Totality of the Program"—i.e., promising everything to everybody—that was perhaps useful, but it was neither decisive nor necessary. . . . When the party abandoned its program this did it no damage.

Its method consisted of the amplification of methods used by all collectives, using flags, symbols, uniforms, marching columns, keeping step, and music to spread a feeling of unity which shaped a mass out of individuals. The decisive influence was that of the leader upon the mass.[15]

Führers apart, Germany was full of confidence men, gurus, charlatans, astrologers, alchemists and miracle workers of various kinds. Some were ordinary frauds: one of the best known cases is that of Max

Klante, who persuaded the Berlin public that he could pick winners with almost monotonous regularity, since he had access to stable information. That some should have believed him is inevitable, but that the people of Berlin should have believed him on such a scale that he could buy a large villa in the suburbs and keep horses in training himself seems scarcely credible. His system was simple. He offered anyone investing with him a return of 600 percent a year, to be secured by his successful betting. He used modern publicity and public-relations techniques to advertise his service—which got off to a good start. When the early clients found they were indeed getting 600 percent, they told others and the Klante bandwagon started to roll. So quickly did the business grow that long after he was no longer bringing off betting coups at 6–1 a time, he was able to pay his old customers out of his new subscriptions. Inevitably the whole system collapsed and most people lost a lot of money. However, the fact remains that numerous people were prepared to believe (a) that someone would do them the favor of making their money multiply six times in a year, and (b) that it is possible to predict the outcome of a horse race.

Max Klante was a people's con man. The case of Fritz Haber is very different, and perhaps even stranger. Haber was a distinguished scientist. In his search for an artificial fertilizer, he invented the explosive which permitted Germany to continue fighting the war without the help of imported saltpeter. He also invented poison gas by another mistake. In the 1920s he devoted much time and effort to the attempt to extract gold from seawater, and enjoyed much official support for the project. When, in the course of his research, he discovered that he had misplaced a decimal point in his early calculations, he had a nervous breakdown.

Haber could not really be described as an alchemist, but Fritz Tausend actually made the serious claim that he could manufacture gold, and for some time he was taken perfectly seriously in official circles. Again it was a case of people believing what they want to believe. The government backed him in the hope that his techniques might solve the reparations problem. Ludendorff, too, gave him financial support. Eventually the "demonstrations" he laid on were seen to be deceptions and he went to prison in 1929, but not before he had been taken seriously by persons who ought to have known better.

More extreme claims still were made by the Austrian autodidact peasant Schappeller, who claimed to have invented a new source of energy, "Space Energy," which would transform life on earth, make its controller the lord of creation, provide infinitely cheap power and create diamonds out of stone, gold out of mud. He too won support in high places, sufficient to enable him to purchase the castle which dominated the village of his birth and carry out expensive restorations. Part of the support came from the ex-kaiser himself, who provided Schappeller with large sums. After his protégé was exposed as a charlatan, the ex-kaiser outlined his motives for supporting him. It was not, he said, that he had any ambition to rule the world: "He wished to liberate himself from the heavy burden of guilt which the collapse of Germany had inflicted upon him through his participation in an undertaking which would render his old empire apt for social renewal."[16]

Occultism and clairvoyance also enjoyed a tremendous vogue at the time, sometimes with ludicrous results:

A case due to come before a Berlin court tomorrow arises from a spiritualistic seance in 1920, at which the medium announced that Ludwig Uhland (who died in 1862) would give a demonstration. A pencil was then removed from a closed satchel, and a few moments later the occupants of the dimly lit room found themselves, it is stated, in the possession of a poem entitled "Wiederkehr," written on stained yellow paper, in handwriting resembling that of the poet and signed L. Uhland—1920. The poem is said to have been accepted as authentic by two hundred experts.

Those present at the seance bound themselves to silence, but one of them, an author, has now begun proceedings against the medium for the restitution of the manuscript, which, he states, was originally delivered into his hands.[17]

The judge reserved his decision, and refused to allow the spiritualists to give the evidence of dead people through mediums.

Erich Jan Hanussen was one of the most popular occultists and clairvoyants of the early 1930s. He was a charlatan with a good mind-reading act and considerable hypnotic powers. A member of fashionable Berlin, he used to give public demonstrations of hypnotism in night-clubs; he was also protégé of Count Helldorf, a senior Nazi who later became Berlin's chief of police. After the Nazis came to power, he became their magician and astrologer until it emerged that, far from being the Danish baron he purported to be, he was a German Jew. A few days after the discovery, he was found shot dead in a forest outside Berlin. However Hanussen lives—or at least his stage name does! Today in Berlin there are posters advertising the fabulous occult and clairvoyant powers of one Erich Jan Hanussen.

Stranger than run-of-the-mill charlatanism was the case of a certain Weissenberg, a Berlin prophet regarded by many as a saint and a miracle worker. Weissenberg claimed to raise the dead—by means of cheese. He treated a small child with curds, and when it died maintained that it was not really dead: a liberal application of cheese to head and foot should restore it. The cheese was applied and time passed. After a week the body was forcibly removed, although the parents, trusting Weissenberg's judgment, maintained that the child was still alive and that the police had killed it by interrupting the treatment. Weissenberg went on to conduct religious meetings, attempting to raise the dead. His public was middle-aged, working class and gullible, and his meetings produced scenes of quite extraordinary mass hysteria. He would begin them by asking for contributions for the community he had founded, New Jerusalem. Then Sister Grete Müller, one of his assistants, would enter into a trance. She spoke with the voice of "Old Bismarck," who would urge all present to subscribe to New Jerusalem. The crowd would begin to get hysterical, then Weissenberg would walk among them laying on hands and calming them. They would then suppose themselves to be historical persons from Wilhelm II's circle, and would all shout and scream together. Despite the fact that Weissenberg went to prison, his sect grew and grew and, of course, considered him a martyr.

It was a time when Germany was literally full of persons describing themselves as spiritual leaders. Some of them were noble, holy and rather remarkable men. R. Olday describes such a guru, "The Old Man," who preached a gospel of peace in the Hamburg slums and commanded a considerable following. Others were more exotic. Indeed the most exotic false prophet of them all was the utterly remarkable Muck Lamberty, who spread something akin to a medieval religious hysteria wherever he went. Leading a "New Troupe" of dancers, singers, players and followers who had come to him from the Youth Movement he moved from town to town, preaching pantheism, ecstasy and the fire of the spirit. He and his band would literally dance into a town, and when they arrived everyone would dance with them—policemen, mayor and fire brigade. Eyewitnesses confirm that when, for example, they entered Erfurt they got the whole town dancing and singing with them in a joyful condition of mass hysteria.

Lamberty was an interesting kind of Pied Piper, for he was a racist and an anti-Semite, preaching the need for high racial purity. This may explain why he and his troupe were so welcome in the future Nazi stronghold of Thuringia. Lamberty practically took over the province, with a castle, Leuchtenberg, placed at his disposal; and he was even invited to preach from the cathedral pulpit—on mystical texts such as "Wir wollen wieder ins Blaue!" His Nietzsche-esque celebrations of Dionysiac ecstasy were brought to a halt, however. Two "Virgin Marys" in his commune, each claiming to bear the new Messiah by Lamberty, complained to the local authority that he was holding courts of love in his castle. A hearing of a distinctly medieval kind was held and Lamberty was formally banished. However short-lived his reign, though, his mixture of racism, ecstasy, leadership, dancing and medievalism do not seem altogether harmless, particularly when one recalls the Nazi leader's wife and her belief that the Nazis had the chance "to turn history into myth."

180

Perhaps the most telling case of strange gods and leaders, and one that takes us to the very heart of conservative Weimar, involves a simple act of deception that got out of hand. The story of Harry Domela is that of a German "Inspector General," and like Gogol's play of that name it is a monument to small-town gullibility. But with one difference: it is true.

The young Domela had spent a year in Berlin living on his wits. He was often penniless, in and around a criminal fringe of vagabonds and down and outs. He moved on to Hamburg where his luck changed appreciably. He made some money playing cards and decided to pay a visit to Heidelberg. There he made friends with members of one of the smartest student corporations. An actor by nature, Domela had suggested that he was a young gentleman, Baron Korff, traveling round Germany for his pleasure. He was immediately accepted at face value, and entertained liberally and frequently by students who found him no end of a fine fellow. His memoirs, incidentally, give a fascinating outsider's view of the remarkably ritualistic and taxing patterns of entertainment in their fraternity houses.

Domela enjoyed himself thoroughly and was pleased to be able to pass for what he was not, but he was much too sensible to believe that the deception could last forever. He knew the game was up when an officer asked him about the regiment in which he purported to have served. He answered evasively, but his interlocutor made it quite clear that he did not believe him for a moment. However, instead of concluding he was an impostor, the officer informed Domela that he had been "identified," although his secret was safe. The officer then informed the bemused con man that he, Domela, was really of course His Royal Highness Prince William of Prussia traveling incognito!

Domela conceded, reluctantly, that there might be something in it. From that moment his life changed. He moved from one first-class hotel to another, without ever having to pay a bill. He would occasionally and graciously accept a small gift or loan, but on the whole he would content himself with free board and lodging. When he moved on, word would precede him that a mysterious and august personage would be taking the train. He was met by the stationmaster, who would pass him on to the hotel manager. Often the mayor would pay him an unofficial visit, and insist on his going to the local opera—in the royal box. A tactful audience would pretend that he was not really there. Sometimes the guard would be turned out for his inspection. Once he accepted an invitation to shoot on an estate in East Prussia upon which he had worked as a laborer not so very long before. Old ladies curtsied to him, old gentlemen bowed; he was even presented with a dachshund. The mayor of Gotha insisted on showing him round the town, since a young

181

prince ought to know about town planning. The CO of the Erfurt garrison saluted him in public although he was in civilian dress and the colonel was an officer in the republican army.

The story is a splendid testimonial to the collective gullibility of the age, and its respect for an authority which had abdicated all power some eight years earlier. It is also a fascinating study in the psychology of royalty. In his memoirs we see Domela not only feeling an increasing disgust at the obsequious treatment he receives, but coming to take it for granted, while feeling at the same time something very close to irritation at the loss of liberty and restriction of movement which are among the burdens of any member of a princely house. Yet despite his growing dislike of the kind of Germany he discovered, he could not bring himself to leave the game until he was about to be unfrocked. He then attempted to join the French Foreign Legion, only to be arrested at the railway station. He was sent to prison for a short sentence, and there he wrote his memoirs, which set most of Germany laughing, and left a handful of students, hotel managers, mayors and stationmasters feeling rather subdued.

Domela's story rings with the higher lunacy of great farce, yet it is also a wretched tale. If a poor little amateur impostor like Domela, with no resources, could deceive so many people in high places for so long, small wonder that another, greater impostor, with a political party and a propaganda genius to support him, and ample funds at his disposal, would prove able to deceive the whole of the nation for more than a decade.

No less important than the irrationalist movement was the role played by various manifestations of violence. The whole society had an uncomfortably violent feel to it, particularly in Berlin. As Alec Swan put it:

There was always a feeling of violence about Berlin, which was not true of other capital cities. You felt that the rule of law was skin deep and people were capable of a greater degree of physical violence than one was accustomed to live with elsewhere. You felt that you could easily be arrested; and that if you were, there was no knowing what might become of you. It was a town in which it seemed remarkably easy to get shot, beaten up or generally maltreated.

Violence started with official violence. Swan was profoundly shocked by regular newspaper reports describing the army or the police going into action in the streets of Berlin—against strikers or Communists. Their assaults were described with all the dash and admiration for the heroic boys in gray usually reserved for the dispatches of war correspondents trying to keep up morale on the home front. A regular Berlin headline of the age might read: "Police obliged to open fire on a demonstration—ten dead.''[18] One cannot help questioning the nature of the obligation.

Christopher Isherwood, as we have seen, found the dark part of Berlin "very dark indeed, a kind of sinister jungle''; and there, too, acts of remarkable and idiosyncratic violence could occur. The Berlin underworld was in many ways unique. It was highly organized into clubs, the "Ringvereine," which were criminal associations with patriotic names such as *Immertreu* or euphemistic ones such as "The Harmless Thirteen." They had considerable group solidarity, as the following news-story suggests:

An affray between criminals and members of the Hamburg Carpenters Guild occurred on Saturday night in Berlin, near the Schlesischer Bahnhof, a district of ill-repute. A number of Hamburg carpenters were gathered in a café when several members of a criminal organization arrived. They had been to the burial of a colleague and were dressed in dinner jackets and silk hats. A brawl followed in which two of the carpenters were hurt. The aggressors disappeared and the café was closed. Later four more carpenters arrived, and at the same time thirty-five taxicabs with reinforcements for the original aggressors.[19]

The *Verein* in question was *Immertreu*. In the ensuing revolver fight one carpenter was killed, others wounded, and the café wrecked. Members of the *Verein* were eventually brought to a trial, in the course of which someone stole the fur coat belonging to Frey, their defending attorney. *Immertreu* never found the culprit, but they bought Frey a new fur coat.

There was more to the Berlin underworld than mere violence, however. It also had a peculiar kind of clumsy poetry—the dinner jackets and silk hats, the thirty-five taxicabs—and that poetry is very much a part of the feeling of the age. It comes out most strongly in one of the most famous arrests that the Berlin police have ever made. One summer a *Verein*, whose alleged basis for association was an interest in boating, rented an island on one of the lakes outside Berlin. The members were armed and hard to get at, since they controlled the hire of all boats to and from the island. The police hit on the idea of masquerading as a singing *Verein*, and wrote asking for leave to serenade them. Leave was given and the police choir duly arrived by steamer. They landed, sang a couple of songs, and then proceeded to draw their revolvers and arrest the entire audience.

Even prison life seemed to have a different feel in Germany. A long-term occupant of Sonnenberg prison, which was run according to the "soft" principles of penal reformers, wrote to a newspaper to complain:

Slackness, disorder, and injustice. . . . The prison authorities do not further the maintenance of law and discipline when they countenance and even

encourage the rowdy elements in the prison; when they tolerate insults
against the state, the nation's officers and even other prisoners.[20]

Yet towering over this idiosyncratic but, on the whole, understandable climate of urban violence was a pattern of crime of an altogether
different nature: pathological, sickening actions with almost mythic
significance. The fact that it could happen at all casts its own light upon
the climate of the Weimar age: "Hardly a month passed without some
terrible murder becoming known. In many cases ordinary criminal
instincts were combined with sexual perversions typical of the day."[21]

There was the case of Piter Kürten, the Düsseldorf murderer, who
killed innumerable victims from his school days on. In later life he killed
children, burying their bodies on the outskirts of town. He eventually
started writing to the press telling them where his latest victim was to be
found. The motive was, quite simply, pleasure, and when he finally gave
himself up it was so that his wife might collect the reward. His performance in court was at first horrifyingly detached and matter of fact, but
despite his reserve he shocked the court so profoundly that he saw the
enormity of his deeds reflected in their faces, whereupon he stopped
talking and hid in the dock. Kürten was guillotined.

Karl Denke was a peasant mass-murderer who came to grief when he
failed to kill one of his intended victims with the first blow. A fight
ensued in the course of which help arrived, and Denke, a quiet, religious
man, was arrested. He hanged himself in his cell that night. A search of
his house revealed innumerable bloodstained garments, including fifteen
jackets bound together with human skin, 351 teeth, braces of human
skin, a barrel full of bones, a dish full of human fat, and a large quantity
of smoked human meat in jars. Denke had been selling it as goats' meat.

Haarmann of Hanover was perhaps the worst of the three. He was a
homosexual who would pick up boys, take them back to his home and
have sex with them. Often he would reach a state of sexual frenzy, in the
course of which he would murder them, sometimes by biting their throat
out. He would sell their meat, preserved or otherwise, to butchers and
food manufacturers. Once again, as with Denke, we find that combination of food and violence, which, in various forms, such as the
Weisswurst, threads its way through the history of the age. Haarmann
had been under suspicion of mass murder for a long time and tried to
brazen it out, walking openly about the town in a dark suit carrying an
umbrella. He was a friend of the chief of police, having probably been an
informer, and the chief was reluctant to prosecute. The city grew
increasingly hysterical as more and more recently buried bones were
unearthed. He was eventually arrested and found guilty of twenty-seven
murders. As Rom Landauer has said: "Indeed human nature could
assume no lower forms."[22]

"The Republic with a hole in its heart" never enjoyed widespread popular support. It is astonishing to realize that pro-republican parties had their first and only majority in the 1919 election, when people voted for parliamentary democracy rather than a system of soviets. The very idea of liberalism was profoundly unsympathetic to many Germans. E. Mowrer, one of the most intelligent observers of Weimar Germany, believed that as a race the Germans hated common sense, reason and liberal values, all of which they regarded as dreadfully bourgeois. They nursed a passion for irrationality—principles beyond mere reason—which made them loathe a republic begot by reason out of defeat, that made a point of playing down ceremonial and personality, and that required one to vote not for a face but for a list. Moreover, the forces opposing the Social Democrats declined to fight reason with reason; this in itself would have been a betrayal."Whoever fights liberalism with its own weapons has become liberal," wrote Hans Zeher in *Die Tat*, October 1931, while Spengler suggested that the last fight of Western civilization against the forces seeking to corrupt it—i.e., capitalism and materialism—would be "the fight of blood against money."

Official republican politics was a colorless business. Violet Markham was astounded at the monotony, order and lack of oratory to be found in political meetings of the early 1920s. Speakers simply read out prepared speeches, and hecklers had to mount the platform to make a point. She was equally amazed at the Germans' tolerance of long boring speeches. Politics, moreover, was depersonalized to the point where it was not possible to get the party list of candidates for a particular electoral area, let alone for the Reich. Hitler's impact becomes more understandable when one grasps the nature of the competition. When Count Kessler discussed Hitler's success with a leading republican, he blamed it upon the republic's failure to make any appeal to Youth or Heroism: those who sought heroics turned elsewhere.

Herr Wallenberg blames the colorless quality of republican politics upon a certain German thoroughness. He considered German democracy to be a peculiar kind of growth. Its architects had observed and analyzed what had happened in other and older democracies, and then, proceeding from fundamentals, set out to demonstrate that they could build a better and more perfect system by working from first principles. The theory was perfect, but the practice made for a gray, anonymous state, free of any glamour or leading principle which could provide a rallying point to a nation long accustomed to rallying. Not only did the republic lack all emotional conviction, even more important it lacked a republican right wing. The right was either fascist or monarchist; the idea of a "conservative republican" was a contradiction in terms. In the meantime, the Communists, the second largest party in Weimar

Germany's last election, were quite as antirepublican as the right.

The weakness of the republic was increased by the fact that young energy flowed into the arts not into politics. One old Jew from East Berlin who was a good Communist told me that well-to-do middle-class Jewish families actively discouraged their children from playing any sort of political role in the republic. Those who disobeyed were frequently disowned, treated as pariahs. His view would seem to suggest that the most talented gene pool in Germany played no part in republican politics. This had by no means always been the case. Walther Rathenau, the first foreign minister of the Weimar Republic, was a Jew. In 1922 he was gunned down in his car on his way to work by a band of right-wing extremists, including Ernst von Salomon who was imprisoned for his part in the action. Von Salomon later wrote that it was precisely because Rathenau was both an excellent foreign minister and a Jew that he had to be killed. His assassination is perhaps the most notorious of all the political murders that studded the early years of the Weimar Republic.

It is perhaps arguable that the lack of political participation was, in fact, part of a more widespread failure of the intelligentsia to stand behind their new republic. Thus Max Weber and Thomas Mann, two of the most distinguished authors to have survived the war, may both have endorsed the republic, but neither did so with any conspicuous enthusiasm. At no stage was there anything approaching a distinguished republican "establishment." Moreover, it is striking that Germans of the Weimar generation tend to describe themselves as "good democrats," an abstract expression, where, if pressed, an Englishman might well talk of a belief in Parliament, and an American speak of his Constitution. In contrast a Weimar German would speak of "democracy," an abstraction, and it was the nebulous nature of that abstraction which rendered it so vulnerable to pressure.

The democratic idea itself had a kind of feebleness born of decency. Wallenberg suggested that the kind of radical policies initiated by Roosevelt's New Deal would have been totally unacceptable to many good democrats simply because they flouted nonessential democratic principles. This respect for the technical aspect of the rule of law was such that it took a Hitler to put through policies which appeared to get Germany out of the depression. One day at the height of the slump, Wallenberg's father suggested that the government should abolish or reduce unemployment benefits and put the unemployed to work building roads. His son, a "good democrat," was horrified, but today he realizes that more actions of that kind might have stopped Hitler from coming to power.

The most telling condemnation of the style of Weimar republicanism comes from the Nazis themselves and the word they used to express the whole "evil" of the regime: "*System*," the Weimar period being the "*Systemzeit*." The Hitler people used the term as a blanket indictment of the persons and principles which had betrayed Germany. This is because the very idea of democratic institutions and a rule of law securing inalienable rights defended by a constitution was profoundly abhorrent to so many Germans. "*System*" suggests a society ruled by law. But what the Nazis, and many idealists, wanted was a society governed according to principles above the law itself; this was the basis of Hitler's defense at his 1924 trial. Democracy had no charm for a nation too full of persons of widely varying complexions and idealisms, all ready to bend or smash the rule of law in the interests of "a higher moral issue" — and anyone who felt he was wrong to do so was just part of the abhorred *System*.

Pro-republican forces may have been weak, but the anti-republican faction was full of conviction. The republic, from the outset, had failed to detach itself from its past. On the rostrum of the Reichstag the speaker's and ministers' chairs continued to bear the imperial and royal insignia: the crown and black eagle. Of course, it is notoriously difficult to fulfill a revolution's promise of radical change for the better; the examples of France and Russia spring to mind. Alexis de Tocqueville suggested that social habits and institutions shape the hearts and minds of a nation so powerfully that a mere change in mode of government is unlikely to make for a long-lasting alteration in the social climate. True of France, how much truer is this of Weimar Germany, where the members of the old administrative establishment in law, civil administration and education were actually kept on by the revolutionary government that had overthrown the régime to which they had pledged their allegiance!

Professor Reiff's old law tutor lamented to him bitterly at the time:

How can you possibly hope to institute a new republic when all the old legal and administrative establishment are still in their old positions? You cannot turn a nation round over night and create new institutions when the persons who have to operate them grew up in the atmosphere of the old ones.

The republic, then, enjoyed the services of a monarchically minded judiciary, which explains the extraordinary disproportion in sentencing throughout the period. Right-wing assassins tended to be discharged or given light sentences (Hitler got fortress arrest), whereas the usual fate of the left-wing extremist was to be "shot while trying to escape."

University and high schools too were largely staffed by old-régime teachers who became increasingly monarchical as their world and its values collapsed around them. They felt they had a sacred mission to bring up the young according to the old ways. Moreover, the student corporations were also radically antirepublican, although they were too socially secure ever to side with the Nazis. One student, a member of

Saxo-Borussia, named Ludwig Freiherr Heyl-Worms, explained that the role of such corporations had become a central one, since the disappearance of the officer caste made them now the sole supporters of the monarchical tradition.[23] Whether or not they were pro-Nazi, there can be no doubt that such attitudes made those students ready to assent to the eventual destruction of the republic.

The army was, of course, equally antirepublican. Its commanders were determined to transfer the best of Prussianness, both attitudes and cadres, into the new republic, which had pledged itself to serving military interests.[24] Because the president was commander in chief of the Reichswehr, the army swore a personal oath of allegiance to the man, not to the state. This was a minor point as long as the man in question was an ex-saddler; it became crucial when the man had once been commander in chief of the Imperial Army.

The republic made no attempt to keep the army in check. It had relied on its support against "Red terror," and was never positive that it might not have to call upon it again. In the meantime Reichswehr officers were paid salaries at one degree higher than their civil-service counterparts, and the army continued to enjoy much of its traditional prestige. Sefton Delmer, who knew Berlin better than most foreigners, once made the mistake of going to a fancy-dress ball with a toy sword and a spiked imperial helmet. He was nearly lynched, and compelled to leave. When I asked him whether, with all his experience of Germany, he should have been surprised at his reception, he replied, "I was, nevertheless. I did not think they would be quite so primitive." In retrospect it is obvious that he was lucky to escape unscathed.

It is difficult to account for the tolerance of the republican "revolutionaries" towards forces within their own administration that declared themselves openly against the régime. One suspects it derives from a combination of weakness and decency. At all events, it makes for a strangely half-hearted defense of republican principles. On August 11, 1927, Count Kessler asked the manager of a smart Berlin hotel why he had put out no flags to celebrate the anniversary of the republic, only to be informed that flags had been expressly forbidden by the management. The republican flag—black, red, gold—was known by many as "black, red, mustard," or even "black, red, chicken shit." Many German embassies, the representatives of the republic abroad, preferred to display the flag of the merchant marine which, strangely, sported the imperial colors of black, white, red.[25]

One anniversary a republican colleague of Professor Reiff's, who lived on the Hohenzollerdamm, hung out a republican flag. His neighbor, an aristocrat who had been political secretary at the Imperial War Ministry, stuck a broom out of his window in response. The republican called the police, who were calmly informed that the broom's owner belonged to a "Chinese Club" and this was their sign. The republican took the amateur Chinaman to court, only to come up against the republican judiciary. The judge's view was how dare he provoke his neighbor by displaying the flag of his republic? The case was dismissed.

Which flag to fly was a burning issue throughout the period, and the saddest of all the flag stories has no hint of right-wing brutality or republican heroics. It concerns an attempt to provide republican sympathizers with a little color, and in its Germanic combination of method, lunacy and ridicule it is a perfect rendering of the sad hole in the republic's heart, or how to blow your nose on a national emblem:

Herr Dr. jur. Ludwig Oppenheimer has patented a model called the Reichsbanner handkerchief. The patent is for handkerchiefs or display hand-kerchiefs with the Reichsflag colors—black, red, gold. The colors are either a narow stripe along the corner (Form One) or a flag with the colors placed on one corner (Form Two). . . .

The invention is intended to register the patriotic feelings of every German. The intention behind Form One is that the colors appear from the breast pocket, behind Form Two that the flag appear as a worthy emblem whenever the handkerchief is brought out for normal use.[26]

ABOVE: *A cabaret act satirizing nudism. The notice reads "Area reserved for middle class nudist colony."*

BELOW: *Women wrestlers—Hitler was much taken by them on his first visit to Berlin.*

ABOVE: *The German army practices with models on manoeuvres in 1928 because the terms of the Versailles Treaty did not allow for the use of real tanks.*

BELOW: *Selling horsemeat sausages, 1920.*

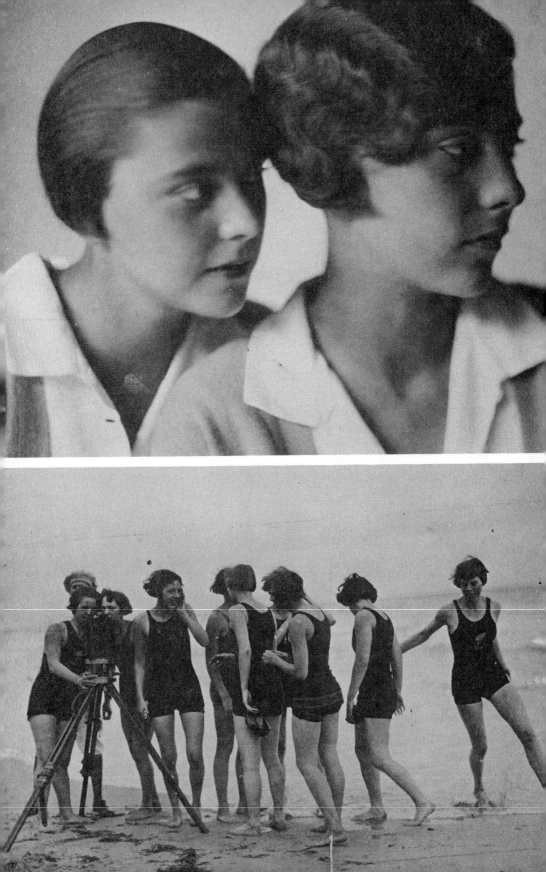

Berlin ladies.

The original caption to this picture reads: "Hitler with an SA unit during the time of struggle."

194

11
The Final Years

WEIMAR'S "FINAL YEARS" date from early 1925, shortly after its sixth anniversary. Although the republic would survive until early 1933 and indeed still had most of its "golden twenties" to come, with the death of its first president, Friedrich Ebert, on February 28, 1925, writing began to be perceptible on the wall. It was writing of a strange and characteristic kind. In the presidential elections to find a successor to Ebert no candidate secured an absolute majority on the first ballot. The procedure called for a second ballot: whoever obtained the most votes would be duly elected. The Deutschnational party tried to persuade Field Marshal Paul von Hindenburg to run for president. He refused at first and changed his mind only after pressure from the ex-kaiser. On the second ballot he got 48.3 percent of the votes; the Social Democrat, Marx, came second with 45.3 percent; and the Communist, Thälmann, trailed behind with 6.4 percent. It was a truly Weimarian result. That Hindenburg should have secured nearly half the republic's votes need come as no surprise. His political position was known:

I am too inveterate a monarchist not to prefer that form of government to the best of republics, in any situation whatsoever, since the latter will always have more deficiencies than the former, for it lacks the strong center that only a throne can create. Germans, and Prussians in particular, are not suited by Jacobite bonnets, which always have fool's bells attached to them.[1]

It is equally characteristic of Weimar that this inveterate monarchist should have been brought to power by the Communists. The party was and remained bitterly opposed to the *System*, and official Comintern policy was to fight social democracy tooth and claw. Consequently, rather than withdraw their candidate after the first ballot and instruct their members to vote for Marx, they managed to split the anti-Hindenburg vote sufficiently to let him in. Even today good Communists of the time refuse to criticize the decision, although younger and more questioning Marxists concede that the failure of the party to join the

Social Democrats, or "Sozis" as they were disparagingly known, was a fatal error. Theodore Wolff commented on the result:

Yesterday's election was an intelligence test in front of a world audience of pitying horrified friends and sneering enemies, a test which nearly half the electorate failed. What, goes the general verdict, can one do with a nation that learns nothing from its misfortunes and again and again, ten, twelve times over, allows itself to be put in a halter and led by the same leaders?[2]

Yet 48 percent of Germany wanted a hero and father figure for its president. They would agree with Hindenburg's contention that republics in general and theirs in particular lacked a strong center, and they hoped that "the Old Gentleman" would provide one. It must be said in their defense that as one looks through photographs of the political figures of the Weimar period there are only three faces that project any kind of political charisma: Goebbels, Hitler and von Hindenburg alone stand out from an otherwise gray and unexciting mass.

For Hindenburg's entry into Berlin, the army and the Stahlhelm had formed rank after rank to greet him. State Secretary Meissner thought the antirepublican presence embarrassingly large and asked the Reichsbanner organization to turn out too. Unfortunately they were rather short of republican flags. Hindenburg was asked to authorize payment from a discretionary fund in order to buy more flags and, much to Meissner's relief, he agreed.

As Brecht watched the new president drive down the Siegesallee in a gray open car, he was heard to observe, "At the end of the first quarter of the twentieth century of the Christian era they brought a man into the city and paid him the highest honors because he had never read a book."[3] It was Hindenburg's boast that the only books he had ever read were the Bible and the army manual.

The "Old Gentleman" was rather afraid that the Communist deputies would shout him down as he took his oath. However it was made clear to them that the Reichstag was only a Reichstag after the oath was taken: then and only then would they enjoy parliamentary immunity. As a result they were relatively quiet.

Hindenburg wore civilian clothes for the ceremony. After his inauguration he wished to inspect the republican guard of honor, and asked whether it would be in order to put on his Iron Cross. "You are in charge now," came the answer, and Meissner rapidly produced the decoration which was hung round the new president's neck.

The early years of his presidency were a time of calm and relative prosperity. Germany had recovered from the nightmare of inflation and political unrest. Nevertheless the scars, indeed the wounds, remained. Herr Wallenberg believes that one of the republic's greatest errors was

196

its failure to assist the economic recovery of the middle classes who had lost their savings during the period of inflation. Their enduring poverty and sense of betrayal was enough to prevent them from constituting the kind of stable center which the republic so sorely lacked. The calm of those years was no more than apparent or relative calm. True there were no civil wars, yet Germany was as full as ever of civil warriors: Communists, Stahlhelmers, Reichsbanner marched and counter-marched without too many serious clashes. Yet a sense of insecurity was ever present. It came through in small details, such as a dream dreamed by journalist Ernst Feder:

June 24, 1926. A dream. I am sitting with my father and have to lecture at 7.30. We look at the clock: 7.45. My father: "Do the clocks run on time under the fascists?"

"But, father, there is no fascism in Germany."[4]

The source of such a nightmare might be found in an occasion like the Stahlhelm Nuremburg rally of 1926. The Frenchman Henri Béraud was there, and the first thing he noticed was a sign on every pillar of a café requesting customers to refrain from beating up Jews and Frenchmen.

On the morning of June 29, at 6 A.M. Nuremberg was woken by fanfares. Old soldiers associations had come from all over Germany in various costumes including eighteenth-century dress, wearing three-cornered hats over shaven skulls. . . . There were peasants out of Werther with red coats, white stockings and broad-brimmed hats, buckled shoes and copper belts. There were village pastors too, with long coats down to their heels, and persons wearing plumed shakoes. . . .

The demonstrators were all in uniform. Most of them wore the military cross. Some in civilian clothes had military hats. Others had their bodies swathed in scarves like beadles. There were also veterans of the war of 1870 in ancient uniforms.

They were soon a hundred thousand strong, wearing Stahlhelm insignia in their lapels. . . .

Gradually officers, and medals, accumulate to the sound of martial music. And it gave you a bit of a shock to see again, in daylight, the squat little bugles, the marching boots, the Boche canteens in their field-gray covers, and the heavy visorless helmets, the helmets of Verdun.

Soon there came trucks decorated with branches and loaded with soldiers. They came shouting and singing, calling out as if they were going over the top. There were officers on the seats, and you should have seen the condescension with which they viewed the free citizens of the German republic.

Soldiers past and present joined a procession with students wearing pink green and blue, with thigh boots and gauntlets, brandishing their rapiers. Then came a sort of battalion of old senior officers with huge mustaches and

197

round bellies, wearing civilian clothes and military hats, fiercely carrying their umbrellas at the port. They marched in time, making their heels clatter. . . . Nobody laughed. Far from it. The double rank of old men marched along calling out "Zwei" every second pace at the top of their voices.

The trams had stopped all the way along the Koenigstrasse. Passengers waved their hats. People applauded from windows or waved long banners. All the bands played at once. As the generals passed they were saluted, and looked coldly, in military fashion, at the ranks which they appeared to be reviewing.

Then the flags came out: the kaiser's flags embroidered with imperial Ws, fascist flags with skull and cross bones, white flags with black swastikas, Stahlhelm flags bordered with crepe. There was not a republican flag to be seen.

When the crowd beheld these emblems it cheered and cheered. The marchers answered with a wave. The soldiers sang. Young people fell in behind them, or hung onto passing trucks. "Zwei"s rang out resoundingly with a bark which cannot be described. And the women waved their hand-kerchiefs, looking on in ecstasy; old men, their eyes moist with emotion, shouted "Hoch" in broken voices and with trembling beards.[5]

The French observer viewed proceedings with a blend of amusement and alarm. He did after all remember Verdun. Yet it was not easy to take the new German militarism seriously: Sefton Delmer's costume was a case in point. One of the first foreign correspondents to understand the increasingly violent mood of Germany was Norman Ebbutt, Berlin correspondent for *The Times*. He would file occasional short pieces which, if read carefully, made it all too clear that the old Germany had not died in 1918. It had gone to sleep for a few years, and now it was waking up.

A memorial to U-boat officers and men killed in the war was unveiled in Kiel on a date coinciding with a sinking in 1914 of three British cruisers. Der Tag remarks that it will perpetuate the tradition of the Imperial Navy and will transmit to posterity the unforgettable will to sacrifice of the U-boat crews.[6]

On another occasion he wrote:

The "Kaiserbund" Association announces the opening of a fund in honor of an occasion which "a victorious Germany would have celebrated as a national festival," namely the seventieth birthday of the former kaiser.[7]

Alec Swan realized that German militarism was to be taken seriously after the astounding experience of an acquaintance, a rather callow young Scottish left-wing journalist. One day when the Reichswehr was engaged in "heroic" operations against the Berlin Communists, the journalist had sauntered up to a platoon commander, with his hands in his pockets, to ask what was going on, only to be told, "Stand at attention when you talk to a German officer!"

The failure of his putsch had almost buried Hitler, and the prosperity of the mid-twenties nearly completed the task. However, during this time he consolidated his position in Munich society, where he was still considered something of a "rough diamond." It was with some trepidation that Baldur von Schirach introduced him to his father, chief administrator of the Weimar Theater, only to have his father find Hitler the most knowledgeable Wagnerian outside professional circles that he had ever met.[8]

At this stage in his career, Hitler considerably underestimated the breadth of his potential appeal. When von Schirach asked him to campaign for the Nazi student association in 1926 he was most reluctant, pointing out that he would never get more than 10 percent of the intellectual vote. Von Schirach considers that he made some of his finest speeches in the mid and late twenties. He was more controlled and professional than he had been in earlier years. When he made a speech he relied on nine or ten cards with slogans or block notes on them, doing all he could to avoid sounding like a lecturer. He was very aware of the need for the right props and was specific about what kind of table and podium were appropriate to the hall in question. He was also most careful about how he was introduced.

He always opened quietly and warmed his audience up. The strident Hitler caught on film was speaking at the climax of speeches intended for a mass audience. But to understand the impact of those passages, one must take them together with the gentler preliminaries.

Some years later Alexandra Bodryeva was to meet Hitler, and on one occasion was actually invited to join his party on the platform at one of his speeches. When she appeared, there was a roar of "Women out, women off the platform." She was told to go off, creep back on hands and knees, and remain kneeling behind those seated on the platform. Hitler began to speak, and though she was kneeling in acute discomfort, and had a command of German that was a great deal less than perfect, she told me that she simply lost all sense of discomfort and of the passage of time itself. There was no question of her responding to his political message—her German was not up to it anyway; it was something much closer to an overwhelming response to a piece of great but totally unfamiliar music.

A quiet beginning would give the impression that Hitler was a thinking man. The slow first half hour was usually devoted to historical exposition. He would use foreign words to indicate that he was educated. As he came to contemporary issues he would warm up and accelerate. The first burst of applause would come now, after half an hour's speaking. This would warm him up and now the sentences would come cascading out, always tightly controlled. Then he would grow quiet again, and again warm up to a crescendo, going faster and faster. After ninety minutes, his set speaking time, he would have the audience applauding his every utterance.[9]

Yet for all this oratory the Nazi movement remained essentially a Bavarian down-home phenomenon until late 1926, when Hitler made the most important appointment of his life: he gave Goebbels the post of Gauleiter of Berlin, a position which he would hold till death. When he arrived in "Red Berlin"—after Moscow, the strongest Communist stronghold in the world[10]—he found the SA a disreputable and disorganized rabble. He applied his genius for propaganda to the task of making it impossible not to be aware of the Nazi presence in the capital. It was he who was responsible for turning National Socialism from a provincial into a national movement. He set out to "conquer Berlin," and the era of the street fight had begun. The paramilitary groups which had been content to march and countermarch just a year ago were now at each other's throats. That steady erosion of law and order which characterizes the latter years of Weimar Berlin had been set in motion

Goebbels reduced the membership of the Berlin SA to a hard core of the faithful. He reorganized the administration and finances, and defined strategy. The party's immediate task was to be recognized, no matter how: "The Berliners may insult us, slander us, fight us, beat us up, but they must talk about us."[11] In order to gain publicity, "we meant to conquer the street. On the street we had to go for the masses, and that was our only road to political power."

Goebbels set out to provoke the Communists. On February 11, 1927, he hired one of the Communists' regular meeting places, the Pharus Hall in "red" Wedding, for a Nazi demonstration. In the ensuing battle, bottles, chair legs and brass knuckles held the floor, while those on the platform defended themselves with water bottles. When the police stopped the fight, Goebbels displayed the Nazi wounded on the platform. At the next meeting, more economically, he used actors to play the part.

He took provocation a stage further with a characteristically mocking twist. The RotFrontKämpferBund had designed a musical instrument, the *Schalmei*. It was built like a series of car horns, was very cheap to make, and made a "wild warlike honking sound."[12] The Nazis took the instrument over, and young SA men, led by such heroes as Horst Wessel, went marching and honking through Red Berlin. It grew increasingly difficult to tell one demonstration from another. Nazis and Communists played the same instruments, and indeed had adapted to their various ends the same collections of soldiers' songs: "You could never say for sure what kind of marching would be coming round the corner as you only heard the singing."[13] To an English eye, the Nazis and Communists looked remarkably alike:

Bodies of both Communists and Nazis were to be seen every weekend, parading in uniform, with a band at their head. They frequently came to blows. I wondered at first how they contrived to distinguish their enemies from their friends in those fracas, for their uniforms were remarkably similar, the only difference being in the brassards they wore. On closer investigation I found the Nazis were mostly of middle-class origin, and the Communists nearly all working-class youths. But as regards outward appearance there was little to choose between them.[14]

In the late twenties street fighting and confrontation were confined to working-class quarters of the capital. People living in Berlin West read about them often enough, but never saw them. It was not until 1930 that one began to notice SA men in the more fashionable parts of town. The fighting itself was a very confused affair, involving Reichsbanner, the Communist party and the National Socialist party. Christopher Isherwood found little to choose between them. In his view, all the people in uniform were simply "thugs and hustlers, spoiling for a fight. Often members of the criminal classes, they shifted from one allegiance to another with remarkable ease." The Germany he knew was fond of violent solutions and without respect for the rule of the law long before the Nazis came to power. Such opinions invite one to see the Nazi takeover not as the inexplicable phenomenon that it has so often been suggested to be, but as the logical political crystallization of a climate of violence and "appeal to principles beyond the law." I asked him about street fights, of which he had seen many.

As with so many other things, one is always on the outside; they always seem to be taking place somewhere else. Or else they are right on top of you, taking place so suddenly that they have already moved on before you have time to stop being surprised.

Sefton Delmer also saw his share of street fighting, although as he put it, "It was not something to stay and watch." When the fighting began, passers-by cleared the streets as soon as they could. "They used revolvers, truncheons, brass knuckles, anything of a lethal nature."

"Did the police steer clear?" I asked him.

"No. They would join in on the side of the right wing."

Horst Wessel was a pimp killed by a colleague, Ali Hoehler, but he had been a Nazi street fighter before he went in for minding prostitutes. He had also written a little poem published in Goebbels' *Der Angriff*. Goebbels found a tune for the poem. His genius promoted Wessel's death into a martyrdom, while his song became the Nazi anthem:

Die Fahne hoch, die Reihen fest geschlossen
SA marschiert mit ruhig festem Schritt.
Kam'raden die, RotFront und Reaktion erschossen
Marschieren im Geist in unseren Reihen mit.

201

> The banner raised, the ranks firmly closed
> SA marches with calm and steady pace.
> Comrades that Red Front and Reaction have gunned down
> March in spirit with us in our ranks.

The stirring music to which the poem was set seems less appropriate when you hear that it was once the tune of a 1900 Viennese cabaret song.[15]

One aspect of the anthem tends to go unnoticed. It is a reminder of the radical socialist claims of the movement, for its enemies include Red Front and Reaction. Quite who the reactionaries might be is hard to say, but it reminds us that the NSDAP presented themselves as a revolutionary party which sought to break with Germany's immediate past—and many people believed them. Frau Boucholz-Starck, who came from an aristocratic background, was not a Nazi, unlike her sister. But, she said, "we thought socialism was good and national socialism could only be better."

The year 1928 was important for Hitler and his movement. His party polled 800,000 votes in the election and won twelve seats in the Reichstag. One was allocated to Goering because of his splendid war record. His friends wryly observed that he was "the only man ever known to rise by means of a parachute." Another of the seats went to Goebbels. It was a good year in other respects for Hitler. He had been dreadfully short of funds, but in that year he made contact with Hugenberg, the media baron and Stahlhelmer. They were specifically united by their opposition to the Young Plan, an arrangement which laid down the future pattern of reparations payment. It had been negotiated, on the German side, by Foreign Minister Stresemann, whom Hitler described in private as "the greatest German politician since Bismarck." It was his intention to bring about Germany's full reintegration into the international community. Hitler, Hugenberg and Seldte, the founder of the Stahlhelm, organized a "National Committee for German Resistance to the Young Plan." Hitler could count on some measure of Hugenberg's not inconsiderable support in the future.

In retrospect all German right-wing organizations may look much alike, but there was a world of difference between the NSDAP and the Stahlhelm. The latter consisted of older men, war veterans, monarchists, who wished to restore the old order. They were backed essentially by big business. The Nazis were younger, and many of them believed in the idea of National Socialism, whatever that idea might be. They were radical and, in one sense, left wing, seeking to end the rule of big business and private enterprise. Many of the rank and file were genuinely appalled by what they regarded as Hitler's cynical betrayal of their cause in his quest for funds. He had aligned himself with the enemy.

There was an attempt to oust Hitler from the party leadership by the so-called "good" Nazis, the Strasser brothers Otto and Gregor. It failed. Goebbels, originally a Strasser man, crossed over, and despite a second bid for leadership in 1932, the Strassers, who have sometimes and inaccurately been termed the leaders of the Nazi left wing, were finished. "Left wing" is inaccurate since it implies the existence of a coherent party policy with delicately modulated views. There never was a coherent and consistent Nazi policy; various people believed various things, while Hitler's sole aim was power. Indeed, the sheer absence of a coherent party line enabled him to broaden the scope of his appeal and reach idealists of many complexions. Goebbels always felt that a coherent policy was something of a nuisance, impeding the true course of propaganda.

Hitler now began to enjoy substantial financial support because industry looked to him to keep the Reds in check. There was, in fact, a Red peril of sorts, in that May 1929 saw something remotely approaching an attempt at a Communist uprising in Berlin. But as Sefton Delmer, who was there, said, "I do not think one could call it an uprising, more of a muscular spasm." The "spasm" began when the Communists held a May Day parade despite a police ban. It was probably an attempt to provoke a state of actual civil war—certainly that is how the Prussian government saw it. "Actual" because there was a standing joke of the period, which was not funny, that went as follows: "Are we going to have a civil war?" "We've got a civil war already."

In Wedding the Communists turned blocks of flats into fortresses, and some eight thousand police with carbines, tear gas and armored hose cars turned out. There was heavy fighting with innumerable baton charges. Sefton Delmer remembers the scene:

In no time at all the police had jumped down from their lorries and were charging along the street, swinging their rubber truncheons at anyone who got in their way. At the same time, another posse of police charged from the far end. But quite a few people without rosettes, harmless passers-by, were left moaning and groaning on the pavement with fractured arms and shoulders, and some of them with broken skulls.

Now the women started shouting down at the police from the dingy windows above. . . .

A few minutes later I was being swept along in a fleeing crowd across the Bülowplatz, known as the Red Square of Berlin. . . . We were right to run. For at one end of the square was an overturned van. Police were firing at it, and from behind it Communists were firing back. I was lucky not to be hit. Bullets zipped up the gravel in little spurts of dust round me as I ran. A few yards from me a schoolboy fell badly wounded.[16]

203

After a series of clashes, which saw thirty-three civilians killed and many wounded, and an abortive attempt at a general strike, the spasm of "*Blutmai*," as it was called, petered out.

Goebbels's genius for provocation and propaganda may have turned the NSDAP from a local party into a national one. Communist unrest may have earned the party the support of industry, but the surge of support that brought Hitler to power came finally from factors quite beyond his planning or control. Wall Street's Black Friday had its drastic repercussions throughout the industrial world, but nowhere were those repercussions as severe as they were in Germany. Its short-lived prosperity had been based very largely on the considerable foreign investment that had come into the country in the late twenties. When the crash came, foreign investors pulled the plug out. Germany experienced the slump more acutely than any other industrial nation, and by the end of 1929 there were 3 million unemployed. Industrial wages were 10 percent lower than they had been in 1914. There was an enduring and acute poverty which took many memories back to the terrible winter of 1918–19. An American journalist touring Berlin at the time found that the horse-meat restaurant had become a major feature of working-class Wedding, yet few customers could even afford horse-meat sausage. He visited the best part of a dozen restaurants, and noticed that perhaps one customer in ten had even a glass of beer. Indeed beer consumption was 25 percent lower than prewar figures.

By 1932 the number of unemployed had risen to 7.5 million, and 17 million, almost one-third of the population, were supported by the dole; all were short of food. The stockmarkets closed in the winter of 1931 and trading did not begin again until the following spring. Cities such as Cologne and Duisberg could not pay the interest on their loans. Munich could not meet its city payroll needs. Prussian civil servants were obliged to accept cuts in a salary which they now received in five or even six instalments a month, but school and university graduates were the worst hit. Since they had never worked they could draw no dole money. Attempts were made to occupy them, for example they were given mass public chess instruction; and in Berlin special tables and chairs were set out for the unemployed to play cards.

The mood of resigned and quiet hopelessness which the depression inspired can be seen in a description of the summer camps which the unemployed created outside Berlin, camps such as Kühle Wampe. The unemployed and their families would move out in the spring and return only in the autumn:

Only the father went into town to collect his dole money. The more unemployed there were, the bigger the camps grew. Visitors were amazed at their quietness. You saw men sitting in front of their tents just staring out over the water. The rows of tents were neatly laid out, with street names and house numbers, and the space between the tents was decorated with patterns of slate.

There was nothing romantic about camp life—it was a clean, adult and neat misery, Prussian in its straightness and its precision. The foresters and the police were amazed at the discipline of the inhabitants. There was seldom any fighting or quarreling, acts of robbery or violence. Every tent town had its mayor and a small parliament. The children had their playground, and the fires on which the women cooked were laid out neatly with slates.[17]

There was a general feeling of hopelessness, accompanied by a total lack of confidence in the ability of the government to do anything about the situation. One can understand all too easily how Hitler the Savior came to power in the light of one German woman's telling observation that the nation was prepared to make great economic sacrifices *if only they had a government strong enough to make the sacrifices worthwhile*: "Out of nothing comes nothing."[18] The Weimar republic was unable to mobilize the nation's spirit of sacrifice: a spirit that Hitler was finally to exhaust.

The NSDAP broke through in the elections of 1930 when they polled nearly 6.5 million votes and secured 107 seats in the Reichstag, making them the second largest party in the country. Earlier that year the Prussian state had banned all uniforms in the hope that this would check the street fighting. Overnight the SA reappeared wearing white shirts, with bottle tops in place of insignia. When the Nazi deputies entered the Reichstag on October 13, 1930, they wore brown shirts in defiance of the ban and their entry was accompanied by savage anti-Semitic action on the streets of West Berlin.

The deadly passivity of the republicans emerges in the words of one of their deputies, a certain Kadorff. He talked with terrible resignation to journalist Ernst Feder: "I am beaten. I have spoken out against the Nazis in the Volkspartei, and now they've won. At least write me a decent obituary."[19] Feder's account of the SPD reaction to the rise of the Nazis unwittingly expressed their hopelessness. The party itself was riddled with intrigue and mutual suspicion, while the republicans as a whole seemed passive and helpless. They behaved like onlookers, only to be treated as victims.

Hitler had problems with his own deputies. They drafted a policy paper which proposed the nationalization of banks and the pegging of interest rates at 5 percent. They submitted it to Hitler who was outraged; such socialist measures would alienate his new backers. He made them retract their proposals at once, and that, says von Schirach, is the moment that Hitler moved from party leader to Führer. From then on he rejected any party policy and happily repudiated views he had put forward in the past. Following Goebbels's view that no policy is the best policy, Hitler relied henceforward not on policy but on personality, supported by propaganda.

But the personality did not always impress. Sefton Delmer, it will be recalled, found Hitler "a very ordinary man." Another journalist, Bella Fromm, found him and his SA men ludicrous. It was the clothes. In an age when good tailoring was a matter of considerable importance, the spectacle of SA men at official receptions appearing terribly proud of their ludicrously overcut britches would have been comical were it not also very alarming. Hitler himself used to appear at first in a dreadful morning coat, although she concedes that as he improved his position he also found a better tailor. At one reception she started to walk away as she saw Hitler approach the group with whom she was standing. He immediately went out of his way to shake her hand and attempted to charm her by staring intently into her eyes. She was totally unimpressed by the act.

Yet the method usually worked, for it was founded on a great instinctive sensitivity toward what others might be feeling. Hitler had an extraordinary knack of sensing which member of a small group was ill at ease or positively hostile, and would make a point of trying to charm that person.

Alexandra Bodryeva first met Hitler at Berchtesgaden. Guests usually put up at the local inn and waited to be called to his presence. She remembers going to her room last thing at night, looking down the corridor and seeing a long line of jack boots put out to be cleaned. Next morning she was invited to breakfast with a party of other guests. They waited at one end of a long room for Hitler to make his entrance, whereupon they all gave the *Hitler Grüss*; all, that is, except for Alexandra Bodryeva, who found it a strange way of greeting one's host. Immediately afterward, she felt dreadfully embarrassed by her omission. Hitler, who had no idea why she felt bad, sensed that embarrassment from the far end of the room, walked across, singled her out from the rest of the group, kissed her hand and devoted many minutes to putting her at her ease.

There was something fundamentally vulgar about Hitler's charm, the intensity of his stare in particular; yet it made converts. A police commander tells of one of his men, on duty at the Sportpalast when Hitler was speaking:

A man of whose integrity and republican convictions I was almost a hundred percent sure. He had been posted by the entrance gate when Hitler arrived. When he alighted from his car he evidently mistook the republican giant for one of the bodyguards assigned to his personal protection. He strutted up to him and grabbed his hand. While holding it in his famous straight-forward he-man grip, he gazed into the police officer's eyes with that fatal hypnotizing and irresistible stare, and it swept the poor officer right off his feet. Clicking to attention, he confessed to me this morning. "Since last night I am a National Socialist. Heil Hitler."[20]

The slump had virtually destroyed parliamentary democracy. The 1930 elections saw a massive increase in the Nazi vote, and the Communists too made very considerable gains. More and more people were turning away from moderate parties and voting for antirepublican radicals. It should be recalled that the Communists were quite as opposed to the *System* as the Nazis, and in that respect Communists and Fascists had much in common. A young German or Frenchman of that generation in search of an alternative to the political and social world he had inherited could turn to fascism or communism with an almost equal ease, for each offered idealistic and radical solutions. It was the radicalism, the rejection of a rotten old world, that was the common denominator of their appeal.

Parliamentary democracy was also rejected by the government. In 1930 Hindenburg had appointed the Catholic Heinrich Brüning, a member of the Center party, as chancellor. He proposed deflationary measures to meet the slump and failed to get his legislation through the Reichstag. It was dissolved, and the 1930 elections duly took place. But essentially, the early 1930s were years of government not by the Reichstag but by emergency decree, a power conferred upon the president by article 48 of the constitution. The power was exercised ceaselessly throughout 1931. To all intents and purposes the parliamentary system was finished.

Germany by this time was already infused with the sense of an ending. One could now see SA uniforms in the center of Berlin, when two years before that would have been inconceivable. Jewish stores had their windows smashed, and Jewish businesses desperately tried to move with the times. Ullstein, the Jewish publishers and newspaper proprietors, tried to Aryanize their staff in a pathetic attempt to adjust; and they were not alone. In other words, Hitler and his policies, which for so long had seemed to so many people no more than a joke in questionable taste, performed by a motley collection of Bavarian thugs and louts, had now become a political reality. Weimar politics were dead and the future lay with the radicals. One question remained: did the future lie with Hitler or the Soviet Union?

When Ilya Ehrenburg returned to Germany in 1931 he was struck by the sense of doom. It came across in small, rather ordinary encounters:

A middle-aged German with cropped hair and a high collar was in the railway compartment reading a thick newspaper. He told me he was a

207

commercial traveler in patent notebooks. I asked him when we were due to arrive in Berlin. He removed a timetable from his wallet. "At thirty and a half minutes past eleven." Then he picked up his paper again and said calmly, "It's the end, the end of absolutely everything."

The publisher of the radical paper Neues Tagebuch . . . *invited some authors to dinner. Everything was as usual: crystal glasses, good wine, flowers, conversation. Suddenly the host said, just like the commercial traveler, "But you know, all this will soon be finished."*[21]

Hitler's increasing credibility helped him to widen his power base. At a meeting in Harzburg in October, Nazis—including industrialists such as Hugenberg and von Thyssen, and soldiers like von Seeckt—came together to form the "Harzburg Front" to fight communism. The non-Nazi right saw Hitler and his party as the most effective counter to the Red peril, while the army had its eye on the SA as an ideal auxiliary fighting force that could eventually be incorporated.

In the meantime the army got Hitler wrong. By the autumn of 1931 Gerneral Schleicher, who had less than three years to live before his assassination on the Night of the Long Knives, found Hitler "an interesting man and outstanding speaker with plans so fantastic that he needed bringing down to earth." Von Hammerstein, chief of the High Command, considered him an "unimportant but perfectly decent fellow."[22] In general, so-called informed circles believed that he posed no kind of threat, since the army would and could restrain him; this was at a time when most of the army's NCOs possessed as a matter of course tin matchboxes with swastikas upon them.[23]

President Hindenburg had mixed views on the subject of Hitler. He would never proceed against the Nazis until Germany was allowed to re-arm, because he felt that he needed them to check communism. He also realized that Nazi-Communist clashes were a perfect excuse to justify a strong standing army. However, for all that, he would never allow "the Bohemian corporal" into the government. Hitler had his own views on Hindenburg: "I respect the old gentleman, but he has no idea what's happening. He thinks I'm just a Bohemian corporal and a disruptive element. He puts me on the same level as Thälmann [the Communist leader]."[24]

By 1931 Hitler was fooling most of the people, and beginning to gain support from reasonably intelligent and unprejudiced persons. Count Kessler met a banker, Eduard Heydt. He had been approached by the French ambassador, who wanted to make informal contact with the Nazi leadership. He had turned to Heydt because of the latter's connections with von Thyssen and the Hohenzollerns. Although Heydt was not a party member in December 1931 he could see only two alternatives: Nazis in the government, or military dictatorship. Of the two, he preferred the former. In his view the Nazis had taken too much money from industry, both Gentile and Jewish, for them to implement any "socialist" policies, and presumably their Jewish backers would be able to control their anti-Semitism.[25]

Hitler was indeed receiving the support of the Hohenzollerns. "Auwi," Prince August Wilhelm, a prince of very little brain, worked in the party's Munich headquarters, the Brown House, and his son, Prince Alexander, was a simple stormtrooper. The family as a whole backed Hitler, although the crown prince's sympathies were with the Stahlhelm. They were very far from disinterested supporters. Hitler's ability to be many things to many people had enabled him to make them suppose that he planned to restore the kaiser. Indeed, when he came to power, the Nazis were distinctly embarrassed for some weeks by the presence in Berlin of the ex-kaiser's wife who had come, as it were, "to collect."

By the end of 1931 the Nazis had become the leading party of the right, with the support of big business and to some extent the aristocracy. Many intelligent people felt that a Nazi government was the only way out of the country's troubles. For such persons Hitler was an ordinary politician. Those who could see more seemed content to sit back and wait for a slaughter which they felt to be inevitable. One army general, clever enough to see things as they really were, summed up the situation:

Machine guns, I fancy, are the only language Hitler could really manage to understand. To speak that language it is true good nerves are required, and above all the courage to cooperate with the working classes.

And nobody in high position had that nerve and that courage. The tragedy of it.[26]

In 1932 Hindenburg's term of office expired. He presented himself for re-election, and it is one of the greater ironies of Weimar Germany that he should have been supported by a political spectrum extending from German nationalists to socialists. The man who had been the enemy of democracy in 1925 was now considered by the democrats to be the only credible political alternative to Hitler. I asked Professor Reiff whether at the time people were conscious of the irony. They were not, he replied; yes, it would have been nice to have run a good Social Democrat for the presidency, but everybody agreed that Hindenburg, the Old Gentleman, was the only candidate who could stop Hitler and support the constitution—and to stop Hitler was the paramount aim. Reiff recalls campaigning for the Old Gentleman. The meetings were the biggest and best attended he ever saw in Germany. He also recalls the problems created by the sheer breadth of Hindenburg's support, when it came to finding an electoral slogan which would suit them all. The socialists'

"Drink a schnaps and vote for Hindenburg"[27] sounds suitably bland.

Hindenburg failed to secure an absolute majority on the first ballot, and a second vote was required. General von Seeckt advised his sister to vote for Hitler the second time. "Youth is right."[28] Hitler felt that time was on his side, even after Hindenburg was duly re-elected: "By the time I'm 85 [Hindenburg's age], Herr von Hindenburg will have been long gone. Our time will come."[29]

Hitler was wrong to see a live Hindenburg as an insuperable obstacle. Although he may have appeared to be an immovable mass, he was in fact nothing of the sort. He had a certain well-known capacity for letting the side down. Indeed betrayal ran in the family of the "Pétain of Germany," as Arthur Koestler has referred to him. In 1806 a Prussian major was sentenced to death for delivering the fortress of Spandau into the hands of the French without a fight: his name was Paul von Beneckendorff und Hindenburg.[30] As Admiral von Schröder, once commander of the marine corps in Flanders, observed when he learned that the "Sozis" were backing Hindenburg:

Why, what more do you want! The kaiser made him his commander in chief, and he let the kaiser down. Ludendorff won his battles for him and he let Ludendorff down. Ebert put him in a place of honor and he let Ebert down. The right-wingers made him president and he let the right-wingers down. Now the left-wingers are going to make him president. And the very devil must be in it if he doesn't let them down too. The Old Gentleman is consistent in that respect.[31]

Yet he attempted to make a reasonable start. Three days after his re-election he banned the SA and the SS. Unfortunately, the NSDAP was well prepared. Its members had been warned in advance of police raids on their HQ, and knew the police code word GREIF. They cleared their offices. By the time the police arrived, there was nothing left to raid.

A month later Hindenburg dismissed his defense minister Groener, who had been responsible for the move against the Nazis. He also dismissed Brüning and his government, appointing in their place the strangest of all the Weimar cabinets, under the aristocratic, well-dressed, but feeble and irresolute Franz von Papen. Known as the "Barons' cabinet," it was largely recruited from the Herrenklub, Berlin's most exclusive club. Von Papen's object was to start a "conservative revolution" with a view to restoring the monarchy. Once again the republic was graced with an antirepublican leader, and a man after Hindenburg's heart. Von Papen was most sympathetic to the president's demands, which included no more cooperation with the unions and an end to what he termed "agrarian bolshevism," by which he meant the attempt to stop the vast subsidies paid out to support the large and poorly run estates of the Prussian junkers.

Von Papen had been appointed on the advice of General Schleicher, and it was he, the "Field-Gray Eminence," who became the new minister of defense. Schleicher was an intelligent and unscrupulous intriguer. "Political morality has nothing to do with human morality," he once observed.[32] He expected to be the real power behind von Papen, who would be easily led. But whoever the driving force, the performance of the new government was staggeringly inept. They issued a statement of policy which left Count Kessler aghast. He felt that it made the kaiser's government seem enlightened by comparison. They proposed to abolish social security, to combat *Kulturbolschewismus*, to prepare the German nation for the coming war by re-Christianizing it and reestablishing the moral leadership of the junkers. All other parties and attitudes were rejected as unpatriotic and morally subversive. Kessler thought it the most stupid official paper to be issued in a hundred years. "It bears the stamp of the general staff in its psychological blindness."[33]

Leadership of this caliber was quite incapable of uniting a country which, as someone put it, was like a set of dumbbells—"only the extremes have weight."[34] The suspension of the SA and SS had brought a little calm after the preceding twelve months, when Berlin street fights had resulted in 182 deaths. However, in June 1932 Hindenburg allowed the Nazis two resounding victories. He dissolved the Reichstag and lifted the ban on the SA and SS.

Chaos immediately broke out all over Germany. Street fighting, murder, harrassment reached unprecedented heights to plunge the country into a state of unofficial civil war. Here is a brief list of the more violent events in early August:

August 1—Attack in Königsberg on a Prussian district president and a city councillor. The latter died of wounds. Two KPD, two SPD leaders seriously wounded. Three newspaper offices bombed.

August 2—Bombs planted in various towns in Holstein. Shooting in Marienburg. Grenade attacks in Liegnitz and Goldberg.

August 3—Mayor of Norgau shot dead. A synagogue in Kiel bombed. A Nazi killed in Kreuzberg.

August 4—Two policemen killed in Gleiwitz. Department store bombed in Ortelsburg. A land-title office burned in Labiau county.

August 5—A bank bombed in Lotzen.

August 6—A grenade attack on a chemist's house in Lyck. A Communist's house shot up in Tilsit. Grenades in Breslau, Gleiwitz, and Königsberg. Bombing and shooting in Kiel. Dynamiting in Braunschweig.

August 7—Reichsbanner leader killed in Lotzen. Catholic newspaper office and social security building bombed in Ratisbon. Twelve acts of violence in Silesia.

August 8—Twenty acts of violence in Silesia. Two deaths. Newspaper

211

offices attacked in Stettin. Reichsbanner member found dead in Liobschütz county. Nazi blown up by own grenade in Reichenbach Silesia.[35]

That same day in Potempa, Silesia, five Nazis broke into a hovel where [a Communist] slept with his aged mother. While the old woman stood terrified against the wall, she saw her son murdered in the flashes of a pocket torch. He had an eye poked out with the blunt end of a billiard cue, his throat trodden in with a boot heel, he was shot, stabbed and bludgeoned, and in all received twenty-nine wounds.[36]

Although sentenced to death, the "Potempa six" were reprieved by von Papen and subsequently released by Hitler. Commenting on the sentence of death, Rosenberg, the Nazi "ideologue," wrote:

Bourgeois justice weighs a single Communist, and a Pole at that, against five German war veterans. In this example is mirrored the ideology of the past 150 years, displaying the mistaken substructure of its being. . . . The unacceptability of this attitude explains the world view of National Socialism. It does not believe that one soul is equal to another, one man equal to another. It does not believe in rights as such: it aims to create the German man of strength, its task is to protect the German people, and all justice, all social life, politics and economics must be subordinate to this goal.[37]

There were countless other acts of violence, on smaller or larger scales. Bloody Sunday in Altona, a district of Hamburg, was one. On July 17, 1932, the Nazis marched through a Communist slum quarter —with the permission of the socialist mayor—to provoke a fight. They were fired on from rooftops and windows, and duly fired back. Trams were halted and shot up, barricades were erected. The local police needed reinforcements, a searchlight and two armored cars before they could restore order. There were fifteen killed and many wounded. "The principle casualties came from an overcurious public."[38]

Yet alarming as such set pieces were, certain intimate acts of violence appear, in retrospect, more disturbing still, for they show just how deeply ingrained the habit of killing had become. Weimar was the age of the mass murderer: Denke, Kürten, Haarmann. Nazis and Communists had no difficulty in taking human life. Indeed murder seems to have come easily to people from every walk, so much had it become part of daily life. This is borne out in the dreadful story of two gentlemen who prefer to remain anonymous since they are today both persons of distinction in their respective professions. In those days they were students. By 1932 they felt so impotent in the face of the Nazis that they relieved their frustrations by taking to the roofs of Berlin, every weekend, with rifles, and aimlessly taking pot shots at uniformed SA men as they walked through the streets.

Besides resorting to organized violence, the Nazis went in for careful

212

persecution and preparation. In Dresden a Social Democrat housing co-operative was obliged to organize its own roster of vigilantes to protect residents from violence. More alarming still, at election time, party members could be seen carefully noting what flags and posters each home displayed, as a "note for future use." One politician was heard to observe that he did not mind the abuse or the anonymous phone calls at four in the morning, but he did wish that the Nazis would stop sending him packets of excrement through the post. Journalists, Jewish ones in particular, were harassed. Egon Jameson, an Ullstein man, would get phone calls informing him of the death of his mother. He would find himself denounced for trafficking in drugs, or find his car tires slashed.

One day Jameson was invited to lunch by an old friend, Ernst Udet, a World War I fighter ace. Udet is a figure who is constantly cropping up in accounts of Berlin in its golden twenties, whether he is stunt flying, driving racing cars, or simply being a very good and charming friend to many people. When the Nazis came to power he was eventually given the job of running aircraft production for the Luftwaffe. Since his whole life revolved around aircraft, he leaped at the chance to do so. A combination of increasing horror at Hitler's policies, and increasing pressures upon his restricted powers of organization and planning made that extraordinarily brave, decent and honorable man take his own life in 1941. He deserves to be remembered.

Over lunch at Horchers that day Udet told Jameson that his name was on a Nazi death list. Jameson's first reaction was to begin planning how to dispose of certain incriminating documents. He borrowed a car and a movie camera and asked the actor Peter Lorre to drive with him to the coast. There they set up the camera and started to try to light a bonfire. "What are you doing," asked a suspicious SA man. "We are shooting the new Peter Lorre film," replied Jameson. Lorre gave the man his autograph, and said they were having trouble with the fire, could he help? The man duly obliged and much incriminating material went up in the smoke.[39]

On July 20, 1932, there occurred one of those events which give rise to endless "if only" speculation. The state of Prussia had always had a socialist government and a republican-minded police force that had tried hard to contain the SA, even though the murder rate was running as high as twelve persons a day. It has been alleged by a mildly questionable source that shortly after the ban on the SA and SS was lifted, Hitler demanded that the Prussian police be removed from socialist control in order to protect his SA.[40] At the same time we know that von Papen and Schleicher were mounting a plot against the legitimate government of Prussia. In a conversation in the Herrenklub, they allegedly agreed that it would be advisable to deliver Prussia to the Nazis, or at least to appear to accede to Hitler's demands.[41] Although there must be some doubt about this alleged appeasement of Hitler, there is no doubt at all about what happened next. Von Papen announced to the leaders of the Prussian government, Braun and Severing, that they were dismissed. Henceforward he would govern personally as "Reichs Commissar for Prussia."

Braun and Severing had been warned that von Papen was to proceed against them. They had ample time to take preventive measures. They could have barricaded themselves in their offices, defended by their own state police. They could have called for a demonstration, a show of republican strength, even a general strike. When the confrontation with von Papen actually happened, Braun did none of these things. He did not even vote in favor of the Prussian ministers withdrawing to discuss a plan of action. Von Papen was greatly relieved by Braun's docility. He had not been at all sure that he could get away with his illegal action. Braun then replied, with dignity, that he would yield "only to force," losing much of that dignity when he asked "force" to arrive at 8 P.M. as opposed to 6 P.M. because he had a meeting. "What time would you like the force, Herr Minister?" went a current joke.[42] When it did come, it consisted of two men and an NCO.

There can be no doubt that Braun and Severing displayed that meekness which marked so many of the decent political figures of Weimar. They vacated their office rather easily, it is true, but what should they have done? A German's answer to the question "Should they have resisted?" reveals much about his politics and temperament. Those whose opinions have been profoundly colored by their politics or by sheer shame for their recent history will say, to a man, that of course they should have fought. There might have been a civil war, but that would have prevented Hitler from coming to power and avoided the death roll of World War II. It is the argument of decent men, but it could scarcely have impressed itself upon Braun.

More practical persons suggest that a fight was impossible. Whether one thinks it possible or not depends on one's assessment of the various forces available to the republicans. They had the Reichsbanner, and possibly the Prussian police. Conceivably, the Communists would also have joined them. Against them were the SA, the Stahlhelm and the German army—whose oath of allegiance was to Field Marshal Hindenburg. Moreover, although it is often said that the police as a whole were prorepublican and anti-Hitler, it is by no means certain that they would have come out against the government of the Reich. When I asked Sefton Delmer whether the police had been sufficiently republican to support Braun in a civil war, he told me, "That's nonsense. Not all nonsense in so far as their republicanism goes. It is nonsense if it meant that they might have come out against the government on behalf of republican principle."

Yet von Papen and Schleicher *were* nervous. I have listened to a recording of von Papen's broadcast to the nation, telling them what he had done, and it was a dreadfully hesitant performance: that of a weak man trying to overlay a fundamental nervousness by speaking with a confidence he does not feel. Indeed, von Papen had every right to be frightened. Dürsteberg, a leading Stahlhelm figure, says that even a republican demonstration and strike would have had a very considerable effect. Assent or civil war were thus not the sole alternatives open to Braun. Yet a sense of decency combined with a lack of political moral fiber made the "good guys" lie down and get trampled once again. Heinrich Mann put it more cruelly, blaming the trade-union background of the socialists for their failure:

The Sozis failed because of their scorn for the intellect. They had now paid the price for the repression of intellectuals and the promotion of trade unionists. Severing lacked the intellect to resist.[43]

It must be said, however, that Weimar's intellectuals did not resist much either.

The July election campaign was a particularly savage one. The rival parties were all on a civil-war footing and had all sunk to the same level of violence:

A state of virtual anarchy prevails in the streets of Germany. . . . Brown shirts were everywhere in evidence again, and now four private armies, equipped at the very least with jack knives and revolvers, daggers and brass knuckles, were shooting in the squares and rampaging through the towns. Processions and meetings, demonstrations and protest, festivals and funerals, all wore the same face but a different uniform—except that the SS and SA of the Nazis, and the Red Front of the Communists marched more obstreperously, the Sozi Reichsbanner more fatly, the Stahlhelmers more sedately. The Reichswehr, the one legal force, was least in evidence, even though it was, in a sense, the private political tool of Hindenburg.[44]

The army, incidentally, was a hundred thousand strong. There were also a hundred thousand police, while the various private armies together numbered four million.

Every party adopted the same electoral methods, Hitler's methods: uniforms, military music, catchwords and whirlwind plane trips. The mood of the country was violent and the electorate wanted extreme, not reasonable, solutions. Schoolgirls painted swastikas on their fingernails and shrieked "*Heil Hitler*" in class.

The universities were also radical. As one rector put it:

Formerly students studied in order to obtain a philosophy of life. Now they

215

arrive with positive convictions about everything, usually entirely unfounded, and refuse to listen to anything but a confirmation of their adolescent pipe dreams.[45]

Perhaps the worst indication of the mental level of the student population comes through in one of the favorite Nazi student chants of the period, a rejection of Weimar and indeed of all political decency in the interests of strong leadership: "Wir scheissen auf die Freiheit!" ("We shit on freedom!") cried the generation which would soon be burning its books.

To this generation Hitler presented himself as the patriotic unifier of a divided country. He had altered the quality of his oratory, making it more sophisticated:

This was the same Hitler speaking, a little heavier, his hair thinner, his voice hoarser, but not the same speech. Gone was the invective of his earlier rabble-rousing orations. He never spoke the word Jew, nor did he pause to attack individuals. With an almost disdainful self-assurance he launched out on a high philosophical plane, rising into ever more rarefied regions of almost abstract theory as he spoke. No need now to stoop to the level of the dullest dolt among the crowd, as before he had done with deliberate purpose. Even if his passionate periods about a dying epoch, state concepts, world outlooks and the imminent Nazi millennium went over their heads, they were clearly moved.... He spoke with the freedom, the fire, the certainty of a victorious leader who knows that he is followed by millions to whom his most obscure parable will seem like an inspired prophecy. The work of electioneering was finished; this demonstration was a superlative finishing touch, a seal set on thousands of rallies which had been held in every corner of the Reich in the last week. And so with millions straining to catch his words, Hitler dared to soar.[46]

As he soared, however, he also mocked the *System* and presented an alternative to it—a united Germany which had sloughed off divisive democracy:

Our opponents complain that we National Socialists, and I in particular, are intolerant and intractable. They say we refuse to cooperate with other parties. They even suggest that National Socialists are not German since they refuse to cooperate with other parties! I want to make one thing clear. They are right, we are intolerant! I have set myself one task, namely to sweep those thirty parties out of Germany.[47]

In the July elections the Nazis got over 13.5 million votes and became the most powerful party in the Reichstag. The Communists made gains, too. Hitler was expected by many of his supporters either to make a direct bid for power, or to accept a post in the government. He rejected the first course out of hand:

"Don't you see? Don't you see that I need the old cab horse [i.e., Hinden-

burg]? *Say what you will, his prestige is still priceless, a fabulous reputation that must be exploited. Here's a symbolic picture I don't intend to miss: Hindenburg represents the Old Germany and I the New; the Old Germany reaches out its hand to the New—the Old Field Marshal of the World War and the Young Corporal from the trenches pledging themselves to the swastika at the tomb of Frederick the Great.*[48]

Yet things did not go Hitler's way immediately. He called on Hindenburg and suggested he be appointed chancellor. However, he failed to impress the cab horse. For once nerves seem to have robbed him of his charm:

Hitler enters, makes an abortive attempt at a profound bow, and fumbles with his hand behind his back to shut the door which, of course, has already closed behind him. Then, noticing his lapse, he grows red in the face, and makes uncertain steps towards the Old Gentleman, who is standing in the middle of the room. But at the very start he stumbles over the carpet. Hardly had Hitler straightened himself from his devout reverences when he prepared to launch into one of his great public speeches. But Hindenburg made a sweep with his arm and Hitler collapsed into terrified silence.[49]

The new Reichstag assembled on September 12. It was a bizarre and moving occasion. The opening address was always given by the senior deputy, in this case an elderly Communist, Clara Zetkin, who was desperately frail and ill. She had come from Moscow to give the speech.

She was dying and her powers were failing fast, but somehow she had memorized a fierce revolutionary oration. . . . Propped on a stick, swaying, gasping for breath. . . . With that speech the voice of the German masses was heard for the last time for many, many long years to come.[50]

She sounded dreadfully old, straining, trying to speak clearly as an orator, but it was still a voice full of an old woman's weakness and sickness. The speech ended on a haunting and hopeful note, looking forward to a better future and ringing with unintended gallows humor: "I open the Reichstag in accordance with my duty as the oldest member, in the hope that despite my present ill health I will live to open the first council-congress of Soviet Germany."[51]

Von Papen, in fact, dissolved the Reichstag immediately after that opening speech, despite the Nazi-Communist attempt to force a vote of no confidence in the government. There were to be new elections, the fourth that year, in November. Shortly afterward Goebbels made a speech which summed up the political situation as it must have appeared to many Germans that autumn:

Things cannot go on as they are. There must be a change. We have the choice: from here on into Bolshevist anarchy or from here on into National Socialist order and discipline.[52]

The future lay with Nazis or Communists, Social Democracy was patently bankrupt. To understand how it came about that so many people voted for Hitler, enough to bring him to power legally and constitutionally, one must remember that if as a German in 1932 one recalled the "Red terror" of 1918–19 and perhaps knew enough about Soviet Russia to be prepared to do anything to avoid a Soviet Germany, the Nazi party was the only party that would stop Germany from going Communist; or so it would have appeared. "Better Nazi than Red" was an argument which made many turn to Hitler.

In 1932 only the extremes had weight. Between them these two totalitarian parties had an absolute majority in the Reichstag. No legislation could go through without the support of one of them. Only dissolution and the prohibition of both parties would have avoided the otherwise inevitable alternative of doing a deal with one or other of them. They were both bitterly opposed to the *System* and without them the system was hamstrung.

One of the consequences of their opposition was a considerable degree of Nazi–Communist solidarity. This is certainly apparent in their concerted opposition to democratic elements in the Prussian Diet.[53] Indeed, it has been suggested that the party wanted the Nazis to come to power, in the hope that this would create a proper and united Communist-led opposition, which would ensure that the Nazis did not stay there for long. That was Stalin's own idea, typical of his devious sense of cunning and tactics. The idea did not work at once; it had to wait till 1945 and the formation of the People's Democratic Republic before it paid off.

One of the strangest consequences of Communist–Nazi collaboration was the Berlin transport strike of November 1932. It was jointly organized by both parties in concert, in the face of trade-union opposition. The unions had lost all authority over their members, who listened to their party leaders and not union chiefs. Even today it is difficult to get some East German Communists to admit that there ever was a transport strike. "There was no such thing," they tend to answer with a slightly sheepish smile, and for good reason. One observer recalls strange sights: "Near my house a group of strikers demonstrated on the street corner. Communists and Nazis arm in arm, the ones shouting "Red Front" whilst the others waited for their turn to cheer Hitler."[54] As so often in the history of Weimar we find a blend of tragedy and farce.

The next elections took place on November 6. Surprisingly, the Nazis lost two million votes. The center parties lost votes, too, but the Communists gained ground. Between them the Nazis and Communists still had an overall majority—in a Reichstag that had not enjoyed a pro-republican majority since 1920. However, many considered that these elections marked the end of the Nazi party, which was also doing badly in local elections. To make matters worse, in addition to the great expense of fighting, the four campaigns in 1932 had rendered the party virtually bankrupt. In the wake of the elections, the *Manchester Guardian* informed its readers: "Although not quite out of the wood yet, the German Left appears to have got over the worst of its troubles."[55]

In the meantime Schleicher found that he had not succeeded in running the government from behind the scenes, and so he began to plot against von Papen. He suggested to Hindenburg that von Papen's policies might precipitate civil war. He had recently commissioned a study which proved that the army would be unable to cope with that eventuality. At the same time he promised the president that he would be able to split the NSDAP by making a deal with its "left wing" led by Gregor Strasser. Reluctantly, Hindenburg called on von Papen to resign. He was immensely fond of his "Fränzchen" and presented him with a photograph of himself, with the inscription *"Ich hatt' einen Kameraden,"* the first line of a famous and sentimental military song about death, glory and the Fatherland. Von Papen's "ignoblest hour," however, was yet to come.

The election results might have given heart to the *Manchester Guardian*, but most people understood that it was all over. By the end of 1932 Klaus Mann, Thomas Mann's son, had lost more friends through suicide than by any other cause.[56] The actor Max Hansen, who had once had a hard time in the profession but was now a star, used to open his house to all friends and colleagues each Christmas Eve. Christmas 1932 was to be the last party. All Berlin was there, and someone sang a song from a show about to open:

> *Vielleicht gewöhnt man mit der Zeit*
> *Sich an die Zeit.*

"Perhaps in time one grows accustomed to the times,"[57] but no one seemed very convinced. The Nazis were already making it virtually impossible to perform in cabaret. They had closed down the film based on Remarque's *All Quiet on the Western Front*. A few days later the Communist Volksbühne was also to close. A technician who worked there told me that the entire company understood that it was quite pointless to try to go on. Gerda Redlich was working in Nuremberg at the time.

I remember doing The Dream. *All of a sudden we were not allowed to use Mendelssohn's music. It was no longer lovely music, it had become Jewish music. We had a director who was anti-Hitler, and said, "All right, no Jewish music, but I have no other music. You all have it in your ear, don't you?" We went through all the actions as if the music were playing. There was no wedding march, but we walked in the rhythm. The silence was uncanny, and the audience giggled hysterically. It lasted two nights, then we had stinkbombs. I had had enough, and I left. That was my last experience of German theater.*

From the safety of Switzerland Paul Nikolaus, one of the most famous and bravest of *conférenciers*, summed up the mood of the time in his suicide note:

Joking apart for once, I am taking my own life. Why? I couldn't go back to Germany without doing it there, and I am afraid that I am in love with my country. . . .

Good-bye. Tell Hansen I liked him a lot — liked — how funny that still sounds. . . .

Say good-bye to everyone who likes me; no point in mourning. Laugh when you think of me; that is the finest piety. I leave my comical body to medicine; I hope it's accepted although the appendix is missing. . . . Final greetings, Nikolaus.[58]

At the end of 1932 the 85-year-old Hindenburg wrote to his "Dear young friend" Chancellor Schleicher, to thank him for "the quietest year since he had been president."[59]

President Paul von Hindenburg.   *A Nazi demonstration, 1930.*
BELOW: *The Stahlhelm ceremony in 1932. Franz Seldte is second from left.*

ABOVE: *A Rotfront demonstration—note the* schalmeien.
BELOW: *Campaign posters for Hitler and Hindenburg, 1932.*

Hitler during election campaign, 1932.   Hitler speaking in the Sportpalast, 1930.
BELOW: *The first Nazi deputies enter the Reichstag, August 30, 1932.*

Max Hansen.

A Berlin slum during a rent strike, 1932.

BELOW: *January 1, 1933—the Nazis demonstrate outside the communist headquarters on the Bülowplatz.*

Hitler, 1933.

John Heartfield's photomontage entitled "Millions stand behind me"—a comment on Hitler's support from big business.

12

The Final Month

VON PAPEN HAD no intention of being driven permanently out of office by
Schleicher. He looked around for a means of removing the general.
Through an intermediary he persuaded Hitler that Schleicher was the
man who had turned Hindenburg against him; however the president
had now seen through the ruse and von Papen's position was growing
daily weaker. He suggested they join forces.

On January 4 von Papen met Hitler, secretly, in the house of a
Jewish banker and stock-exchange man, Kurt von Schröder. After a
two-hour talk it was agreed that they should form a right-wing coalition,
combining Nazis and the Stahlhelm. Hitler would be chancellor, but
would include von Papen and two Stahlhelm conservatives in his
cabinet. The conservatives believed that they were using Hitler as a
means of coming to power. Although many dates may be suggested for
the day on which the Weimar Republic died, there is little doubt that
this was the day on which the Third Reich was born.

Hitler now proposed to use the Nazi—Communist vote to obstruct
Schleicher's every move, leaving him effectively paralyzed and helping
to provoke a constitutional crisis, since the machinery of government
had broken down. January was a doom-laden month filled with wild
rumors and an ever-increasing sense of unease. There was an alleged
plot to send the entire German navy to Holland to bring the kaiser back.[2]
Sefton Delmer told me that he had never heard the rumor himself but
this certainly did not mean that it wasn't true. It was a time when any
lunacy could become political reality overnight.

The high point of the Berlin social season, the Press Ball, took place
on Saturday January 28 that year. It was the Weimar Republic's
positively last public appearance. The dancers at the Press Ball knew
they had come to the end—and there was not much sound of revelry
that night. For Professor Reiff, who was there, Press Balls had been the
highlight of his particular experience of the golden twenties, and he

found the ball of '33 a very different occasion. There was a strange blend of nervous excitement and extreme depression. In the vast, brightly lit, crowded halls, with their tiers of boxes, the "élite of Weimar" was assembled, crowds of politicians, artists, intellectuals. Tension mounted when it was seen that the great center box in the main hall—the government box—was empty. Chancellor Schleicher and his ministers had not yet appeared. He and his cabinet had resigned that afternoon, and a new government was being formed, but would it be von Papen again, or would it be Hitler? Carl Zuckmayer remembers:

The mood in the crowded ballrooms that evening was the strangest I have ever experienced. Everyone sensed what was in the air, but no one wanted to admit it fully. . . . People indulged in a macabre blend of somberness and hectic gaiety.

In the Ullstein box, which adjoined the government box, we met our friends, the aviator Ernst Udet and the novelist Bruno Frank. Others came and went. None of the Ullstein brothers appeared; Emil Herz, the firm's managing director, did the honors. He was forever filling our glasses, saying each time, "Drink up, go ahead, who knows when you'll again be drinking champagne in an Ullstein box."

At the bottom of our hearts we were all feeling: "Never again."

Udet and I, who took brandy between the glasses of champagne, were soon in that condition in which one no longer guards one's tongue.

"Look at the tinware," Udet said to me, pointing around the hall. "They've all got their gewgaws out of mothballs. A year ago no one would have been caught dead with that stuff."

Sure enough, on many lapels and dinner jackets you saw the ribbons and crosses of war decorations, which in the past no one would have dreamed of wearing at the Berlin Press Ball. Udet took his Pour-le-Mérite from his neck (he always wore it under his white tie with evening dress) and put it into his pocket.

"You know what," he proposed to me. "Let's take our pants down and dangle our bare backsides over the railings of the box."

To worry my wife . . . we went so far as to loose our suspenders. In reality neither of us was feeling in a jocular mood.[3]

Just after midnight the music stopped. A spotlight moved across the ballroom to pick out the government box, hung with expensive rugs. Schleicher was there. He had just arrived from the Budapeststrasse, through a crowd yelling "Down with Schleicher"—even though the radio had already announced his resignation. He had been chancellor for fifty-eight days. As the news spread through the ballroom the ex-chancellor's reaction was awaited with increasing tension. Music and dancing stopped and as the searchlight found him he got up slowly, raised his glass and said, "*Nu, dann mal Prost meine Damen un Herren.*"

He drank his cynical and ambiguous, bland and yet loaded toast to the end of the Weimar Republic.

The next day, January 29, saw the culmination of a month of intrigue and pressure upon Hindenburg to ask Hitler to form a government. Hitler, meanwhile, was staying at the Kaiserhof Hotel. He always put up there so he could listen to his favorite danceband, Barnabas von Creczy.

Hindenburg was reluctant to turn to a man whose professed intention it was to form a dictatorship, but he had few options left. Besides, very real personal pressures were being brought to bear upon the old man: his son Oskar was anxious that he should bring the Nazis to power. There is every reason to believe that Oskar Hindenburg was being if not blackmailed then subjected to severe pressure by the Nazis, for he was involved in the *"Osthilfe"* scandal. East Prussian junkers had for years been abusing the extremely generous allowances and subsidies granted them by the government, and Oskar Hindenburg was in it up to his neck. Moreover the president was involved in a second piece of chicanery. As Professor Reiff told me, Hindenburg's family had lacked the generosity to secure the Old Gentleman's financial position. They therefore both encouraged and welcomed the gift to him, from right-wing supporters, of the old family estate at Neudeck. It appeared however that to avoid death duties the estate had been put in Oskar's name. Although the precise details of the scandal remain obscure, the smell of stinking fish was strong enough to render Oskar in particular susceptible to pressure.

Sefton Delmer believes that the scandals were significant for another reason: they were symbolic of the kind of corruption in high places which the Nazis would pledge themselves to sweep away. At a dinner party Delmer gave for Goering some weeks later, Goering thought that Delmer would be much impressed by Nazi plans to clean out "the Augean stables of conservative corruption."

There was yet another source of pressure on Hindenburg senior. The facts are again somewhat obscure, but it seemed that Hindenburg was threatened with the possibility of a putsch headed by Schleicher if he failed to bring Hitler to power. What seems to have happened is that Hammerstein, head of the Potsdam garrison, talked with Schleicher on January 29. They agreed that if Hitler didn't become chancellor the country would collapse and there would be a general strike, even perhaps civil war. In such an eventuality the army would find itself fighting both the right and the left. Hammerstein called on Hitler at 2 P.M. to ask him whether Hindenburg would really invite him to form a government, or whether he was going through some sort of pretense. At 4 P.M. that afternoon Hitler still could not say.

Hammerstein went on to a horseshow and called on Schleicher afterward. He was joined by Werner von Alversleben Neugattesleben, the younger brother of the president of the Herrenklub. An often foolish man, von Alvensleben was a fine horseman and had ridden round Aintree in a prewar Grand National. He was sent off to Hitler to discover whether or not he now knew anything more about his appointment, but he returned without a clear reply, and the evening broke up. Then he seems to have acted on his own initiative. He intimated to Sefton Delmer that Schleicher and Hammerstein were planning a putsch: the Potsdam garrison was about to march on Berlin and sweep Hindenburg from power. Delmer passed the story on to the Nazi leadership, who in turn allowed it to reach the ears of Hindenburg.

Even today Sefton Delmer is not certain of von Alvensleben's actual role. He feels it quite likely that he was "playing it both ways," running both with Schleicher and with the Nazis (who, incidentally, would later send him to prison for allegedly plotting with Schleicher). He told Delmer indignantly that the putsch story was a totally unfounded invention of his own to help the Nazis, who had proved distinctly unappreciative of the service. But whatever von Alvensleben's actual role may have been, the rumor decided Hindenburg, and Sefton Delmer is sure of one thing: namely that by passing the rumor on: "I am in fact the man who put Hitler in power." It must be said that he bears his responsibility with good grace.

Hammerstein and his family deny that there were plans for a putsch, and it is indeed hard to conceive of the army marching against Hindenburg. Moreover, Hammerstein insists that he and Schleicher wanted Hitler to come to power. Other sources suggest that the army wished to prevent him from so doing, desiring to take over and rule Germany itself.[4]

Von Papen is said to have made his own contribution at 7 A.M. on the morning of January 30. "If a new government is not formed by 11 A.M. the army will march," he allegedly told Hindenburg.[5] Von Papen had made his plans to "contain" Hitler some days earlier. On January 26 he had had talks with Seldte and Dürsterberg, the leaders of the Stahlhelm, to persuade them to join a government led by Hitler. Seldte, who was promised a cabinet post, agreed. Dürsterberg had his doubts, but Hugenberg assured him that with Hindenburg as president and commander in chief, von Papen as vice-chancellor, Hugenberg in charge of the economy and Seldte as minister of labor, "Hitler would thus be contained."

Hitler was due to receive the chancellorship from Hindenburg at 11 A.M. on January 30. Shortly beforehand he was waiting in the presidential chambers with Hugenberg and von Papen, who congratulated him on his appointment. Hitler announced to them that there would be new elections as a vote of confidence in his cabinet, knowing that the Nazis would now recoup their November losses and that he would be able to ditch the non-Nazi elements in his government. Hugenberg grew alarmed and declared that in those circumstances he would not agree to serve under Hitler. A serious argument ensued. Hugenberg was immovable, and for the moment Hitler needed him. Just then State Secretary Otto Meissner, burst in:

Gentlemen, the oath of allegiance was set for 11 A.M. It is now 11.15. You cannot keep the Reichspräsident waiting any longer.[6]

Hugenberg gave in. The niceties of form and protocol proved too much for him; he yielded to the overwhelming pressure of embarrassment.

Proud, triumphant and henceforth a victor, Hitler strutted up the stair behind his underling, to the Old Gentleman who was waiting for him on the first floor. History was taking its course.[7]

Hitler was very pleased. He had heard of no objections to his appointment, which he described as "the least bloody revolution in history."[8] Later that day he left the Kaiserhof Hotel where he had been staying in order to take up residence in the Chancellery. As he entered that building as chancellor for the first time, he remarked to Goebbels, "No one gets me out of here alive."[9] Of all his promises that is one of the very few that he kept.

The news of Hitler's appointment took various people in different ways. An Ullstein director, Kurt Safranski, had had rather a good Press Ball. He got home at dawn and slipped into deep and protracted sleep. When he finally came round, he sat up and gazed at his wife. "Any news?" he asked. "Not much," she replied sarcastically. "Hitler has been appointed chancellor."[10]

Baldur von Schirach was driving through Cologne in *"Räuberzivil,"* civilian clothes approximating a uniform, and the standard gear of all private armies: shirt (brown) and a windbreaker. He stopped at a crossroads and was surprised to see a policeman on traffic duty salute him. He assumed that he had been mistaken for somebody else. At the next intersection he had to stop again and again he was saluted. He turned off and drove to the nearest Hitler Youth Office where he learned that Hitler was now chancellor.

Klaus Mann had already decided that it was time to leave:

On January 30, 1933, I left Berlin early in the morning, as if driven away by evil forebodings. The streets were calm, clear and empty when I rode to the station. I looked at them, but not carefully enough. I did not realize that it was for the last time.[11]

There was nothing "calm, clear or empty" about the streets that night, however. Indeed, the city saw mass hysteria and jubilation without parallel in its history. The mood was a compound of triumph, aggression and strange exultant relief. Complete strangers embraced one another, saying, "At last we are saved." It was as if the German nation believed itself to have been released at a stroke from political chaos and economic misery.

No one who saw the *Fackelzug*, the torchlight procession, that filed through Berlin for five hours that night, will ever forget it. For the Stahlhelm leader Dürsterberg it was strangely disturbing:

History teaches us about mass hysteria. But I had never believed it possible that our steady, disciplined nation could become so aroused. Anyone who experienced the torchlight procession will remember hundreds of thousands of people with torches, singing and whooping in an indescribable state of ecstasy up the Wilhelmstrasse where Hitler stood on a balcony, triumphantly receiving calls of Sieg Heil *from his fanatical followers. The Old Gentleman and the underling [i.e., Meissner] were obliged to look on from a side window. The Berliners, usually so level-headed, witty and skeptical were in a state of collective delirium. The* morituri te saluant *[those who are about to die salute you] of Rome's gladiators celebrated its return in the twentieth century.*[12]

The demonstration was spontaneous—an SA man remembers:

On January 30, as evening falls over the capital, the Wilhelmstrasse is a seething, red, clear burning sea of torches. No one alerted the sections. No one summoned the hundred thousand. No one had purchased the torches; no one had given the order to march. It was their own hearts that alerted them, bought torches and marched out.

For on this day Führer Adolf Hitler became chancellor and leader of the Reich.[13]

So spontaneous was it, indeed, that the whole proceedings had to be restaged subsequently for the benefit of the newsreel cameras.

Helena Boucholz-Starck's sister burst into the family flat and told everyone to come to Unter den Linden. *"Es gibt was Tolles auf der Strasse."* ("There are amazing goings on in the street.") As Helena watched she sensed that she was seeing a new beginning. Something strange and quite unpredictable was happening. There was an uneasy atmosphere, but Hindenburg was there. He was the father of the family, of the nation, and as long as he remained nothing much could go wrong. He was to be trusted. She did not feel frightened by the passing torrents of SA men, for, as she said, "One always attributes one's own motives and characteristics to other people if one has nothing else to go on." She assumed them to be balanced and level-headed moderates.

Maurice Bonn was not so sure. As he saw the SA march he was both alarmed and puzzled. They did not use the Prussian goosestep, but a loose swinging gait that seemed strangely familiar. Suddenly he got it:

it was based on the march of the Deutschmeister, Vienna's crack regiment. The recognition made history fall into place for him. The south had finally triumphed over the north. The Prussian order was ended and Hitler was "Austria's revenge for the Battle of Sadowa."[14]

Hedda Adlon saw the procession begin at eight o'clock:

Densely packed columns streamed out of the darkness of the Tiergarten and passed beneath the gaze of the Goddess of Victory on the Brandenburger Tor. Bands marched between the columns, their big drums beating the rhythm while they played military and old Prussian marches. But as each band crossed the Pariser Platz where the French embassy was situated, they stopped whatever they had been playing and with a preliminary roll of drums broke into the tune of the challenging warsong, "Siegreich wollen wir Frankreich schlagen." ["Victorious we will crush the French."]

When Hitler heard how the crowd was behaving, Goering asked him what he would have done had he been the French prime minister. He replied without hesitating. "I should have marched."[15]

Not so for the French ambassador, who was actually there. A. François-Poncet watched the proceedings "with a heavy heart, in the grip of strange forebodings," but perhaps he did not know enough about German marching songs to appreciate the situation fully. His account does not mention the music.

Ernst Udet was without illusions. Watching the procession from the Adlon, he turned derisively to Hedda Adlon and described the SA as "Germany's hurrah *canaille*."

Hindenburg found the procession altogether bewildering. Who were these people marching past in their thousands? "Did we really take all those Russian prisoners at Tannenberg?" he is alleged to have asked.

For years now Hitler's stormtroopers had been tightening their grip on Berlin, gradually moving in from the working class districts to the west end and the smarter parts of town until now, as the procession went through the *Regierungsviertel* itself, their takeover was complete. Berlin the wild and exuberant city with its artistic and sexual extravagance was finished. It had succumbed to pathological behavior of a different kind as the torch bearers of the *Fackelzug* spontaneously set the tempo of the new Germany.

Douglas Reed leaves us with the final picture of that strange day:

Berlin was buzzing like a beehive from morning till night, the nerves of four million people were quivering like harp strings. Only the very ill, very poor or deeply enamored were not moved on this day by lively hopes or fears for the future.

I walked down Unter den Linden to the Wilhelmstrasse, thinking back to Armistice Day 1918, and forward to what might be coming. I felt this was the final breakdown of peace.

233

The Brown Shirts were hilariously jubilant. The last trench had been taken, the brown armies had the freedom of the streets, even of the coveted Bann-meile, that square mile of streets in central Berlin where the ministries and other government buildings are situated, within which political demonstrations had never been allowed.

I stood at a window of the Foreign Office that night and watched them tramping endlessly past, the Brown Shirts, while their bands played "Fridericus Rex" and the "Horst Wessel" march. Hour after hour they poured with their torchlights through the once forbidden Brandenburger Arch into the promised land of Unter den Linden and the Wilhelmstrasse, marching with the triumphant ecstatic air of soldiers taking possession of a long beleaguered city. Opposite me were two palaces — the old and the new chancellor's palaces, one a gray ponderous building in the Wilhelmian style of architecture, the other a clean-cut four-square building, a typical product of the Germany of 1918–33.

Behind a lighted window of the old building stood a massive old man. The night air was chill and they wouldn't let him have the window open. His dim old eyes saw the river of torchlights flowing past, his ears heard the crash of the bands and the tramp of the stormtroopers.

I saw him nod his head continually as the bands blared and the Brown Shirts marched past, throwing their heads back and their eyes right to salute him. But they were not there to honor him. His day was done. The salute to the old man, dimly seen behind the lighted window, was perfunctory.

Fifty yards down the street in the new palace was another window, on a higher level, open, with the spotlights playing on it, a young man leaning out . . . [A Jewish colleague] found beauty in the scene — the tumultuous brazen music, the tramp, tramp, tramp, the ceaseless cheering of the crowds, the blazing torches, the bellowing of the loudspeakers, the old man behind the lighted window, and the younger man who leaned out of the spotlit window saluting.

"Hitler looks marvelous," he said.

The old and the new. Field Marshal and Bohemian Corporal. Hitler and Hindenburg, Tramp tramp tramp, blare blare blare. Hour after hour they came tramping through the Brandenburger Tor down the Wilhelmstrasse. Die Strasse frei, die Reihen fest geschlossen, Hoch, Hoch, Hoooooch![16]

ABOVE: *Hitler sets off to see Hindenburg.*

BELOW: *The crowd, seen through the windscreen of his Mercedes, congratulate Hitler on his appointment.*

Hindenburg congratulates Hitler.   The Nazi headquarters in Berlin, 1933.
BELOW: *A Hitler Youth demonstration in the Sportpalast, 1933.*

ABOVE AND BELOW: *The crowds salute Hitler.*

"A last chance."

Chronology

1918
Oct. 28 Sailors mutiny in Kiel.
Nov. 7 Revolution in Munich.
Nov. 9 Scheidemann proclaims a republic.
Nov. 10 The kaiser flees to Holland.
Groener talks to Ebert on a secret line.
Nov. 11 Armistice signed in Compiègne.
Dec. 16–20 Mass meeting of the workers and soldiers soviets.
Dec. 30 Foundation of the German Communist party (KPD).
Foundation of the Stahlhelm Bund.
Eight-hour working day established by law.

1919
Jan. 5 Mass demonstration in the Tiergarten.
Foundation of the German Workers' Party, later the National Socialist Party (NSDAP); Hitler is member no. 5.
Jan. 5–12 Heavy fighting in Berlin. Noske's men move in on Jan. 11.

Jan. 15 The murder of Karl Liebknecht and Rosa Luxemburg.
Jan. 19 Elections to a National Assembly to be held at Weimar; republican majority result.
Feb. 11 Ebert elected president.
Feb. 21 Murder of Kurt Eisner.
March/April Heavy fighting in Berlin, the Ruhr and central Germany.
April 7– May 2 Soviet republic in Munich.
June 28 Germany signs the Treaty of Versailles.
Aug. 11 The Weimar Constitution becomes law.

CULTURAL EVENTS
Opening of Reinhardt's Grosses Schauspielhaus (Nov. 28).
Walter Gropius, L. Feininger, Gerhard Marcks found the Bauhaus in Weimar.
Hans Vogt, Josef Massolle and Josef Engl patent their sound film process (the Triergon Process).

1920
Feb. 15 The last horse-drawn streetcar in Berlin ceases to run.

March 13	Ehrhardt division enters Berlin (Kapp Putsch).
March 17	Ehrhardt division leaves Berlin.
March/May	"Uprising" in the Ruhr. The Red Army is destroyed by the Reichswehr.
June 12	Fishing in lakes and rivers of Berlin by hand grenade forbidden by law.

CULTURAL EVENTS
Opening of the UFA Palast am Zoo.
Das Kabinett des Dr. Caligari, starring Conrad Veidt and Werner Krauss, directed by Robert Wiene.
Der Golem, starring Paul Wegener.

1921

March	Communist uprising in Saxony and Hamburg.
May	Freikorps check Polish rising in Upper Silesia.
Aug. 18	550 marks = 1 dollar.
Aug. 26	Murder of Erzberger — held responsible for the Versailles Treaty — by members of secret right-wing "Organization Consul."

CULTURAL EVENTS
Opening of the Avus track (Auto Verkehrs und Übungstrasse), Berlin Wannsee.
Fridericus Rex, parts I and II, starring Otto Gebühr, directed by Arzen von Czerèpy.

1922

April 16	Treaty of Rapallo.
June 24	Assassination of Rathenau.
July 5	550 marks = 1 dollar.
Dec. 31	7500 marks = 1 dollar.

CULTURAL EVENTS
Wilhelm Furtwängler takes over the Berlin Philharmonic.
First public performance of a talkie in the Alhambra, Berlin.
Dr. Mabuse der Spieler, directed by Fritz Lang.
Nosferatu, directed by F. W. Murnau.
Fridericus Rex, parts III and IV.

1923

Jan. 11	The French occupy the Ruhr.
Jan. 22	22,400 marks = 1 dollar.
May 24	54,300 marks = 1 dollar.
June 11	Berlin streetcar ticket costs 600 marks.
Sept. 3	Berlin streetcar ticket costs 400,000 marks.
Sept. 26	Abandonment of policy of passive resistance in the Ruhr.
Oct./Nov.	Separatist movements in the Rhineland.
Oct. 12	4 billion marks = 1 dollar.
Oct. 19	Berlin stockmarket goes on strike.
Nov. 8	Hitler putsch in Munich.
Nov. 20	4,200 billion marks, 4.20 Rentenmarks = 1 dollar.

CULTURAL EVENTS
First public radio broadcast for entertainment (Oct. 29).
Arthur Moeller van den Bruck publishes *Das dritte Reich*.

1924

April 1 (NB)	Hitler condemned to five years' fortress arrest.
Sept. 25	Zeppelin ZR III visits Berlin.

CULTURAL EVENTS

Grosses Schauspielhaus becomes a variety theater (Oct. 22).

Thomas Mann publishes *The Magic Mountain*.

Der letzte Mann, with Emil Jannings, directed by F. W. Murnau.

Die Niebelungen, directed by Fritz Lang.

1925

Feb. 24	Refounding of the NSDAP after Hitler's release.
Feb. 28	Death of President Ebert.
April 26	Hindenburg elected president.

CULTURAL EVENTS

Beginnings of television—first public broadcast will take place in 1928.

Josephine Baker appears in Berlin.

Die freudlose Gasse, with Asta Nielsen, Werner Kraus, Greta Garbo, directed by G. W. Pabst.

1926

Sept. 28	Germany enters League of Nations.

CULTURAL EVENTS

Gropius moves the Bauhaus to Dessau.

Metropolis, with Brigitte Helm, directed by Fritz Lang.

1927

Aug.	First Nazi Nuremberg rally.

CULTURAL EVENTS

Otto Klemperer takes over orchestra at the Kroll Opera, Berlin.

Alfred Hugenberg takes over UFA, 60 million marks in debt.

Berlin, Symphonie einer Grosstadt, directed by Walter Ruttman.

Der Alte Fritz, with Otto Gebühr, directed by Gerhard Lamprecht.

1928

CULTURAL EVENTS

Opening of *The Threepenny Opera* (Aug. 30).

Erich Maria Remarque publishes *All Quiet on the Western Front*.

1929

May 1	*Blutmai*, the Communist rising in Berlin.
July 9	Hugenberg, Hitler and Seldte unite to oppose the Young Plan.
Oct. 3	The death of Stresemann.
Oct. 24	"Black Friday" on Wall Street.

CULTURAL EVENTS

Thomas Mann wins the Nobel Prize.

Graf Zeppelin goes round the world.

First TV broadcast in Berlin.

Completion of new UFA sound stages in Neu Babelsberg.

Menschen am Sonntag, directed by Robert Siodmak.

Die weisse Hölle von Piz Palü, with Leni Riefenstahl, directed by Arnold Franck.

Fräulein Ilse, with Elizabeth Bergner, directed by Paul Czinner.

First German talkies.

1930

March 30	Brüning forms a cabinet.
June 30	Last French troops leave German soil.
Sept. 14	Elections, Nazis increase their representation from 12 to 107 seats in the Reichstag.
Dec.	4.8 million unemployed.

CULTURAL EVENTS

Max Schmeling becomes heavyweight champion of the world.

Ernst von Salomon publishes *The Outlaws*, an autobiographical novel about the killing of Rathenau.

Alfred Döblin publishes *Berlin Alexanderplatz*.

White Horse Inn produced by Eric Charell.

The Blue Angel with Marlene Dietrich, Emil Jannings, Hans Albers and Rosa Valetti; screenplay Carl Zuckmayer and Karl Vollmoeller, directed by Josef von Sternberg.

Die drei von der Tankstelle, with Lilian Harvey and Willy Fritsch, directed by Wilhelm Thiele.

1931

Jan. 1	Five million unemployed.
July 13	Collapse of the Danat Bank. All banks, savings trusts and stock exchanges closed by law.
Oct. 11	The "Harzburg Front," union of all right-wing groups.
Oct.	National Socialist Student organization gains a majority in the Union of German students.

CULTURAL EVENTS

Graf Zeppelin journeys to the Arctic.

Dreigroschenoper, with Lotte Lenya, Carola Neher and Rudolf Forster, directed by G. W. Pabst.

Der Kongress tanzt, with Willy Fritsch, Lilian Harvey and Conrad Veidt, directed by Eric Charell.

Mädchen in Uniform, with Hertha Hiele and Dorothea Wieck, directed by Leontine Sagan and Carl Froelich.

1932

Jan. 1	Six million unemployed.
April 10	Reelection of Hindenburg.
April 13	Banning of the SA and SS by Brüning.
May 30	Hindenburg dismisses Brüning.
June 1	Von Papen's cabinet of barons.
June 14	Lifting of ban on SA and SS.
July 20	Braun and Severing dismissed.
July 31	NSDAP get 37.8 percent of the vote, 230 seats in the elections.
Aug. 30	Clara Zetkin opens the Reichstag.
Sept. 12	Von Papen dissolves the Reichstag.
Oct. 1	7.5 million unemployed.
Nov. 3	Berlin transport strike.
Nov. 6	Elections. Nazis lose two million votes and 34 seats, Communists gain 42.
Dec 3	Von Schleicher becomes chancellor.

CULTURAL EVENTS

Hans Fallada publishes his *Little Man What Now?*

Cologne–Bonn Autobahn opened.

Die Tänzerin von Sans Souci, Otto Gebühr.

1933

Jan. 4	Hitler meets von Papen at von Schroeder's house.
Jan. 30	Hitler becomes chancellor.

Notes

1 THE COLLAPSE
1 Wolff, p. 122
2 Kessler, p. 92
3 Zuckmayer, p. 174
4 Toller, pp. 73–4
5 Kessler, p. 645
6 d'Abernon, vol. III, p. 80
7 Zuckmayer, pp. 177–8
8 Halkett, p. 109
9 Von Schirach, p. 15
10 Buck, p. 94
11 Toller, pp. 133–4
12 Bernstein, p. 56
13 *Ibid*, p. 18
14 Oldat, p. 54
15 Plesch, pp. 110–11
16 Schacht, p. 149
17 Lenke p. 54
18 Halkett, p. 107
19 *Ibid*, p. 122
20 Tuohy, pp. 23–4
21 *Ibid*, pp. 30–1
22 *Ibid, loc. cit.*
23 Markham, p. 8
24 Jameson, p. 145
25 Baum, p. 218

2 REVOLUTION IN BERLIN 1918–19
1 Baum, p. 202
2 Schacht, p. 155
3 Wolff, p. 130
4 *Ibid, loc. cit.*
5 *Ibid*
6 *Ibid*, pp. 132–3
7 Kessler, p. 24
8 Bernstein, p. 37
9 *Ibid*, p. 38
10 Glombowski, p. 23

11 Tormin, p. 83
12 Schönberger, pp. 107–8
13 Kessler, p. 28
14 Waite, p. 3
15 Fallada, *Iron Gustav*, p. 210
16 Bernstein, pp. 71–2
17 Waite, p. 2
18 Osborne, p. 100
19 Bernstein, p. 114
20 Jameson, p. 153
21 Schönberger, p. 104
22 Kessler, p. 81
23 Bernstein, p. 106
24 Schönberger, p.104
25 *Berliner Tageblatt*, January 1, 1919
26 Glombowski, p. 42
27 Brecht, p. 235
28 Wolff, p. 144
29 *Ibid*, p. 152
30 *Rote Fahne*, January 1920
31 Adlon, pp. 76–7
32 Schönberger, p. 104
33 Kessler, p. 99
34 *Ibid*, p. 107
35 *Ibid*, pp. 110–11
36 *Rote Fahne*, January 15, 1926
37 *The Times*, May 12, 1919
38 Buck, p. 91
39 Kessler, p. 151
40 *Ibid*, p. 158

3 MUNICH 1918–19
1 Zarek, p. 89
2 *Ibid*, p. 45
3 Bonn, p. 199

4 Schönberger, p. 99
5 *Ibid*, p. 106
6 Bernstein, pp. 56–7
7 Niekisch, p. 50
8 Toller, p. 156
9 Schönberger, p. 118
10 Toller, p. 182
11 Mann, p. 47
12 Waite, p. 82
13 Waite, p. 81
14 Manfred von Killinger, Munich 1919
15 Bayer, p. 134
16 Hans Fischer, *Jünger*, p. 162
17 Toller, p. 242
18 Schönstadt, p. 97
19 Toller, p. 248

4 THE KAPP PUTSCH
1 Jünger, E. p. 170
2 *Deutsche Zeitung*, March 4, 1920
3 Morgan, p. 55
4 *Ibid*, p. 57
5 Jünger, p. 179
6 *Ibid, loc. cit.*
7 *Ibid*, p. 181
8 *Ibid, loc. cit.*
9 Pem, p. 15
10 Fromm, p. 16
11 Pem, p. 151
12 Brecht, p. 312
13 Feder, p. 127
14 Morgan, p. 69
15 Waite, p. 166
16 Kessler, pp. 221–2
17 Morgan, p. 77
18 *Ibid*, p. 88
19 Waite, p. 161

20 Hoelz, pp. 130–1
21 Jünger, p. 204
22 Morgan, p. 152
23 Waite, p. 182
24 Heck, p. 18

5 THE RHINE AND THE
RUHR 1919–24
1 The Times (London),
   April 7, 1919
2 Ibid, April 14, 1919
3 Deutsche Zeitung,
   September 25,
   1919
4 Gedye, p. 52
5 Ibid, pp. 30–31
6 The Times (London),
   April 5, 1919
7 Markham, 146
8 Ostwald, p. 26
9 Kessler, p. 225
10 Markham, p. 192
11 Ibid, p. 9
12 Tuohy, p. 42
13 Gedye, p. 20
14 Tuohy, p. 87
15 Ibid, p. 49
16 Ibid, p. 53
17 Ibid, p. 52
18 Gedye, p. 102
19 Ibid, pp. 110–11
20 Tuohy, pp. 92–3
21 Ibid, p. 94
22 Ibid, p. 92
23 Ibid, p. 87
24 Hirschfield, p. 72
25 Tuohy, pp. 159–60
26 Reynolds, p. 83
27 Allen, p. 139
28 Hirschfeld, p. 82
29 Tuohy, p. 112
30 Ibid, p. 260
31 Gedye, p. 128
32 Morgan, p. 211
33 Gedye, p. 162
34 Ibid, p. 222
35 Ibid, p. 189

6 INFLATION
1 d'Abernon, vol. II, p.
   23
2 Ibid, p. 22
3 Ibid, p. 24
4 Bonn, p. 278
5 Buck, p. 143
6 Ludecke, p. 148
7 Zweig, p. 237
8 Ibid, loc. cit.

9 Daily Express,
   February 24,
   1923
10 Ostwald, p. 63
11 Adlon, p. 99
12 Ostwald, p. 130
13 Clark, p. 11
14 Ibid, loc. cit.
15 Ibid, p. 12
16 Schönberger, p. 155
17 Ostwald, p. 181
18 Adlon, p. 98
19 Ostwald, pp. 84–5
20 Tynan, p. 132
21 Ibid, p. 157
22 Zweig, p. 223
23 Tynan, p. 157
24 Lochner, p. 102
25 Ibid, p. 103
26 Got, p. 67
27 Ibid, p. 57
28 Weltbühne,
   November 1922
29 Béraud, p. 82
30 Buck, p. 163
31 Ibid, p. 141
32 Ibid, loc. cit.
33 Béraud, p. 22
34 Mann, p. 77
35 Fallada, Wolf, Among
   Wolves, p. 15
36 Zweig, p. 238
37 Landauer, pp. 77–80
38 Got, p. 53
39 Buck, p. 232
40 Zweig, p. 238

7 THE HITLER PUTSCH
1 Bonn, p. 165
2 Niekisch, pp. 110–11
3 Hanfstängl, p. 51
4 Ibid, p. 61
5 Ludecke, p. 97
6 Ibid, p. 135
7 Von Schirach, p. 20
8 Zarek, p. 135
9 Ibid, p. 149
10 Zuckmayer, pp.
   271–2
11 Ryder, pp. 213–4
12 Ludecke, p. 164
13 Gordon, p. 345
14 Ibid, p. 360
15 Zuckmayer, p. 272
16 Ludecke, p. 175
17 Mowrer, p. 165
18 Bayrische Kurier,
   April 2, 1924
19 Ewers, Alraune

8 BERLIN
1 Koch, p. 120
2 Chancellor, pp. 60–1
3 Ehrenburg, p. 120
4 Ibid, p. 550
5 Halkett, p. 300
6 Ostwald, p. 132
7 Zuckmayer, p. 218
8 Ibid, loc. cit.
9 Kessler, p. 462
10 Zuckmayer, pp.
   274–5
11 Morgan, p. 34
12 Adlon, p. 119
13 Kiaulehn, p. 535
14 Chancellor, pp.
   142–5
15 Jameson, p. 205
16 Landauer, p. 72
17 Ibid, p. 84
18 Morgan, p. 42
19 Kästner, p. 151
20 Ostwald, p. 152
21 Hirschfeld, p. 374
22 Ibid, p. 363
23 Chancellor, pp.
   112–13
24 Hirschfeld, p. 279
25 Chancellor, pp.
   120–1
26 Morgan, p. 204
27 Holländer, p. 82
28 Ibid, p. 84
29 Kessler, p. 576
30 Chancellor, pp.
   136–7
31 Landauer, p. 79
32 Morgan, p. 196
33 Chancellor, pp.
   114–5

9 FILM, THEATER AND
CABARET
1 Pem, p. 214
2 Ehrenburg, p. 401
3 Hirschfeld, p. 302
4 Mowrer, p. 76
5 Adlon, p. 147
6 Holländer, p. 238
7 Adlon, p. 146
8 Plesch, p. 316
9 Kessler, p. 581
10 Hoelzig, Das Grosse
   Schauspielhaus
   (1920), p. 121
11 Koch, p. 58
12 Zarek, p. 124
13 Zuckmayer, p. 263
14 Ibid, loc. cit.

15 *Ibid*, p. 266
16 Aufricht, p. 65
17 *Ibid*, p. 66
18 *Ibid*, p. 68
19 Holländer, p. 131
20 Krell, p. 212
21 A cabaret song in W. Mann, p. 130
22 Koch, p. 149

10 THE SPIRIT OF WEIMAR— A COLLAGE
1 *The Times* (London), September 5, 1925
2 Koestler, p. 283
3 *The Times*, October 24, 1928
4 Lockner, p. 164
5 Linke, p. 63
6 Halkett, p. 151
7 *Ibid*, pp. 274–5
8 *Ibid*, p. 322
9 Ostwald, p. 136
10 *Ibid*, p. 145
11 Kessler, p. 625
12 Olden, p. 20
13 Kent, pp. 111–12
14 *Ibid*, pp. 111–15
15 Olden, pp. 16–17
16 *Ibid*, p. 104
17 *The Times*, October 30, 1928
18 Halkett, p. 303
19 *The Times*, January 1, 1929
20 *The Times*, January 21, 1929
21 Landauer, p. 81
22 *Ibid, loc. cit.*
23 Koch, p. 103
24 Groener, pp. 468–9
25 Weimarer, p. 223
26 Hussong, p. 23

11 THE FINAL YEARS
1 Groener, p. 468
2 *Berliner Tageblatt*, April 7, 1925
3 Zuckmayer, p. 280
4 Feder, p. 60
5 Béraud, pp. 167–171
6 *The Times* (London), September 24, 1928
7 *Ibid*, September 25, 1928
8 Von Schirach, p. 280
9 *Ibid*, p. 48
10 Knickerbocker, p. 5
11 Fraenkel, p. 74
12 *Ibid, loc. cit.*
13 Halkett, p. 306
14 Reynolds, p. 236
15 Hanfstängl, p. 144
16 Delmer, p. 90
17 Kiaulehn, p. 559
18 *Ibid*, p. 164
19 Feder, p. 274
20 Fromm, p. 40
21 Ehrenburg, p. 582
22 Wucher, p. 80
23 Halkett, p. 327
24 Von Schirach, p. 101
25 Kessler, p. 652
26 Klotz, p. 61
27 Mowrer, p. 195
28 Wucher, p. 43
29 *Ibid*, p. 113
30 Klotz, pp. 178–9
31 *Ibid*, p. 29
32 *Ibid*, p. 31
33 Kessler, p. 670
34 Ludecke, p. 359
35 Brecht, p. 63
36 Reed, p. 119
37 *Völkischer Beobachter*, August 26, 1932

38 *Deutsche Allgemeine Zeitung*, July 18, 1932
39 Jameson, p. 281
40 Klotz, pp. 75–6
41 Kessler, p. 691
42 *Ibid*, p. 691
43 Ludecke, p. 337
44 Mowrer, p. 203
45 *Ibid*, p. 132
46 Ludecke, p. 344
47 Tormin, p. 366
48 Ludecke, p. 413
49 Klotz, p. 150
50 Reed, pp. 117–8
51 Tormin, p. 373
52 Wucher, p. 119
53 Tormin, p. 360
54 Linke, p. 334
55 Kent, p. 153
56 Mann, p. 196
57 Pem, pp. 184–5
58 *Ibid, loc. cit.*
59 Wucher, p. 9

12 THE FINAL MONTH
1 Tormin, p. 383
2 Klotz, pp. 178–9
3 Zuckmayer, p. 322
4 Reed, p. 127
5 Dürsterberg, p. 39
6 *Ibid*, pp. 40–1
7 *Ibid, loc. cit.*
8 Wucher, p. 159
9 *Ibid*, p. 155
10 Ullstein, p. 9
11 Mann, p. 206
12 Dürsterberg, p. 41
13 Bade, p. 252
14 Bonn, p. 343
15 Adlon, p. 202
16 Reed, pp. 127–8

Bibliography

Adlon, H. *Hotel Adlon*, London 1958.

Allan, H.T. *My Rhineland Journey*, London 1924.

Allen, S.W. *The Nazi Seizure of Power*, Chicago 1965.

Arnold, K. *Hoppla wir Leben*, Munich 1928.

Aufricht, E. *Erzähle damit du dein Recht erweist*, Hamburg 1966.

Bade, W.A. *Die SA erobert Berlin*, Munich 1934.

Baum, V. *I Know What I'm Worth*, London 1956.

Behr, H. *Die göldenen zwanziger Jahre*, Hamburg 1964.

Béraud, H. *Ce que j'ai vu à Berlin*, Paris 1926.

Bernstein, E. *Die deutsche Revolution. Erinnerungen*, Berlin 1921.

Beyer, H. *Von Novemberrevolution zum Räterepublik im München*, s.d. Munich.

Böök, K. *An eyewitness in Germany*, London 1936.

Bonn, M.J. *Wandering Scholar*, London 1949.

Boucholtz, C. *Kurfürstendamm*, Berlin 1921.

Bracher, K.D. *Die Weimarer Republik im Spiegel der Memoiren Literatur*, London 1955.

Braun, O. *Von Weimar zu Hitler*, New York 1940.

Brecht, A. *Prelude to Silence*, London 1944. *Aus nächster Nähe*, Stuttgart 1966. *Mit der Kraft des Geistes*, Stuttgart 1967.

Brentano, L. *Mein Leben*, Jena 1931.

Buck, P.S. *How It Happens*, New York 1947.

Chancellor, J. *How to be Happy in Berlin*, London 1929.

Clark, L. *Germany Yesterday*, London 1923.

Cros, G.C. *Le coup d'état de Kapp*, Paris 1921.

d'Abernon, *An Ambassador of Peace*, London 1929–30.

Delmer, S. *Trail Sinister*, London 1961. *Weimar Germany*, London 1972.

Domela, H. *Sham Prince*, London 1927.

Düerlein, D. *Der Hitler Putsch*, London 1966.

Dürsterberg, H. *Der Stahlhelm und Hitler*, London 1949.

Eckhardt, W. & Gilman, S.M. *Bertolt Brecht's Berlin*, New York 1975.

Erenburg, I. *Lyudi, gody, zhizn'*, Moscow 1966.

Fallada, H. *Iron Gustav*, London 1969 ed. *Wolf among Wolves*, London 1938.

Fanderl, W. *H.J. marschiert!*, Berlin 1937. *Von sieben Mann zum Volk*, Berlin 1933.

Feder, E. *Heute sprach ich mit . . .*, Berlin 1971.

Feuchtwanger, L. *Erfolg*, Munich 1931.

Foerster, E. *Erlebte Weltgeschichte*, Munich 1953.

Forsthoff, ed. *Deutsche Geschichte seit 1918*, Munich 1938.

Francois-Ponçet, A. *Souvenirs d'une ambassade à Berlin*, Paris 1946. *Friede Freiheit Brot Ein Deutschland Spiegel*, Berlin 1926.

Friedrich, H. *Berlin Gestern Heute Morgen*, s.d. Berlin.

Friedrich, O. *Before the Delúge*, London 1974.

Fromm, B. *Blood and Banquets*, New York 1942.

Gay, P. *Weimar Culture*, London 1968.

Gedye, G. *The Revolver Republic. France's Bid for the Rhine*, London 1930.

Gentizon, P. *La révolution allemande*, Paris 1919.

Giese, F. *Girlkultur*, Munich 1925.

Glombowski, F. *Frontiers of Terror*, London 1934.

Gordon, H.J. *Hitler and the Beer Hall Putsch*, London 1972.

Got, A. *L'allemagne à nu*, Paris 1923.

Groener, W. *Lebenserinnerungen*, Göttingen 1957.

Gruenfeld, M. *Alte unnenbare Tage*, Berlin 1938.

Guedj, M. *Instantanés de Berlin*, Paris 1933.

Haas, W. *Erinnerungen*, Berlin 1960. *Sitten und Kultur in Nachkriegs-deutschland*, Berlin 1932.

Hagemann, O. *Hauptstadt Berlin*, Berlin 1948.

Halkett, G.R. *The Dear Monster*, London 1939.

Haney, W. *Berlin Heute Gestern Morgen*, Berlin 1950.

Hanfstaengel, E.F.S. *Hitler The Missing Years*, London 1957.

Heck, K. *Der Igel in Tübinger Studentenbataillon 1919–20*, Karlsruhe s.d.

Heiber, H. ed. *Deutsche Geschichte seit dem ersten Weltkrieg*, Munich 1966.

Hemingway, E. *Bye-Line*, London 1968.

Hirschfeld, M. *Sittengeschichte der jüngsten Zeit*, Berlin 1931.

Hoelz, M. *From White Cross to Red Flag*, London 1930.

Hoffmann, E. *Kokoschha His Life and Work*, London 1947.

Holländer, *Von Kopf bis Fuss*, Hamburg 1965.

Huerlimann, M. *Bilder aus Berlin*, Berlin 1936.

Hussong, F. *Kurfurstendamm*, Berlin 1934.

Jameson, E. *Wenn ich mich recht erinnere*, Berlin 1963.

Junger, E. ed. *Der Kampf um das Reich*, Berlin 1937.

Junger, F.G. *Spiegel der Jahre*, Berlin 1952.

Kästner, E. *Fabian*, London 1932.

Kallenbach, H. *Mit Adolf Hitler auf Festung Landsberg*, Munich 1939.

Kent, M. *I married a German*, London 1938.

Kessler, Count H. *Tagebücher 1918–37*, Frankfurt 1961.

Kiaulehn, W. *Berlin Schicksal einer Weltstadt*, Berlin 1958.

Klotz, ed. *The Berlin Diaries*, London 1934.

Knickerbocker, H.R. *Germany Fascist or Soviet*, London 1932.

Koch, T. *Die göldenen Zwanziger Jahre*, Hamburg 1970.

Koestler, A. *Arrow in the Blue*, London 1952.

Kortner, F. *Alle Tage Abend*, London 1959.

Kracauer, S. *From Caligari to Hitler*, London 1947.

Krell, M. *Das alles gab es einmal*, Munich 1961.

Krummacher, ed. *Die Weimarer Republik*, Berlin 1965.

Kuehn, R. *Elise von Lützow. Das Freikorps und seine Göttin*, Munich 1938.

Landauer, R. *Seven*, London 1936.

Laqueur, W. *Weimar, A Cultural History 1918–33*, London 1974.

Linke, L. *Restless Flags. A German Girl's Story*, London 1935.

Lockner, L. *Always the Unexpected*, London 1956.

Ludecke, K. *I knew Hitler*, London 1938.

Mann, K. *The Turning Point*, London 1942.

Mann, W. *Berlin zur Zeit der Weimarer Republik*, Berlin s.d.

Markham, V.R. *A Woman's Watch on the Rhine*, London 1920.

Mendelssohn, Peter. de. *Zeitungsstadt Berlin*, Berlin 1959.

Morgan, R.P. *Germany 1870–1970*, London 1970.

Morgan, J. *Assize of Arms*, London 1945.

Mowrer, E. *Germany Puts the Clock Back*, London 1932.

Niekisch, E. *Gewagtes Leben*, Munich 1958.

Noske, *Von Kiel bis Kapp*, Berlin 1920.

Olday, J. *Kingdom of Rags*, London 1939.

Olden, R. *Das Wunderbare*, Hamburg 1932.

Osborn, M. *Der bunte Spiegel*, Munich 1945.

Ostwald, H. *Sittengeschichte der Inflation*, Berlin 1931.

Pedersen, J. *Our Street*, London 1938.

PEM (Paul E. Marcus), *Heimweh nach dem Kurfürstendamm*, Berlin 1952.

Picton, H. *Nazis and Germans*, London 1940.

Plesch, J. *Janós. The Story of a Doctor*, London 1947.

Reed, D. *Insanity Fair*, London 1938.

Reynolds, B.T. *Prelude to Hitler*, London 1933.

Roden, ed. *Deutsche Soldaten vom Frontheer und Freikorps*, Munich 1935.

Ryder, A. *The German Revolution of 1918*, London 1967.

Salomon, E. von. *Das Buch der deutschen Freikorpskämpfer*, Berlin 1938. *The Outlaws*, London 1931.

Schacht, H. *My First Seventy-Six Years*, London 1959.

Schoenberger, F. *Confessions of an European Intellectual*, London 1965.

Schoenstadt, W. *In Praise of Life*, London 1939.

Sinshausen, H. *Gelebt in Paradis*, Munich 1953.

Spender, S. *World Within World*, London 1951.

Straus, R. *Wir lebten in Deutschland*, Munich 1961.

Toller, E. *I was a German*, London 1934.

Tormin, ed. *Die Weimarer Republik*, Dusseldorf 1962.

Tuohy, F. *Occupied 1918–30*, London 1931.

Tynan, K. *Life in the Occupied Zone*, London 1924.

Ullstein, H. *The Rise and Fall of the House of Ullstein*, London 1945.

von Schirach, *Ich glaubte an Hitler*, Hamburg 1967.

Voigt, F.A. *Unto Caesar*, London 1938.

Viertel, S. *The Kindness of Strangers*, London 1969.

Waite, R.G. *Vanguard of Nazism*, London 1952.

Werner, B. *Die zwanziger Jahre*, Hamburg 1962.

Wolff, T. *Through Two Decades*, London 1936.

Wucher, A. *Die Fahne Hoch*, Berlin 1963.

Zarek, O. *German Odyssey*, London 1941.

Zuckmayer, *A Part of Myself*, London 1970.

Zweig, S. *The World of Yesterday*, London 1953.

PICTURE ACKNOWLEDGEMENTS

The photographs in this book are reproduced by kind permission of the following organizations:

Landesbildstelle, Berlin: 45 (bottom), 71 (both), 142 (both), 144 (top right and bottom), 164 (bottom), 168, 190 (bottom), 191 (both), 222 (both), 224 (top right and left).

Märkisches Museum, Berlin: 20 (both), 21 (both), 22, 23, 24, 45 (top), 46 (both), 47 (all), 59 (bottom), 60, 72 (both), 73 (both), 107 (bottom), 108 (both), 109 (bottom), 164 (top), 165, 166, 221 (top left and bottom), 224 (bottom), 226, 236 (top left and bottom), 239.

The Press Association, London: endpapers, 2 (frontispiece).

Ullstein GmbH. Bilderdienst, Berlin: 48, 57 (both), 58 (all), 59 (top), 74, 90 (both), 91 (both), 92, 106 (both), 107 (top), 109 (top), 110, 120, 121 (both), 122, 124, 143 (both), 144 (top left), 145, 146, 167, 190 (top), 192 (both), 193 (top and bottom left), 194, 221 (top right), 223 (all), 225, 235 (both), 236 (top right), 237 (both).

Index